HELL IN THE
THE BATTLE FOR IWO JIMA
PACIFIC

OSPREY
PUBLISHING

HELL IN THE

THE BATTLE FOR IWO JIMA

PACIFIC

GORDON L ROTTMAN & DERRICK WRIGHT

First published in Great Britain in 2008 by Osprey Publishing,
Midland House, West Way, Botley, Oxford OX2 0PH, United Kingdom.
443 Park Avenue South, New York, NY 10016, USA.

Email: info@ospreypublishing.com

Previously published as Derrick Wright, Campaign 81: *Iwo Jima 1945 (Parts 1, 3, and 4)*; Gordon L. Rottman, Warrior 95: *Japanese Infantryman 1937–45 (Part 2)*; and Gordon L. Rottman, Warrior 112: *US Marine Rifleman 1939–45 (Part 2)*.

© 2008 Osprey Publishing Ltd

A CIP catalog record for this book is available from the British Library.

ISBN 978 1 84603 335 3

Page layout by Myriam Bell
Index by Alan Thatcher
Typeset in Goudy and Quay Sans
Originated by United Graphic Pte Ltd., Singapore
Printed in China through Worldprint

08 09 10 11 12   10 9 8 7 6 5 4 3 2 1

For a catalog of all books published by Osprey please contact:

NORTH AMERICA
Osprey Direct, c/o Random House Distribution Center
400 Hahn Road, Westminster, MD 21157, USA
E-mail: info@ospreydirect.com

ALL OTHER REGIONS
Osprey Direct UK, P.O. Box 140, Wellingborough, Northants, NN8 2FA, UK
E-mail: info@ospreydirect.co.uk
www.ospreypublishing.com

Front cover image courtesy National Archives
Back cover image courtesy US Navy

CONTENTS

PART 1
ROAD TO IWO JIMA

ORIGINS OF THE CAMPAIGN

As the final days of 1944 ebbed away the Japanese were facing defeat on all fronts. The heady days of conquest that had followed the attack on Pearl Harbor on December 7, 1941, and the occupation of the Philippines, Singapore, Hong Kong, and the oil-rich Dutch East Indies, were little more than a memory as they prepared to defend the homeland at the inner limits of their defensive perimeter.

After suffering staggering defeats at Midway, the Philippine Sea and Leyte Gulf, the Imperial Navy was impotent in the face of the massive US Task Forces that scoured the Pacific and accompanied every amphibious landing. In the west, British and Commonwealth forces of the Fourteenth Army had pushed the enemy back from the borders of India, and in bitter fighting in some of the worst jungle terrain in the world were driving the Japanese Army along the Irrawaddy River into central Burma.

In the Central Pacific, General Douglas MacArthur's army had advanced through the Solomons and across New Guinea and by October 1944 had invaded Leyte in the Philippines, redeeming his pledge that "I shall return." Through the islands and atolls to the north, Admiral Chester Nimitz's Marines swept onward in their "island hopping" campaign that had begun at Tarawa in 1943 and was to climax at Okinawa in 1945. Seizing only those islands that were essential for the

support of further operations and bypassing and neutralizing the others, the Marines had by August 1944 occupied the main islands of the Marianas – Guam, Saipan, and Tinian.

The unique strategic location of Iwo Jima, midway along the B29 Superfortress route from the Marianas to Tokyo, made it imperative that the island should come under American control. Prior to the occupation of Saipan, Tinian, and Guam, the B29s had been limited to carrying out raids on southern Japan from bases in central China. With the problem of transporting all of their fuel by air over thousands of miles of inhospitable country and the limitations of small bomb loads, the attacks had little impact. But now, with the construction of five huge airfields 1,500 miles (2,414km) from the Japanese mainland, the way was open for the 20th Air Force to mount a massive campaign against the industrial heartland of Japan.

Initially the 20th Air Force had attempted to duplicate the technique that had been so successfully used by the 8th Air Force in their bombing campaign against

The B29 Superfortress bomber was the most advanced aircraft of its day. With pressurized crew compartments, remote-control gun turrets, and a huge range and bombload, it was able to reach the Japanese mainland with ease. Here, rows of brand new aircraft stand outside the plant specially constructed for the B29 program at Wichita, Kansas. (Boeing Company Archives)

Germany – daylight precision bombing. The experiment had failed largely because of unexpectedly high winds as the Superfortresses approached their targets at altitudes of 27,000–33,000ft (8,230–10,058m) in the jetstream. The 20th Air Force commander, Brigadier-General Haywood Hansell, became increasingly frustrated and blamed his crews for the disappointing results; by January, 1945, the chiefs in Washington had decided that Hansell had to go. His replacement was Curtis LeMay, a brilliant technician who had previously been in command of the 3rd Division of the 8th Air Force in England. LeMay was to introduce a new term to the aircrews of the 20th Air Force – "area bombing" – a tactic which was widely used by the RAF throughout the war. He proposed to firebomb the main cities of Japan at low level and by night in a dramatic reversal of Hansell's earlier tactics. LeMay was aware that his career was on the line. He had not informed General Henry "Hap" Arnold, commanding general of the United States Army Air Force (USAAF), of this first low-altitude raid: "If we go in low, at night, not in formation, I think we'll surprise the Japs, at least for a short period. If it's a failure and I don't produce any results then he can fire me," he said.

The only obstacle on the flight path was Iwo Jima. It housed two airfields with a third under construction, and a radar station that could give two hours warning of an impending raid. The USAAF desperately needed to eliminate the threat of fighter attacks from the Iwo airfields and to neutralize the radar station there. With the island under American control there would be the added bonuses of a refuge for crippled bombers, facilities for air-sea rescue flying boats, and more importantly, a base from which P51 Mustang long-range fighters could escort the Superfortresses on the second leg of their long haul to Japan.

At Iwo Jima the amphibious techniques that had been developed over the previous three years were to receive the supreme test as three Marine divisions pitted themselves against more than 21,000 deeply entrenched Japanese troops led by a brilliant and determined commander, Lieutenant-General Tadamichi Kuribayashi. "Do not plan for my return," he was to inform his wife from Iwo Jima. Sadly his words would also be the epitaph for nearly 6,000 US Marines.

Lieutenant-General Holland "Howlin' Mad" Smith, Commander Fleet Marine Forces Pacific, called the battle: "The most savage and most costly battle in the history of the Marine Corps." Smith had fronted every amphibious landing in the Central Pacific from Tarawa in 1943 to the Marianas in late 1944 and was eminently qualified to make such a judgment. As the battle reached its climax, Admiral Nimitz was to add his now famous phrase: "Among the Americans who fought on Iwo Jima, uncommon valor was a common virtue."

CHRONOLOGY

1941

December 7	Japanese attack Pearl Harbor. US declares war on Japan.
December 8	Japanese assault Philippines, Hong Kong, Malaya, and Wake Island.
December 11	Germany and Italy declare war on the United States.

1942

February 15	Singapore falls to General Yamashita.
March 12	General MacArthur leaves Philippines vowing "I shall return."
May 6	All US forces in Philippines surrender.
May 7	Battle of the Coral Sea – first Japanese setback of the war.
June 4–7	Battle of Midway – Japanese lose four carriers; turning point of the Pacific War.
August 7	US Marines land on Guadalcanal in Solomon Islands.

1943

February 1	All Japanese troops evacuate Guadalcanal.
June 30	Operation *Cartwheel* – operations against remainder of Solomon Islands.
November 20–23	Battle of Tarawa – start of Marines' "island hopping" operations.

1944

| February 2 | Marines assault Kwajalein in Marshall Islands. |
| June 11 | US Task Force 58 bombards Mariana Islands. |

June 15	Invasion of Marianas begins at Saipan.
June 19	Battle of the Philippine Sea – destruction of Japanese naval air power.
August 8	Island of Guam in Marianas occupied.
September 15	1st Marine Division (MarDiv) assaults Peleliu in Palau Islands.
October 20	US Army under MacArthur lands on Leyte in Philippines.
November 27	B29 Superfortress bombers firebomb Tokyo.

1945

February 19	Three Marine divisions assault Iwo Jima.
March 26–June 30	Battle of Okinawa.
August 6	Atomic bomb dropped on Hiroshima.
September 2	Japanese surrender aboard USS *Missouri* in Tokyo Bay.

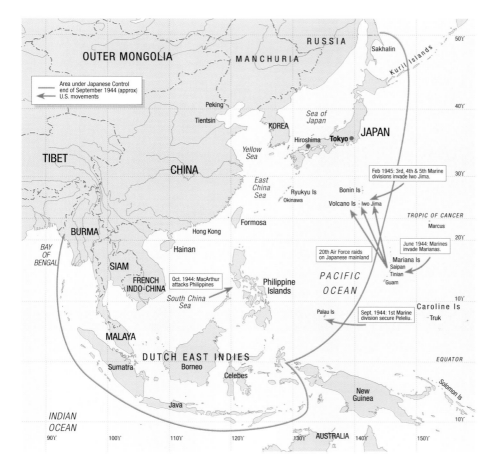

Area under Japanese control, end of September 1944 (approx). In 1941/42 Japan had established a defensive perimeter throughout the Pacific and Southeast Asia, hoping to force the United States to the negotiating table rather than engage in a long, drawn-out conflict. By the end of 1944, however, that perimeter was already in the process of collapsing.

PART 2
OPPOSING FORCES

US MARINE RIFLEMAN

On December 7, 1941, the headline of the *New York Daily News* proclaimed "JAPS BOMB HAWAII" – few people at the time knew where Pearl Harbor was. Thousands of young men flocked to recruiting stations anxious to get into the fight. Many who wanted a crack at the Japanese "before the war was over" signed up with the United States Marine Corps (USMC), counting on a Corps slogan, "First to Fight," to fulfill its promise. For the men of the 1st and 2nd MarDivs this would hold true. By February 1942 the recruiting station lines had dwindled. Those who wished to get into the fight early had already enlisted. Most others, beyond enthusiastic youngsters coming of age, would wait for a letter of invitation from Uncle Sam. Two days short of the anniversary of the Pearl Harbor attack, President Franklin Roosevelt signed an order ending voluntary enlistment of draft age men. By February 1943 intake at Marine recruit depots had reduced to a trickle of 18-year-olds who had enlisted in the Marine Corps Reserve at 17, or younger if they had lied about their age (this was an era in which birth certificates were not always rendered). The Corps' age-old tradition of accepting only volunteers had ended.

Since its formation the Corps had provided ships' detachments, landing parties, expeditionary forces, and naval station guards. In 1933 the Fleet Marine Force (FMF) was established to provide a dedicated expeditionary and overseas base defense force.

Opposite:
A typical Marine Corps recruiting poster offered no illusions as to what Marines did. Many young men were attracted to the Corps because of the promise to get into the fight first. (USMC)

12

LET'S GO GET 'EM !

U.S. MARINES

The USMC was not a second land army, but a specialized amphibious force with its own service elements and air arm to support the US Navy. By 1944 there were over 472,000 Marines in two amphibious corps, six divisions, and a large service force. The US Army had 89 divisions, of which 21 served in the Pacific theater. On the eve of the Pearl Harbor attack, the Corps had consisted of 65,881 officers and men. Ten days later it was authorized a strength of 104,000. There was much to do to bring the two existing divisions and the recently authorized and yet to be activated third division up to strength and achieve the necessary training.

With the mission of supporting the Navy in mind, it was originally envisioned that one Marine division would serve with the Atlantic Fleet and participate in the North Africa landings. The FMF, though, would be entirely committed to the Pacific theater – the ultimate naval campaign. The 3rd MarDiv was activated in September 1942. The need for additional Marine divisions was soon realized. Existing and new units began to assemble on the east and west coasts in early 1943, and in August 1943 the 4th MarDiv was activated. It was followed by the 5th MarDiv in January 1944 and the 6th MarDiv, organized around an existing brigade, in September.

The Marines manning these units were just average American boys, mostly from low- or medium-income families. Some came from the southern states, but the states that contributed the most troops to the Corps were New York, Pennsylvania, Illinois, California, and Texas. The men had spent their childhood and early adulthood under the cloud of the Great Depression. They came from farms, small towns, or big cities: their backgrounds reflected the diverse society of the country they would fight for. These young men, being raised during the Great Depression, had often led tough lives and were used to some degree of privation. Many were as tough as the Drill Instructors (DIs) who would turn them into Marines. Their average age was 18 to 22. They were patriotic, dedicated, and willing to fight for the duration. They took the battle cry "Remember Pearl Harbor" seriously. To the average American, the sneak attack on Pearl Harbor was a worse transgression than all other Japanese acts of aggression combined.

CONSCRIPTION

President Roosevelt declared a "limited emergency" in response to the German invasion of Poland in September 1939. This permitted voluntary mobilization of Marine reservists. The Marine Corps Organized Reserve was ordered to active duty in October 1940 to be followed by the Fleet and Volunteer Reserves. The Marine Corps Reserve as an organization was terminated in order to eliminate distinctions between regulars and reservists – to form a single unified Marine Corps.

NOTICE OF CLASSIFICATION ^{App. Not Req.}

(First name)   (Middle name)   (Last name)

Order No. _____ has been classified in Class _____

(Until _____ , 19_____)

(Insert date for Class II-A and II-B only)

by ☐ Local Board.

☐ Board of Appeal (by vote of _____ to _____).

☐ President.

_____, 19_____   _____

(Date of mailing)   (Member of local board)

The law requires you, subject to heavy penalty for violation, to have this notice, in addition to you're your registration Certificate (Form 2), in your personal possession at all times—to exhibit it upon request to au-authorized officials—to surrender it, upon entering the armed forces, to your commanding officer.

DSS Form 57. (Rev. 3-29-43)

A Notice of Classification or "draft card," which all registered men carried and turned in when conscripted. (USMC)

The President directed the implementation of peacetime conscription in the form of the Selective Training and Service Act in September 1940. The act provided for 12 months of service. All men between the age of 18 and 65 were to register, and those aged up to 45 were liable for induction, although the maximum authorized age of induction was 38. In late 1941, after the President declared a "full emergency," the draft period was extended to 18 months.

Prior to the war and the authorized expansion of the Marine Corps, the draft was of no concern. With the country just coming out of the Great Depression, many young men found the Corps' pay of $21 a month appealing, even with a four-year enlistment, and hungered for travel, challenge, and adventure. Hollywood movies about the Corps enticed others. To many the Corps seemed more attractive than the Army or Navy. They volunteered before the draft caught them, or because they wanted to sign up with the best. Many did not bother to register for the draft and would find themselves receiving warning letters as they fought on South Pacific islands. Seventeen-year-olds could enlist with their parents' or guardian's permission. Some quit high school to join up, and many had not even made it that far in school before they enlisted. Some were attracted by the blue uniforms of the recruiting non-commissioned officers (NCOs), or the image of the "Devil Dogs" of the Great War, or the "old salt" Marines serving in exotic lands during the recent Banana Wars (1898–1934). The influx of volunteers immediately after Pearl Harbor was huge. They soon exceeded the Corps' authorized

A Marine officer swears in young recruits at an Armed Forces Induction Center. Marine recruiting NCOs wearing dress blues stand at the rear of the formation. The American and Marine Corps colors flank the ceremony. (USMC)

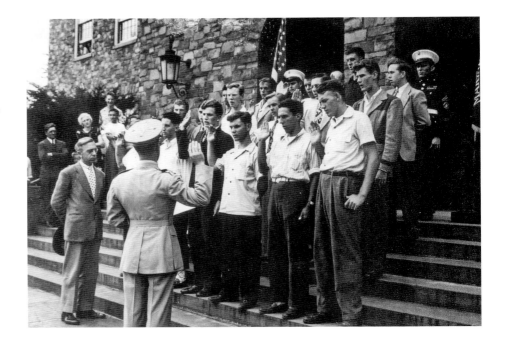

strength. There were examples of entire high school football teams signing up together. The pre-Pearl Harbor volunteers, even if they had been in the Corps only a year, were the "old timers" that brought the traditions and esprit de corps of the "Old Corps" into the new, rapidly expanding force. With the declaration of war, service was extended to the "duration plus six months."

On December 5, 1942, voluntary enlistment in all armed services was ordered to cease. This measure provided a more efficient means of mass induction by not distracting recruiting personnel. There was a final rush to volunteer before the order took effect on January 1, 1943. Even after the order, however, conscripts received by the Marine Corps were in practical terms still volunteers. Headquarters Marine Corps (HQMC) detailed liaison officers to state draft boards, and NCOs to Armed Forces Induction Centers to coordinate the assignment of draftees preferring the Corps. If current Corps quotas did not provide a billet for called-up individuals, the draft boards often deferred the applicants until such openings were authorized. In this way the Corps received 224,000 inductees, whom the Corps called Selective Service Volunteers (SS-V) or, less formally, "draftee-volunteers" or "hand-cuffed volunteers." From the beginning of 1943, recruiters could also sign up 17-year-olds in the Marine Corps Reserve. Some 60,000 enlisted, and on turning 18 they reported for active duty. The four regional Recruiting Divisions were redesignated Procurement Divisions in

May 1943, overseeing the draftee-volunteers, recruiting 17-year-olds, and procuring officers. Each division had six or seven recruiting stations co-located with Navy recruiting stations in major cities. Men classified 4-F (unfit for service) lived with a sense of shame, and there were even occasional suicides.

The draft was conducted by a national lottery system. After draft registration numbers were assigned, a draw was held on October 29, 1940. A total of 365 dated capsules were drawn in random order and the dates announced in newspapers. Each date was assigned a number from 1 to 365 in the order drawn. The 1-As (available for military service) were called in the order their birth date was drawn: most inductees and volunteers were born between 1919 and 1926. This was repeated each year, with the age bracket extended until the draft was canceled in 1947. When their number was drawn, the men received an eight-page questionnaire, used to determine their eligibility for military service.

Camp Elliott, California, with its H-shaped barracks and administrative buildings still under construction. To the right are the tent encampments ("tent city"). Camp Elliott was where West Coast infantrymen were trained, along with tankers. (USMC)

There was a complex system of deferments and exemptions based on physical qualifications, religious grounds, and essential employment, which included those involved in defense industries and farm workers. Draft exemptions were determined by local draft boards; there was usually one board per county, or several in large cities. There were no education exemptions, although college students undertaking Reserve Officers' Training Corps (ROTC) or other officer training programs were deferred. Nor were there exemptions for family hardships such as caring for ill or elderly parents. Inducted conscientious objectors were mostly assigned to medical services.

If selected, a draftee received an Order to Report for Induction and would report to his local draft board. This fateful letter could have been received as few as ten days before the reporting date. At this point it was not certain whether he would actually be inducted. From the draft board office he would be taken by bus or train to the nearest Armed Forces Induction Center (usually at a major city Post Office, federal building, National Guard armory, or local military base) for a simple physical examination and to complete some administrative paperwork. Those who were selected were assembled and, if they desired, were allowed home for a week to put their affairs in order. Most accepted this option, but could be sent straight on to the reception center if they so requested. The others would return the next week and take part in a mass swearing-in alongside men going into other services.

The issue of uniforms was the first step towards becoming a Marine. Here recruits are issued forest-green and khaki service uniforms. The Marine wearing the sun helmet is not a drill instructor, but an NCO guiding the recruits through their first days until assigned to a recruit platoon. (USMC)

The inductee would say his goodbyes after a farewell family dinner, and report again to the induction station. Transportation costs were paid. The young man's volunteering or induction was often announced in the local newspaper. Families with sons in the military displayed a Blue Star Service Banner in their windows, a small rectangular banner with a blue star for each serving son. If a son was lost a gold star was displayed.

Marine recruits were transferred to one of two places by bus or train. If they lived east of the Mississippi River they went to Marine Corps Recruit Depot, Marine Barracks, Parris Island, South Carolina, or if to the west, to Marine Corps Training Center, Marine Corps Base, San Diego, California. They had a change of clothes, a toilet kit, perhaps a few dollars, some meal tickets provided by the induction center, and a sense of apprehension.

There has been a great deal of debate over the differences between the two recruit training centers, an argument that still continues today. The Commandant of the Marine Corps permitted both to develop their own curricula. There were differences in the hours allotted to subjects, with more or less emphasis in certain areas, and a few minor techniques were taught differently. One officer commented that the only real difference was that San Diego ("Dago") taught Marines to jump from a sinking ship with both hands protecting the face, and Parris Island ("PI") to use one hand for face protection and the other to protect the crotch.

There were other differences, of course, but the variance in instruction made less difference than the environment. PI was in a remote area, essentially a big sandbar mostly surrounded by swamps. It was hot and humid, infested with sand fleas, flies, and mosquitoes in the summer, but enduring a cold winter and Atlantic storms. It was 55 miles (88.5km) southwest of Charleston, with the small town of Beaufort 5 miles (8km) distant for the rare liberty. Dago, on the other hand, was in sub-tropical southern California with a year-round pleasant climate. San Diego was immediately outside the gate. Marines training there and at camps Elliott and Pendleton were called "Hollywood Marines," even though Los Angeles was a considerable distance away. There was a degree of competition and resentment between PI and Hollywood Marines.

Many of the Marines who found themselves on the bus to PI or Dago were away from home for the first time, with few having ever been farther from their birthplace than the neighboring county. They were from major urban, suburban, and rural areas, and small towns. Many accents sounded strange to them and the sights they saw were equally as strange as they traveled westwards.

Mass uniform and equipment issue. Recruits freshly shorn of their hair pack their basic issue into sea bags. (USMC)

To modern eyes the Corps was bigoted. It strongly resisted the enlistment of African-Americans and women, and was the last service to accept either. "Colored troops," as African-Americans were then officially designated, were kept completely segregated and were seldom seen by most Marines. Hispanics were integrated into the Corps, but were few in number. Fewer still were Native-Americans – most Marines were not aware of the Navajo Code-Talkers. Sometimes ethnic minorities were singled out for harassment. Men with noticeable physical differences were also often picked on. Those with a college education, or who appeared to come from families of means, seemed to be particularly targeted for harassment by DIs. Eighty percent of a platoon would be teenagers, but there were a few over the age of 20 – they generally proved to be the platoon's unofficial internal leaders, keeping the youngsters in line when they cut-up or "grab-assed" (caused mischief or perpetrated pranks) too much when DIs were not present.

TRAINING

In the spring of 1943 a new batch of recruits rolled into Marine Corps Recruit Depot (MCRD), at the San Diego Training Center, to be astounded by the palm-lined entrance road and Spanish-style architecture. The first few days were a blur. They were turned off the bus by a sergeant, herded into a formation by lining their toes up on a white stripe, and told to ground their bags on their right side. The introduction to discipline was immediate. The recruits or "Boots" (there were worse names) learned quickly never to smile, to look straight ahead, to speak only when spoken to, to answer "Yes, Sir" or "No, Sir." There were no excuses for mistakes or infractions, and they had to pay very close attention to what was being said – "Boots" were already being dropped for 25 push-ups for the slightest transgression. Names were checked off, the recruits were broken down into squads, and then marched into a large two-story stucco barracks. Double-stacked bunks or "racks" lined both walls and an end-to-end double row of bunks stretched down the center, leaving two aisles. Next to each pair of bunks were two olive-drab plywood locker boxes and two 3-gallon (11.4-liter) galvanized buckets. The men were given the opportunity to turn in any contraband items, no questions asked (weapons, knives, straight razors, liquor, obscene materials).

With buckets in hand, they followed the sergeant single file to the Post Exchange (PX) – the "ge-dunk shop." They were told what to place in their buckets: scrubbing and shoe brushes, bath soap, box of laundry powder, toothbrush, toothpaste, safety razor and blades, bag of Bull Durham® tobacco, Zigzag® cigarette papers (they would roll their own, no "ready-mades"), brown boot polish, Brasso® polish, two white bath

Recruits during their two weeks at the rifle range march in formation with the M1903 rifle. Their rifle scorecards are pinned behind the globe and anchor on their sun helmets. (USMC)

towels embossed "U.S. MARINE CORPS" on a red strip, and other necessities. They also bought a copy of *The Marine's Handbook* ("Red Book") for $1. After learning that $15 would be deducted from their $50 a month pay for these PX purchases, they were led to the barber shop. Seated in the chairs, they were asked if they would like a trim around the ears while their scalps were sheared bare.

The recruits' next visit was to the quartermaster. Entering the warehouse-like building, they were confronted with shelf after shelf of uniforms and equipment. Ordered to strip, they were given a cardboard box on which they wrote their addresses and in which they put their "civvies" to be sent home. They were issued with green dungarees, a utility cap, white underwear, and white socks. The quartermasters issuing

Barracks inspection included a full layout of equipment on the bunk ("junk on a bunk") inspection on Saturdays. The Marine wears the khaki uniform with the summer garrison cap while the 1st lieutenant wears the summer service uniform with forest-green wool trousers and the summer service cap. "Boots" were later issued service caps, but without the braid quatrefoil on their crowns. (Howard Gerrard © Osprey Publishing)

the uniforms merely "eyeballed" their clothing sizes. Care was taken, though, for the fitting of leather service shoes or "boondockers." Carrying buckets in their right hands, clothing in the left, and their two pairs of boondockers hanging around their necks, the recruits returned to barracks. They were given padlocks for the locker boxes and drew bedding: two sheets, two wool blankets, and a pillow case. A key was placed on their "dog tag" chain – the tags could never be removed, even to unlock a locker, a task requiring the recruit to get down on all fours to do so. A second key was retained by the sergeant with the man's name on a tag. The men spent the rest of the day learning how to make bunks, stow gear, and the dos and don'ts of barracks life. They could not sit or lay on their bunks until "lights out," when an instructor entered the squad bay. The first to see him would shout "Attention" and they would all remain in that position until told "As you were" or "At ease." The recruits could only smoke when told the "smoking lamp is lit" and cigarettes were extinguished when the "smoking lamp is out." They could not leave the barracks unless told. The squad bay and head (bathroom) were to be kept spotless at all times.

They also learned what it meant to be part of the naval services. The floor was the "deck," the walls "bulkheads," the ceiling the "overhead," stairs were "ladders," etc.

Over the next couple of days the recruits completed more paperwork and signed up for National Service Life Insurance at $6.40 a month for a $10,000 payout, a benefit the service had provided since October 1940. They received a complete physical, a dental examination, and seemingly endless inoculations. They also took a simple mental skills test, and, unknown to them, their paperwork was being examined by classification specialists to determine their fate. Their actual assignment, though, would have more to do with the needs of the service at the given moment, rather than any particular qualifications or skills they might possess.

Many of the recruits had assumed they would spend boot camp in the barracks, but one morning they were ordered to fall out with everything, including bedding, packed in their canvas sea bags and lockers. They

Water survival training included basic swimming (enough to stay afloat and to swim away from a sinking ship), abandoning a ship by jumping, and assisting a wounded man. Here recruits have removed their trousers, tied off the legs, and inflated them. (USMC)

lugged the impossible loads across the broad, blistering drill field to rows of green-painted steel Quonset huts. Platoons of recruits on the drill field shouted a disparaging, "You'll be sorreeee!" One of the new groups of 60 men in ill-fitting dungarees found themselves facing a tough-looking sergeant and two plain, mean-looking corporals wearing starched khaki uniforms and dark olive-drab field or "campaign" hats – these men were their DIs. They quickly learned that Sergeant "Sandbag" and Corporals "Tightlips" and "Barbedwire" held absolute authority of life and death over them. The DIs informed the recruits that they were an insult to the Corps and all the real Marines who had gone before them, and were no doubt here because their god-fearing families had thrown them out in embarrassment. They were now members of a numbered recruit platoon organized into three 20-man squads. After a period of screaming, yelling, and being dropped for push-ups, the platoon was herded into the two 20 x 48ft (6.1 x 14.6m) Quonset huts assigned to them. The head and showers were in a separate building. The men made their bunks and stowed their gear, with the corporals all the time shouting that they were too slow. Seemingly they could do nothing right; they were too slow, too sloppy, and plain dumb. Over the coming miserable days a desire grew to please the DIs no matter what, not to halt the harassment (they knew that would never end) but to prove they had what it took to be Marines. They pushed themselves. A small number were washed out.

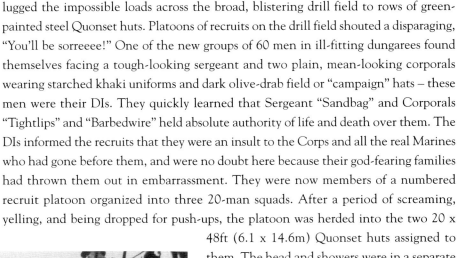

Marines practice descending a simulated ship's side on a cargo net. Note the diamond-shaped rope pattern, making footing difficult. Most landing nets were a square pattern. (USMC)

The DIs are a Marine Corps institution and they are the means by which young men are turned into Marines. Prior to the war there was more time available to train and indoctrinate recruits – up to ten weeks. DIs coached and, in effect, mentored recruits. The instructors were hand-picked and used a fair, but firm methodology. There was harassment, but it was meted out in doses and only when necessary. At the time there was only a small number of recruits, and they were motivated by more professional considerations of duty; they were not driven by a war of preservation. In the early 1940s, however, with an unprecedented influx of thousands of green young men pouring into the Corps, a means had to be found to hammer them into battle-ready Marines; and hammer was the right word. The Corps' training mechanism could barely handle the load. Even training areas, ranges, quarters, support facilities, and equipment were in short supply. Recruits could not be "nurtured" into Marines. It had to be done fast and effectively. DIs were no longer hand-picked, but selected for their gruff appearance, loud voices, and lack of concern over hurting feelings. They were relentless disciplinarians. Many had only been in the Corps for a limited time; some DI corporals had only just graduated from boot camp. In the early days few had combat experience. The old salts, the career Marines with Banana Wars experience, fleet Marines, and "Old China" hands were needed in the combat units to train and lead the first Marines into combat. It would not be until mid 1943, when veterans from the South Pacific were rotated back to the States, that vets began to be assigned as DIs in any numbers. The early, less-experienced DIs were often unsure of themselves, having little practical experience leading men, and they relied on their position of authority to bully recruits and to make up for their own lack of confidence. There were abuses and humiliation, which were often ignored; the job at hand was too critical to allow concern about niceties and there was little time in which to accomplish the job. Boot

A recruit traverses a three-rope bridge. Khaki garrison caps were often worn in training with the dungarees. In 1944 recruits began receiving M1 rifles rather than the M1903. (USMC)

camp had been cut back to three weeks before the war to accommodate the build-up; this was insufficient time to train and condition a recruit to any acceptable level – they were only given a week's rifle and marksmanship training.

Boot was lengthened to seven weeks by the end of 1940 and eight in 1944. The new recruits spent the evening scrubbing down their quarters until lights out was ordered and Taps sounded over the base loudspeaker at 2200hrs. There were seven or eight double bunks on each side of the squad room. The rifle racks were at the back wall and there were two 30-gallon (114-liter) galvanized garbage cans in the center aisle, which were cleaned with brass polish. The DIs had their own rooms in the huts and nothing escaped them. Men were assigned two-hour fire-watch shifts through the night, ensuring that no one smoked, and guarding the racked rifles. They would holystone (soft sandstone block) the deck once a day. Each evening they would wash a set of dungarees, skivvies, and socks.

The lights came on at 0400hrs with DIs screaming for the men to fall out of their racks, amid buckets being kicked across the deck: "Hit the deck!" The dreary-eyed platoon had 30 minutes to wash before falling out in formation. They had to shave even if a razor had never before touched their faces. Roll was called by the glare of a flashlight and they marched to the chow hall. The men sat down on benches at plank tables when ordered, and other recruits, obviously "senior" as they were sun-tanned and fuzz was growing back on their heads, served them platters of eggs, bacon, and pancakes and pitchers of coffee, milk, and orange juice. They were not to speak unless asking for food to be passed. They were told "take all you want, but eat all you take." Most began to gain weight, not just from the food, but also from exercise. They ate a lot of chicken, pork chops, and ground beef, had plenty of potatoes in all forms, and lots of vegetables and fresh breads. On Sunday there was always chicken and on Monday chicken leftovers. There was fish on Friday even though the "Mackerel-snappers" – Catholics – were given wartime dispensation to eat meat. Likewise, Jews were allowed to eat non-Kosher foods. It was a seven-day week, although Sundays were dedicated to church call, administrative requirements, and cleaning quarters, gear, and uniforms.

In formation in front of their huts they were told that here was a landmark day: they would be issued with their rifles. At the armory they each received a .30-cal. M1903 Springfield rifle and a long bayonet. They had to memorize the rifle's serial number by the time they returned to barracks, and there they learned the difference between a rifle and a gun. The first recruit making this error in nomenclature demonstrated the difference by holding the rifle and another more personal piece of equipment in the opposite hand reciting, "This is my rifle, this is my gun. This is for fighting, this is for fun." The day was spent learning to disassemble and assemble the rifle and how to clean it meticulously. They were told they would have to disassemble and assemble it blindfolded, that they must be able to name correctly every single part, and that the rifle would become their best friend. To drop or otherwise mistreat a rifle was a cardinal sin.

MARKSMANSHIP TRAINING, CAMP ELLIOTT

Rifle marksmanship was a cornerstone of Marine training. A great deal of time and effort was committed to turning boys, many of whom had never fired a weapon, into effective riflemen. During their two weeks at the range, living in tent cities, they learned all aspects of musketry and the use of the infantryman's primary weapon. They were given cloth pads to sew on their dungaree elbows and the right pit of the shoulder. "Boots" would pair up and alternate firing and coaching. The coach would talk the shooter through the steps of firing: sight alignment, sight picture, breath control, gentle trigger squeeze, and follow through. Dry fire exercises – "snapping in" – were conducted before live firing commenced. Their rifle scorecards are pinned behind the globe and anchor on their sun helmets. A drill instructor looks on wearing the khaki uniform. Recruits wore an identical uniform, except the campaign hat was no longer issued from late 1942. Instead they would wear a khaki garrison cap. (Howard Gerrard © Osprey Publishing)

The first four weeks were spent at the depot undertaking a great deal of close-order drill, manual of arms, physical fitness drills, bayonet training, obstacle courses, lectures on field sanitation, military courtesies (when and whom to salute), recognizing rank, military law (Articles of the Government of the Navy – "Rocks and Shoals"), and guard duty. Field training was conducted in the form of forced marches, first aid, signaling, gas warfare, cover and concealment, scouting and patrolling. The recruits were taken to the nearby Del Mar Race Track, closed for the duration of the war and now called Camp C. J. Miller, where they were taught combat swimming and water survival. Harassment continued relentlessly. The DIs' goal was to break these young men down to the lowest level and then gradually build up their confidence and self-esteem. They had to work as a team and put aside individual concerns and comforts. The recruits, even though they had to work together, had little time to talk to one another and discover personal details.

Barrack and full equipment layout inspections were held on Saturdays. The early inspections were disasters. DIs raked meticulously displayed gear off bunks with a sweep of the arm and threw locker boxes down the aisles, scattering the contents. The DIs seemed to introduce them to new punishments daily: one DI telling them to dig a 6ft-cubed (1.8m-cubed) hole and another DI telling them to fill it in; running around the drill field or on the spot with the rifle at high port (held at arm's length over the head); holding two partly filled buckets of water in outstretched arms; and ice-cold showers. Some punishments were reserved for specific infractions. Failure to shave resulted in a "dry shave" without lather or water. If the DI wished to make a deeper impression he had another recruit do the shaving. A recruit found with his hands in his pockets had the pockets filled with sand and sewn shut. A "Boot" who could not seem to do things correctly would stand to attention in front of his hut clad in "skivvies" with a bucket over his head shouting, "I am the platoon screw-up" to all passing by. Passing DIs would rap their swagger sticks on the bucket. A man continually causing problems, one who could not get it right, brought grief on the entire platoon. DIs were not beyond group punishment to make the point that they were all in this together. A "blanket party" might be called for, a late-night visit by the nonconformist's platoon mates. A blanket would be thrown over the transgressor and he was held down as others applied fists. Even with the draft the Marines considered themselves a volunteer service. Men could gripe, but only to a point. They would be reminded that they asked for this, they volunteered. In the eyes of the Corps the fact that they were volunteers meant they could be driven harder and more could be expected of them.

A DI demonstrates the parry and long thrust with an M1905 bayonet on an M1903 rifle. The Marine had to knock (parry) the enemy spring-loaded "rifle" away and thrust his bayonet into the rag-filled dummy's vitals. (USMC)

For the fifth and sixth weeks the company moved to Camp Calvin B. Matthews, 13 miles (20km) north of San Diego. They lived in squad tents with wooden decks, a "tent city." Here they focused totally on rifle marksmanship, conducting known-distance (KD) range firing. This was extremely important, as all Marines were (and remain) considered as riflemen first, regardless of specialty. Harassment here was reduced to allow them to concentrate on qualifying as Marksmen, Sharpshooters, or Expert Riflemen, and they would all qualify. As motivation to fire Expert, they would receive $5 extra a month. They also fired the .45-cal. M1911A1 Colt pistol for familiarization. Most Marines have fond memories of this period.

Upon their return to Dago the recruits pulled a week of mess duty and post work details. Yet again they had not seen the PX, had any "poggy bait" (candy), soda, or beer, and liberty was beyond hope. The DIs, however, were starting to treat them somewhat like humans, even joked with them sometimes; the recruits were feeling like they might become Marines. They conducted their first parade in forest-green service uniforms. It was their first time seeing officers. They were given a speech about what they had achieved and the service they would soon provide the country, and they were also given their globe and anchor insignia. They were now Marines because the DIs actually told them so, and even drank a brew with them. This is when the platoon photograph was taken, with the new Marines in their service uniforms and sun

Marines in the frontline seldom attempted to shave, but when pulled out of the line, or the combat zone was secured, they reverted to normal grooming. The steel helmet universally served as a wash basin. (USMC)

helmets, gripping their rifles in their hands, and standing on a five-tier bleacher with their DI front row center, behind the sign bearing their platoon number and the year.

The recruits were quite proud of themselves at this point. They were in the best physical condition of their lives, they were sun-tanned, had put on weight (or lost it if they had been overweight), and had a great deal of self-confidence. Through it all, the recruits seldom spoke of the enemy. There were no propaganda speeches or political exhortations other than the occasional Hollywood movie, which offered more in the way of propaganda than any government effort.

Much to their surprise, the recruits were given a week's leave and they headed home wearing their unadorned khakis via bus and train. This was new to the Corps, as leave after boot camp had only begun to be granted in the spring of 1943; previously they had gone directly to specialty training, then were assigned to a unit and deployed, often without any leave. They all returned at the appointed time, by midnight. They had been sternly lectured about what would happen if they failed to return on time – they were not told they had a 24-hour grace period to return from leave and were dismayed when one man came in a day late and nothing was said. He had been informed of the grace period by an older brother. If an individual failed to report in from leave or liberty at the required time, he was declared Absent Without Leave (AWOL) and was subject to disciplinary action. If he had still not reported in after 30 days, he became a deserter, subject to arrest by the police and sought after by the FBI.

It was after leave that the men learned their future assignments, which had been much anticipated. The Marine Corps had 21 occupation fields, each with numerous individual specialties. Some men found themselves going to Camp Pendleton, 32 miles (51km) north of Dago, for artillery, scout and sniper, engineer, amphibian tractor, or signal training. Most, though, were assigned to the Infantry Training Battalion at Camp Elliott, 12 miles (19km) northeast of Dago.

Camp Elliott covered 32,000 acres (12,928 hectares) on Kearney Mesa, a dry area of scrub brush, rolling hills, and ravines. The infantry students were housed in two-story H-shaped wooden barracks with squad bays in the arms of the "H" and heads in the crossbar. The training was straightforward and practical, and no time was wasted on harassment. The instructors, mostly combat vets, were there only to teach them their trade. The recruits usually had evenings off, plus weekend liberty. The three weeks' training qualified each young man as a Rifleman, Specification Code No.745. He was issued an M1 rifle and would carry it to his next assignment. He conducted more rifle firing integrated into tactical live-fire exercises, and received introduction to squad and platoon tactics, scouting and patrolling, hand and rifle grenades, basic judo and knife fighting, and familiarization firing with all battalion weapons. Other men were trained on the Browning Automatic Rifle (BAR; never pronounced "bar"), light and heavy machine guns (LMGs and HMGs), 60mm and 81mm mortars, or 37mm antitank gun. They were given first and second choices as to which weapon they wanted to train on.

Marine dress blues worn by a 1st sergeant, sporting two service stripes ("hash marks," each for four years' service) and the NCO's 30in (76cm) sword, used in the Corps since 1875. Arguably one of the most appealing uniforms in US service, it attracted many men to the Corps, but few would actually wear it. (USMC)

APPEARANCE

The image an observer would first note when observing these soldiers was the youth of many Marines. They were kids – when the war started in 1939 they were in junior high or had just entered high school. They were lean because of the Depression years and the lack of "fast foods." Their average height was 5ft 6in (1.67m) – the average today is 5ft 8in (1.72m) and average weight has increased. They were proud of their spartan uniforms and went to the expense of having them tailor fitted.

There was not much on their uniforms – no shoulder insignia, name tags, or ribbons. They wore only a silver Marksman, Sharpshooter, or Expert Rifleman badge on the left breast pocket flap, bronze globe and anchor or "bird on a ball" insignia on their collars, and another on the left side of the garrison cap. If qualifying on other weapons, the Marine would wear a Basic Weapons Qualification Badge with bars signifying the weapons and level of qualification. Once assigned to a division he would receive a "battle blaze" for his left shoulder. A private 1st class (PFC) wore a point-up chevron on both upper sleeves – red on forest green on the winter service uniform and forest green on khaki on the summer shirt. Even old salts bore few adornments: more chevrons and diagonal hash marks on the coat's left cuff, one for each four-year hitch. Ribbons were few in number, even for prewar and South Pacific veterans.

The most distinctive Marine uniform was the "blues," the uniform that attracted many young men to the Corps. It was a uniform that most would never wear, as its general issue ceased in early 1942. From that point the uniforms were issued only to Marine Barracks, Washington; Marine Detachment, London; Marine Band and recruiters. Individuals could purchase them, but few could afford blues.

The forest-green winter service uniform, or "greens," was the formal uniform issued to most Marines. No doubt recruits were disappointed to find they would have no blues in their sea bag, but greens were an attractive uniform. The forest green was more appealing to the eye than brownish olive-drab. The kersey wool coat or blouse had epaulettes, Marine-style (Polish-style) cuffs, pleated breast pockets, and large box-style pockets on the skirts. The buttons were dark bronze adorned with the globe and anchor insignia. A 2in (5cm) wide cordovan belt with an open brass buckle was worn with the coat, and was known as the "fair-weather belt." In 1943 a cloth belt with a dark bronze buckle replaced the leather item. A tan wool shirt was worn with the greens in winter. In the summer a khaki cotton shirt could be worn with the forest-green trousers without the coat. Much to the Marines' chagrin, the trousers had only front pockets and no hip pockets (which only officers' trousers boasted). A tan field scarf (necktie) was worn with both shirts. A 3in (7.6cm) long "battle pin" held the collars and scarf in place. Garrison or overseas caps were provided in forest-green wool and khaki cotton for wear with the appropriate uniform. Caps were referred to as "covers," and prior to the issue of the utility cap they were worn in the field. Ankle-high, rough-side-in cordovan service shoes were worn with greens and khakis. These dark-brown shoes were to be highly "spit-shined."

The utility uniform – "utilities" or "dungarees" – was the uniform in which Marines spent the most time. The two-piece dungarees were made of cotton herringbone twill (HBT) in sage green (grayish green). The hardwearing fabric proved to be effective camouflage in the jungle. It was in this uniform that the Marines stormed Guadalcanal; previously they had worn khakis in combat. The coat (shirt) had three flapless pockets on the skirts and left breast. On the breast pocket was stenciled a black globe and anchor over which was written "USMC." Rank insignia were sometimes stenciled or crudely hand-painted in black on the upper sleeves. The front opening was secured by four black metal buttons. The trousers were unusual in that they had both front and hip pockets. The utility cap began to be issued in early 1943. It was inspired by a railroad worker's cap, had a short bill, pleats around the crown, and usually a black globe and anchor stenciled on the front. The tan web trousers belt was 1¼in (3.2cm) wide with a brass buckle and tip, both blackened. This was worn on dungarees, khakis, and greens. Since recruits were issued two belts, they would rub off the blacking on their belt's buckle and tip, which they would Brasso® to a shine. Marines became quite familiar

A typical field uniform: dungarees with helmet, M1 rifle with M1 bayonet, cartridge belt with canteen and first aid pouch, and haversack. Here the leggings are worn unbloused, but they might be worn with the trousers bloused (tucked into leggings), or discarded. (USMC)

with the sharp odor of Brasso®, a canned liquid metal polish applied with a rag and rubbed briskly. Marines would also purchase a Blitz Cloth®, a square of soft cloth impregnated with brass polish. Jeweler's paste was used to polish bronze devices.

RECRUIT, SAN DIEGO

The Marine recruit undertaking boot (1 and 2) wears "utilities" or "dungarees." First issued in late 1941 as a work uniform, they became the Corps' main combat uniform. He is armed with a .30-cal. M1903 Springfield rifle with an M1905 bayonet in an M1917 leather scabbard. The artwork above depicts some of the fundamentals of recruit uniform, such as a fiber sun helmet (3) adorned with the bronze globe and anchor; Marine Corps canvas leggings (7 – Army leggings had eight lacing hooks); service shoes or "boondockers" shod with nylon-cord-reinforced rubber soles (8); and identity or "dog tags" (6) – tags were worn on a cloth- or plastic-covered wire, or alternatively, many men bought a thin chain available in the PX. A detail of the globe and anchor as stenciled on the dungarees' breast pocket is also shown (4). Other issue items include: *The Marine's Handbook* (5). The "Red Book" had 242 pages and described the skills that were essential for a Marine to master. The book became his "bible." Five-round .30-cal. stripper clip with M2 ball ammunition for loading the M1903 rifle (9). Two clips were carried in each cartridge belt pocket. The M1905 bayonet (10) was issued with one of three scabbards: M1910 canvas-covered leather (10a), M1917 leather (10b), or M3 fiberglass (10c). The first two were mainly issued to recruits. (Howard Gerrard © Osprey Publishing)

The tan fiber tropical helmet was worn by recruits during much of their training, especially on the rifle range. A large bronze globe and anchor insignia was fitted on the front. Often, the recruits did not receive the M1 steel helmet and resin-impregnated duck liner until infantry training. For field duty recruits wore tan canvas leggings and rough-side-out dark-tan leather-laced ankle boots with non-slip composite rubber soles.

Undershirts, under drawers, and socks were white. These were often dyed in some shade of green by Marines using Rit® powdered dye. In combat, coffee grounds were used to dye skivvies tan or light brown. Late in the war the Marines were issued with green underwear and tan socks.

All items of clothing were marked in specified locations with the owner's first and middle initials and last name in ¼in (6.5mm) block letters. This was done with a Carter's® permanent marking outfit with rubber letters that could be set in wooden stamp blocks.

Each Marine was issued two 1¼ x 1½in (3.2 x 3.8cm) oval dog tags to be worn around his neck. There was a hole in both ends of the monel alloy, brass, or stainless steel tag. The second tag was attached by a short loop to the lower hole of the first. Prior to 1942 only one tag was issued with an acid-etched right index fingerprint on the back. Five lines of data were stamped on the tags: 1) surname (family name); 2) given name and middle initial (sometimes first and middle initials); 3) six-digit service number and religious preference (C – Catholic, H – Hebrew [Jew], P – Protestant, or blank); 4) Tetanus inoculation date (T. or TET-month/year; e.g. T.4/43) and blood type (TYPE A, B, AB, O); and 5) USMC or USMCR. If the Marine was killed, one tag would remain with the body and the other be turned in to the company command post (CP) to be forwarded to Division of Personnel (Personnel Department from July 1944).

The Marine Corps utilized a complex system of enlisted ranks with numerous specialty ranks in each of the seven pay grades. The basic ranks were private, PFC, corporal, sergeant, platoon sergeant, gunnery sergeant ("gunny"), and master gunnery sergeant. Pay grades 1–5 were NCOs – "noncoms." Corporal and sergeant ranks were "line NCOs," holding leadership positions and identifiable by arches ("rockers") beneath their chevrons. The others were "staff NCOs" with a bar rather than a rocker beneath their chevrons or identifiable by some other device. Originally a 1st sergeant, the senior NCO in a company or battery, could be graded 1–3, but on February 10, 1943, the 1st sergeant became grade 1 only. The 1st sergeant's diamond, which had been used between 1857 and 1937, was restored to the Corps on February 8, 1944.

COMBAT GARB

The Marine in combat was stripped down to the bare essentials. Packs were often left in the company rear to be brought up at night. In the rugged jungle terrain and across broken ground, speed and agility were essential. The Marine wore faded dungarees bearing only the black globe and anchor and no rank insignia. Officers often removed their pin-on collar rank because they attracted snipers. The utility cap was often worn under the olive-drab painted steel helmet. A photo of his wife or girlfriend might be tucked into the helmet webbing. Reversible helmet camouflage covers began to be issued in late 1942. The more commonly used "green-side" was dark green, light olive-drab, and dark and light browns on a pale green backing, while the "brown-side" was dark and light browns, and tan on a sand backing. These same colors were used in other camouflage clothing and equipment. In monochrome photos the "brown-side" appears much lighter than the "green-side." The camo cover became a distinction of the Corps, as the Army used bare helmets or camouflage nets. The shirt was always worn outside the trousers. The Marine discarded the leggings, as they chafed, restricted

Frontline troops received their water in 5-gallon (19-liter) cans. Water was treated with chlorine or halazone tablets before being sent forward. Most water was provided by transport ships' salt water distillers, and troops were cautioned about drinking water found on the islands. (USMC)

An M1 rifle-armed infantry training squad rests after completing a night infiltration course. The Marines behind them wearing gray sweat shirts were the exercise "enemy." (USMC)

circulation, were too hot, and retained water after wading ashore or through swamps and streams. His trousers were unbloused and perhaps rolled up to his ankles. His boondockers were scuffed and scarred, but broken into a comfortable fit. He may have discarded his skivvies altogether, or at least the drawers. They held sweat and did not dry out, causing rashes – "jungle rot." His only gear was a cartridge belt, perhaps with suspenders (not always issued), one or two canteens, a first aid pouch, often a jungle first aid kit, a KA-Bar fighting knife, and a couple of grenades.

A Marine's physical appearance in prolonged combat was near appalling. Weight loss was a given. He was unshaved for days or weeks, his hair grew mangy; the opportunity to bath did not exist. Those fighting in dense jungle were frequently pale or their skin took on a yellow-cast owing to the tiny, bitter, bright-yellow atabrine anti-malaria tablets. A soldier's eyes may have appeared yellow due to jaundice. Small cuts and abrasions might develop into tropical ulcers and coral cuts could become infected. He was dehydrated, making him susceptible to shock, and took salt tablets to counteract the effects of excessive sweating.

EQUIPMENT

The Marines used a combination of Marine and Army individual equipment. The latter came into increasing use late in the war as Army and Marine units conducted frequent joint operations. Army web gear was mostly khaki, with olive-drab gear being

FIELD EQUIPMENT CARRIED BY A USMC RIFLEMAN

The Marine (1 and 2) is prepared to board an amtrac for the run to shore. The M1941 pack system is worn in the marching pack configuration with haversack, cartridge belt, and entrenching tool, the normal assault rig. He is armed with an M1 rifle and the short M1 bayonet. His kit consists of the following: 1-quart canteen, cup, carrier (3). First aid pouch with field dressing (4x4in/10x10cm unfolded) and sulfa powder packet (4). KA-Bar knife and scabbard (5). K-ration meals (6). D-ration bar (7). The enriched chocolate bar was purposely made less than tasty to prevent troops from consuming it as a snack. C-ration (8). The six cans constituting a C-ration provided three 12oz (340g) meat and three bread units for one day's meals in a single carton. Troops complained that the C-ration was too rich and greasy, had too many beans, and lacked variety. Mess kit and knife, fork, and spoon (9). Toilet kit (10), typically containing a toothbrush, toothpaste, safety razor, razor blades, shaving soap tube, shaving brush, steel mirror, bath soap in a plastic box, comb, foot powder, and maybe a sewing kit. The jungle first aid kit (11) originally contained a field dressing, six band-aids, insect repellent, Frazer's athlete's foot solution, atabrine anti-malaria tablets, salt tablets, halazone water purification tablets, and sulfadiazine tablets. The later issue included field dressing, six band-aids, insect repellent, petrolatum, halazone water purification tablets, and a tourniquet. The M1 satchel charge (12) contained eight 2½lb (1.14kg) M2 tetrytol demolition charges, linked by detonating cord ("detcord" or "primacord"). The charge would be detonated by a short length of delay fuse ignited by a waterproof M2 fuse lighter. (Howard Gerrard © Osprey Publishing) introduced in 1943. Marine web gear was tan, a darker shade than Army khaki. It was seldom marked with "U.S." in a high-visibility location as Army gear, but with "U.S.M.C." under flaps or on the back. Collectively, Marines called their web equipment "782 gear," after the quartermaster form on which they signed for it. When a Marine received his gear it was a bewildering pile of belts, straps, bags, and containers. The DIs had the platoon form up at double-arm intervals and dump their gear out of their sea bags. One of the corporals would hold up an item and the sergeant would bellow out its nomenclature. Then they talked the men through assembling and fitting it. It would require a couple of forced marches before it was adjusted to some degree of comfort. Once fully loaded with ammunition, rations, and other gear it would all have to be readjusted and rebalanced.

The M1941 pack system was the basis for load carrying. It consisted of two packs: an upper haversack with integral shoulder straps and a lower knapsack, which could be secured beneath the haversack. A full prescribed haversack load held a set of underwear, socks, poncho, rations, mess kit, knife, fork and spoon, towel, and "ditty bag" (toilet kit). A bayonet and entrenching tool were attached to the haversack. The knapsack held a set of dungarees, another set of underwear, socks, and spare shoes. A third component was the bedroll, consisting of a shelter-half ("pup tent"), three-section tent pole, five wooden tent stakes, tent guy line, mosquito net, and blanket.

Automatic riflemen were trained separately from riflemen, although the latter were familiar with and could operate an M1918A2 BAR. Here an instructor provides advice of the intricacies of stripping this complex weapon. (USMC)

The M1941 pack could be configured in five assemblies:

Light marching pack – haversack without cartridge belt

Marching pack – haversack, cartridge belt, entrenching tool

Field marching pack – marching pack with bedroll

Transport pack – haversack, cartridge belt, knapsack

Field transport pack – transport pack with bedroll

What pack configuration to carry on a given training day was spelled out on the training schedule, along with the uniform of the day. Other 782 gear included an M1912 first aid pouch with a field dressing and sulfa powder or tablets, M1941 suspenders, 1-quart (roughly 1-liter) steel canteen with a metal or black plastic cap, a canteen cup with a folding handle (carried nested on the bottom of the canteen), canteen carrier, M1928 ten-pocket cartridge belt with each pocket holding two five-round M1903 rifle stripper clips or an eight-round M1 rifle clip, and a non-folding M1910 entrenching tool or "e-tool." (Marines soon learned it was never called a "shovel.") From late 1943 a folding e-tool began to be issued. The jungle first aid kit was issued after 1943 in an effort to provide individuals with first aid and preventive medicine items necessary in the tropics. The poncho and shelter-half were olive-drab, but in 1943 reversible camouflage versions began to be issued.

Alternative web gear items were provided to accommodate weapons other than rifles. Automatic riflemen carried an M1936 six-pocket belt with each pocket holding two BAR magazines. Individuals armed with pistols, carbines, and submachine guns used a pistol belt with special pouches: a two-pocket pistol magazine pouch, two to four two-pocket carbine pouches, or three- or five-pocket submachine gun magazine pouches.

WEAPONS

The Marine Corps, first and foremost an infantry force, considered its most important weapons to be those arming its infantrymen: rifle, bayonet, automatic rifle, submachine gun, machine gun, carbine, rifle grenade launcher, and hand grenade. Other weapons were also available to the infantryman: bazookas, flamethrowers, and demolition charges.

The rifle was the Marine's basic arm. While country boys tended to have some experience with firearms, it was by no means near the level of skill required by the Corps. Most city boys had little if any firearms experience. A fair percentage of those familiar with firearms, though, had some degree of experience with bolt-action deer rifles, and they found the "03 Springfield" easy to operate.

An M1 carbine-armed Marine demonstrates the kneeling throwing position with the Mk II "pineapple" fragmentation hand grenade. Grenades proved to be a key weapon on the Pacific islands. (USMC)

The .30-cal. M1903 Springfield rifle had been in use by the Corps since 1908, providing legendary service. The old hands held it in reverence and recruits were expected likewise to regard it highly and learn everything there was to know about it. It was relatively light and compact at 8lb 11oz (3.95kg) and was 43¼in (110cm) long, with a five-round magazine loaded by stripper clip. A slightly improved version, the M1903A1, was put into production in 1939, and in 1942 the M1903A3 was standardized to speed up production. While better finished and more refined than the Japanese Arisaka rifle, the two weapons were not dissimilar in capabilities. The Japanese 6.5mm round had less penetration and knockdown power, but their 7.7mm was about equal to the US .30-cal. Their rifles, though, were longer, and in the hands of smaller troops were a bit more awkward to handle in the jungle.

The Springfield armed the Corps through Guadalcanal. In early 1943 the semi-automatic .30-cal. M1 Garand rifle began to replace the "03." By late 1943 the FMF was completely armed with the M1. To the old timers the introduction of the M1 foretold the doom of the legendary Marine Corps marksmanship. They decried the M1 as too heavy and bulky at 9lb 8oz (4.32kg; it was only a half-inch longer than the M1903), for being inaccurate, and too complex for dumb recruits to understand. The M1, however, proved to be a highly effective weapon, being fast to reload with an eight-round en bloc clip, and pumping out a higher rate of fire than an enemy armed with a five-shot bolt-action rifle. An M1-armed Marine could snap off 15–18 aimed shots in one minute, compared to an Arisaka-armed Japanese soldier's eight to ten rounds. While the rifle was a bit heavier than they would have liked, most Marines thought very highly of the M1, deeming it rugged and reliable, and they took extremely good care of it, as their lives and the lives of their buddies depended on its functioning.

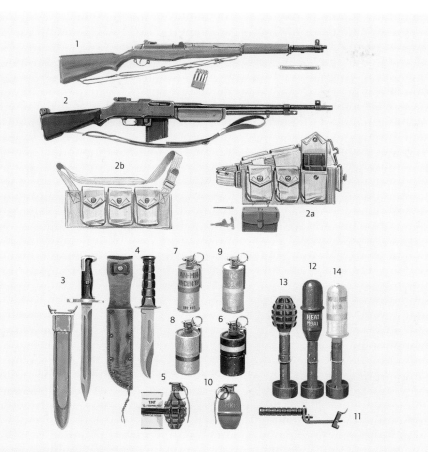

THE INFANTRYMAN'S WEAPONS

The rifle squad was armed with two basic weapons, the .30-cal. M1 Garand rifle (1) fed by an eight-round clip (this one with armor-piercing ammunition, as commonly used in combat) with an oiler tube carried in the butt trap, and the .30-cal. M1918A2 Browning Automatic Rifle (BAR) (2), here with its bipod and flash suppressor removed and a takedown tool and extractor for ruptured cartridges. The automatic rifleman carried a six-pocket belt with 12 20-round magazines and a leather spare parts and tool case (2a) while his assistant carried a slung belt with six magazines (2b). There were also supplementary weapons: M1 bayonet in an M7 fiberglass scabbard (3), KA-Bar fighting knife with its leather sheath (4), and a variety of grenades. The grenade types included the Mk IIA1 fragmentation (5), here with a ½lb (0.23kg) TNT charge taped on for pillbox busting, Mk IIIA1 offensive (6), AN-M14 thermite incendiary (7), and M15 white phosphorus (8), AN-M8 white smoke (9), and Mk 1 illuminating (10). The M7 grenade launcher (11) enabled M9A1 antitank (12), M17 fragmentation (13), and M19 white phosphorus (14) grenades, to be fired from the M1 rifle. (Howard Gerrard © Osprey Publishing)

With the rifle came a more basic weapon, the bayonet. The Japanese possessed a well-earned reputation for bayonet fighting, which they practiced for long hours, and the Marines were determined not to be outmatched. The 16in (40cm) bladed M1905 and M1942 bayonets were used on both the M1903 and M1. The 10in (25.4cm) M1905E1 and M1 bayonets began to be issued in 1943 to make them more usable at close-quarters. The Japanese had a 15½in (39.4cm) bayonet and a longer rifle, but their small stature limited their reach somewhat, and this was additionally countered by the typical Marine's longer reach. The M1 carbine was not provided with its M4 bayonet until almost the war's end. Springfields remained in use into 1944, as M7 rifle grenade launchers were not initially available for the M1 rifle, and stayed in use with ships' detachments, Marine barracks guards, and training and service units for some time. Rifle squads retained an M1903 with an M1 grenade launcher. The launchers gave the squad the ability to project grenades farther than hand-thrown grenades. Grenade types included M9A1 antitank, M17 fragmentation, M19 white phosphorus, and colored smoke and signal flares. Fragmentation hand grenades could also be fitted to a tailboom adapter and fired by grenade launchers. The M8 launcher was provided for the M1 carbine in 1944.

A weapon actually seeing wider use than the M1 rifle was the .30-cal. M1 carbine. A Marine division in 1943 had 8,000 rifles, but over 11,000 carbines. Officers, weapons crewmen, artillerymen, and most service and support personnel were armed with this light, compact weapon – a better alternative to the pistol. In fact, from April 1943 pistols were no longer issued to infantry and artillery regiments, being completely replaced by carbines. The semi-automatic carbine was fed by a 15-round detachable magazine. (The semi- and full-auto M2 with a 30-round magazine did not see combat in World War II.) The "baby Garand," as it was sometimes known, was initially popular and much sought after by Marines.

Machine gunners were trained on both the air-cooled M1919A4 light machine gun and the water-cooled M1917A1 heavy machine gun, pictured here. The brass water jacket end cap has been painted for camouflage and a blank adapter is fitted on the muzzle. (USMC)

It was light, compact, had a high-capacity magazine, and also looked slick. Once used in combat it was found wanting: while reliable enough it lacked range, penetration, and knockdown power. It used a smaller .30-cal. cartridge than the M1 rifle, BAR, and Browning machine gun, little more than a pistol round. Another problem was that it sounded like a Japanese 6.5mm rifle, so could attract friendly fire. From early 1944 the squad's three assistant automatic riflemen were armed with carbines, but these weapons were soon replaced with M1 rifles. Squad and platoon leaders were armed with carbines, but many units replaced these too with rifles or submachine guns. While both the rifle and the carbine were designated M1, Marines called the rifle simply the "M1" and the carbine just the "carbine."

Thompson submachine guns were not common in rifle platoons: in 1943 a division had a pool of 78. The Thompson had long been in use by the Corps, who had found it useful in the Banana Wars, but it was little used in the Pacific. Three versions of the .45-cal. "Tommy gun" were employed by the Corps, the M1928A1, M1, and M1A1. They used 20- and 30-round magazines and were heavy, almost 11lb (5kg), and complex to disassemble and assemble. Its penetration through bamboo and brush was limited and it unfortunately also sounded like a Japanese 6.5mm machine gun.

The .30-cal. M1918A2 Browning Automatic Rifle was the second most important weapon in the squad. Two were assigned, and, from early 1944, three. It was heavy at 19lb 6oz (8.9kg), and bulky at 4ft (1.22m) in length. The flash suppressor was often

Marines check a dugout for by passed enemy. This was a continual effort. Positions cleared of the enemy by assault troops had to be constantly rechecked – enemy stragglers and infiltrators sometimes re-occupied them. Likewise, discarded enemy and US weapons had to be rounded up to prevent their recovery by stragglers. (USMC)

removed to reduce its length by 3in (7.6cm), and detaching the bipod knocked off 2lb 8oz (1.14kg). Its 20-round magazines were heavy and deemed too small for sustained fire. It was accurate, though, and offered two rates of fire: the high 500–650rpm rate and the low 300–450rpm, the latter allowing single shots to be squeezed off. Yet the gun was complex and difficult to maintain. Marines were thankful that regulations prohibited white-glove inspections and timed disassembly and assembly. It was too easy to lose and damage the many small parts.

The hand grenade was another essential weapon. Grenades included the Mk II and Mk IIA1 "pineapple" fragmentation, Mk IIIA1 offensive "concussion" (½lb/0.23kg TNT) for blasting pillboxes, AN-M8 white smoke for screening, AN-M14 thermite incendiary for destroying enemy equipment, M15 white phosphorus (WP), and Mk 1 illuminating burning for 25 seconds at 55,000 candlepower to illuminate a 100-yard (90m) radius area. The WP was especially useful for knocking out pillboxes and attacking troops in uncovered positions. Burning WP particles showering into positions stuck to whatever they came in contact with. Panicked soldiers hit by WP might try to wipe the sticky substance off, burning at 5,000°F (2,760°C), only to smear it over a wider area as it burned through them. M16 and M18 colored smoke grenades were used to mark positions and provide simple signals. The M16 came in red, yellow, green, violet, orange, blue, and black. The M18 generated a more vivid smoke cloud more rapidly and was issued in only the first four colors. Colored smoke rifle grenades, and hand grenades, fitted to rifle grenade adapter tailbooms, were used to mark targets for tanks. Marines would remove the fuse and scrape out half the smoke compound, as the full load obscured the target. A basic load of "frag" grenades was two per man, but it was common to carry a "double-dose," a double load. Grenades were used in such enormous numbers that during some island fighting their use rate far exceeded forecasts and an emergency resupply of grenades had to be flown in, sometimes depleting depot stockpiles. A common technique was to "cook-off" frags, that is, pull the arming pin, release the safety lever, count to two or three, and chuck it into a firing port. Because the grenade had a 4.5–5-second delay the enemy did not have time to recover it and toss it out.

Using demolitions was an important skill. Each platoon had a trained demolition corporal in anticipation for a raiding mission. Raiding was not to be an infantry role in the Pacific, but the emphasis on demolitions served the Corps well, owing to the enemy's extensive use of pillboxes and caves. The two most common demolition items were the ½lb (0.23kg) TNT block, issued 100 in a wooden box, and the satchel charge. Multiple TNT blocks could be taped together, placed in sandbags or in other bags, or

Quartermasters inspect KA-Bar fighting knives, virtually a symbol of the Corps. The man to the right is checking the edge of a hospital corps knife. (USMC)

linked together with detonating cord, and detonated by a delay fuse ignited by a friction fuse lighter. Marines sometimes taped a TNT block to a frag grenade as a more potent pillbox popper. Satchel charges contained eight 2½lb (1.14kg) M2 tetrytol demolition blocks linked together by detonating cord at 8in (20cm) intervals as an M1 chain demolition charge. The 20lb (9kg) of explosives, slightly more powerful than TNT, were usually sufficient to destroy pillboxes. Another assault technique was to tape demolition charges to 81mm mortar shells and chuck them into caves.

Flamethrowers – "Zippos" or "Blowtorches" – did not see much use until the November 1943 Tarawa assault, but they proved invaluable for defeating pillboxes and caves. The M1A1 flamethrower was heavy – 70lb (32kg) with 4 gallons (15 liters) of thickened fuel. It was quite a load for a man to carry. An assistant operator would carry a 5-gallon (19-liter) refill fuel can and a spare compressed-gas propellant tank. The range with thickened fuel was up to 50 yards (46m), but in practice it was shorter. In a continuous burst the flamethrower could burn for eight to ten seconds, but two-second bursts were normal. Rather than waste fuel by burning it as it was fired at targets, operators would sometimes "wet-down" the pillbox with a spray of un-ignited fuel and then WP grenades or Molotov cocktails were thrown. It is an understatement to say flamethrower operators led dangerous and often short lives. The Japanese would put the hated weapon under intense fire (detonation of the fuel tanks seldom occurred, that is a Hollywood invention). Heat exhaustion from bearing the load was common.

The 2.36in M1A1 antitank rocket launcher was another key weapon. The "bazooka" or "stovepipe" was introduced in time for Tarawa and for the first time infantrymen had a light, portable direct-fire weapon capable of knocking out a tank or pillbox with a shaped-charge warhead. It had a range of 250 yards (226m) although more practical ranges were 50–70 yards (46–64m).

Flamethrowers and bazookas did not have dedicated crewmen; instead specially trained riflemen were assigned. The two weapons were pooled at battalion level and there were sufficient numbers to provide one per squad, although the Marines did not always use this many. Two more weapons found at company level, however, were provided with dedicated crews. The .30-cal. M1919A4 Browning LMG was a tripod-mounted weapon, of which three were assigned to the weapons platoon. Normally one would be attached to each rifle platoon. There were also three 60mm M2 mortars, the company commander's "hip-pocket artillery." These operated as a section under central control and could deliver high-explosive (HE) and WP rounds out to 1,985 yards (1,814m).

There is one final weapon that was important to the infantryman, the KA-Bar fighting knife, virtually a symbol of the Corps. The Union Cutlery Company offered its heavy-duty fighting knife to the Corps in 1942. The Marines adopted it and other companies also manufactured it, but it became popularly know as the "KA-Bar." The name came from a customer's endorsement, a fur trapper who crudely wrote that his rifle had jammed and he used their knife to kill a wounded bear attacking him. In thanking the company the trapper described using the knife to "kill a bar." The way his writing was scrawled across the paper, it looked like "ka bar." The quartermaster general advised against its adoption, claiming it was too expensive for the good it would do, and that too many Marines would be injured by their own knives. Fortunately the commandant ignored the recommendation.

BELIEF AND BELONGING

Faith in the Corps and loyalty to squad and platoon were the primary motivating factors for most Marines. Some veterans compare their indoctrination and compulsory dedication to the Corps to brainwashing, but few bear any regrets. They understood the necessity for cohesion, and the sense of belonging this instilled. Marines did not fight for America, the flag, democracy, or their families: they fought for one another, for their comrades, and the Corps recognized this.

Their motivation against the Japanese was another thing. It was basic – veterans simply said the "Japs," or "Nips" as they called them, were doing a wrong that had to be righted. If the enemy wanted to die for their emperor, the Marines would help them. The more the US troops heard about the Japanese, the more determined they were. Young Marines liked to win, and they did not like to see buddies killed. By 1945 the stories of the Japanese being supermen had been thoroughly dispelled. Nor did the stories of Japanese snipers, atrocities against Americans, and the fact that the Japanese never took prisoners, frighten them. The Marines felt they were better trained and equipped, and that right was on their side.

It was the old hands, the old salts among the NCOs and the prewar Marine officers with long service in Latin America, China, and at sea with the fleet, who instilled the traditions of the service that were so important to making the new Corps what it was. Nonetheless, they endlessly bemoaned the demise of the "Old Corps" prior to the 1940 expansion.

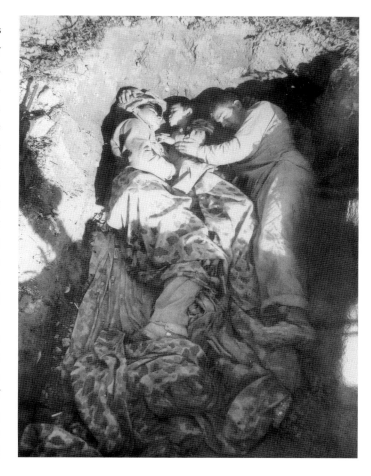

Behind the lines, two-man sleeping holes were dug as protection from artillery, mortars, and the occasional air attack. It was not uncommon for Marines to take children into "protective custody," probably thinking about their kid brothers at home. (USMC)

There is no disputing that life in the Corps was rough and demanding. The Corps came first, over family and self. Only the barest concerns were paid to comfort and diversions. The hours were long, the work hard, and the discipline harder. They hated Army "dogfaces" only because they were told by their NCOs that they were worthless, that they lacked pride and tradition. They really had no idea about the Army, having never worked with soldiers and only having seen some on leave, mainly antiaircraft and coastal artillery troops while on liberty.

The Marine's squad was his immediate family, a dozen men in whom he developed absolute trust. His platoon became an extended family under the guiding eye of its patriarch, the platoon commander, and even more so, the platoon sergeant, usually an old hand with prewar experience in exotic lands. The company commander, the "Skipper" or "Ol' Man" (usually in his mid 20s), oversaw his fiefdom aided by the

1st sergeant ("Top"). The Marine was imbued with a sense of total loyalty to his unit and the Corps. There is an old saying, "Once a Marine always a Marine." There is more truth to this than mere hype.

ASSIGNMENT TO UNIT

Following their successful completion of training, the new recruits would be assigned to a unit. The experience of each recruit varied according to the specific unit – its location, culture, focus etc. As an example, we can look more closely at the regiments that would comprise the 4th MarDiv. The regiments were organized prior to the creation of the division. The Corps had planned for three wartime divisions, but the escalating war resulted in the need for more. The first regiment to be activated was the 23rd Marines in July 1942 at New River, North Carolina. In February 1943 it was reassigned to the yet to be activated 4th MarDiv. In May 1943 the 23rd Marines was split to create the 25th Marines. This was a common practice, achieved by preparing two rosters and splitting every unit in half down to squad level. The old regiment's current commander would not know which roster he would draw, something decided by the flip of a coin with the commander of the new regiment. The next month, 14th and 20th Marines were raised, the future division's artillery and engineer regiments.

Folding cots were used in tent cities, here with a mosquito net rigged. A cot's taut canvas was akin to sleeping on a board and in cold weather was chilly unless insulated with layered blankets, which also served as padding. (USMC)

In July and August the four regiments moved by train to Camp Pendleton, California. There they joined the 24th Marines raised in March 1943. The 24th was organized from an unusual source. The 1st–3rd Separate Battalions (Reinforced) had been raised between October 1942 and February 1943 at Camp Lejeune to train infantrymen. They were shipped to Camp Pendleton and formed the 24th Marines. The 4th MarDiv was activated on August 16, 1943.

Each Marine was generally assigned to a unit in which the men were familiar with one another and were comfortable with their chain of command. The outsider, by contrast, knew no one. To make matters worse, the Dago recruit's new comrades would have trained at Parris Island and come from the eastern United States. Their attitude towards the new Marine would not be unlike that of students from a rival high school on the other side of town. He was not only a new man, but he was green, having just come out of training, and would have lived the despicable "soft life" the Hollywood Marines enjoyed at Dago. A new Marine would have to prove himself all over.

The 24th Marines had the benefit of not being split or providing large cadres for new units. It focused on training without too many disruptions. There were a few personnel shifted to other units within the regiment, while others were sent off to specialist schools and a few volunteered for Officer Candidate School (OCS). The specialist schools – division schools – provided one- and two-week courses on demolitions, scouting, machine guns, mortars, bazookas, flamethrowers, and antitank guns. Unit training progressed from squad to platoon, company, battalion, and finally regimental exercises, along with Command Post (CP) exercises to fine tune staffs. Sprawling Camp Joseph H. Pendleton provided the necessary maneuver space and ranges. It was on the coast 32 miles (51.5km) north of Dago, with plenty of beach space to practice amphibious landings. The Marines would come to know Pendleton's semi-desert hills and canyons well. The 200-square-mile (518 sq.km) former ranch had only been acquired in 1942 and facilities were still under construction. Regardless of the echelon of training underway, the squads and platoons practiced their skills, movement formations, fire and maneuver, patrolling, and living in the field. Small-unit training included night attacks, pillbox assault, and rubber-boat training. The Marines undertook small-arms firing both on ranges and as part of unit maneuvers – live-fire exercises – in which supporting weapons were employed. These included practice on moving-target ranges.

Individual training was not ignored. There were organized sports, plus training in hand-to-hand combat, bayonet and knife fighting, scouting, map reading, compass land navigation, map symbol identification, first aid, water survival, gas mask drills,

A company mail clerk picks up his unit's mail at the 4th MarDiv Post Office on Saipan. Mail call was one of the most anticipated events for deployed Marines. (USMC)

signaling techniques, hand and rifle grenades, demolitions, barbed wire breaching, and familiarization with all weapons within the company. There were full-equipment forced marches up to 25 miles (40km). While the artillery regiment moved to Camp Dunlap some 100 miles (160km) to the east for range firing, the infantry organized into Regimental Combat Teams (RCTs), and with engineers, pioneers, medical personnel, joint assault signalmen, and amphibian tractors (amtracs) they boarded transports in San Diego and conducted practice amphibious landings on Pendleton's Aliso Beach. Later the entire division loaded aboard transports and conducted landing exercises supported by live naval gunfire, several times, on San Clemente Island. They knew this was a rehearsal.

While the days were mild to hot, the nights were cold, and extra blankets were issued for the unheated tents. When there was no night training scheduled, troops had free time for movies at the six theaters, milk shakes at the PX, beer, sandwiches and snacks at the enlisted club ("slop chute"), arguments, card games, billiards, crap games, fist fights over the most trivial incidents (more for letting off steam and reinforcing unit reputations), and weekend liberty. There were endless talks about their lives and hopes, likes and dislikes, unfair policies, how they would run the Corps, talk of families, school day pranks, women, and what they would do after the war. Just about everyone had a nickname. It was not uncommon for veterans to remember their squad buddies only by nicknames or last names at the most. Many nicknames were attributable to physical characteristics (Four-Eyes, Red, Blackie, Leftie, Curly, Big…), character traits (Joker, Lover Boy, Slugger), or ethnic or cultural background (Wop, Dago, Wetback, Redneck, Hillbilly, Chief, Ski, Pedro, Dutch, and many more). These racial epithets may be difficult for today's readers to understand, but they were accepted and not considered offensive if used among buddies.

Liberty was special; the division's almost 18,000 men knew they were soon bound for "duty beyond the seas." Some felt they were on borrowed time. Others were going to enjoy what time they had before shipping out. Traveling by bus, train, or hitchhiking, they flooded into San Diego, Los Angeles, and Oceanside beyond the main gate. Liberty was granted for 24 or 48 hours; seldom was a 76- or 96-hour liberty given. Friday afternoons at 1700hrs they hit the showers, cleaned up, and made certain their uniforms were shipshape. Bars, night clubs, boxing matches, and movies were popular. Professional prostitutes ("street-walkers") and amateur equivalents ("victory girls") at $3–$10 were plentiful, as was a cheap local wine called "Dago Red." Contracting a venereal disease was a chargeable offense. It was the Marine's responsibility to use condoms and visit a prophylaxis station or use a pro-kit after his "date." "Short arm" inspections were conducted, with Marines falling out wearing only raincoats and jock straps for inspection by medical personnel. A toilet stall in the head was reserved for those contracting VD.

They crawled back by midnight on Sunday and fell in for reveille in various states of alertness. Most of the east coast Marines soon forgot their animosity toward their Hollywood Marine brethren, especially when it was found that they were not really issued sunglasses. The new antagonists were the sailors and Marines comprising the Shore Patrol (SP). Any misconduct on liberty brought them charging in, followed by fist fights and arrests. SPs showed no favoritism regardless of their parent branch.

CONDITIONS OF SERVICE

The inside of a barracks was something a Marine seldom saw, as his life was designed to keep him busy elsewhere. While his training unit may have been assigned a Quonset hut, a wood-frame and tar paper hut, or wooden or even brick barracks with indoor head, his squad more likely lived in a squad tent in a remote part of the base. They spent so much time in the field living under two-man "pup tents" that Marines often forgot what a four-sided room looked like. On larger bases, tent cities or simple wooden barracks housed infantry and other units in scattered sub-camps. These were self-contained with headquarters and administrative buildings, mess halls, warehouses, dispensary, PX, movie theater, chapel, slop chute, and NCO and staff NCO clubs (highest three grades).

Life in the field was preferred by many Marines. There was not so much spit-shine and the priority was on training, not work details and harassment by NCOs. If not living in pup tents, they lived in tent cities among neat rows of squad tents, divided by grid pattern into company streets. The eight-man pyramid tents were 15 x 15ft (4.5 x 4.5m), square in shape with wooden decks. Their sides could be rolled up in hot weather, but this exposed them to the persistent dust. Even with the sides up the sun made them uncomfortably hot, but the Marines spent little time in them during the day. The Marines slept on folding canvas cots or sometimes regular barrack bunks, and lived out of their sea bags. It was a continuous battle to keep uniforms, gear, and quarters clean. With the rains the dust turned into a particularly gummy mud that was no less troublesome than the dry dust.

Marines were encouraged to write home, and likewise families were urged to write frequently to their servicemen. Aboard ship and overseas, postage was free except for

En route to an island objective, Marines spent much of their time undertaking innumerable tasks to prepare for action. Here Marines belt .50-cal. machine-gun ammunition, inserting tracers every fifth round. (USMC)

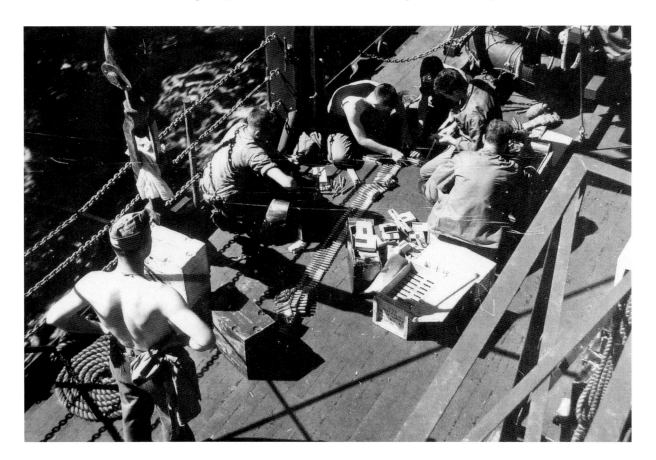

parcels. Of the many lectures Marines received, one was concerned with safeguarding military information. They were cautioned not to write about unit location, strength, equipment, military installations, transport facilities, convoys (particularly their routes

"DUTY BEYOND THE SEA"

In the days before a landing, part of the time aboard ship was spent undertaking individual preparations. Many men unclipped M1 rifle ammunition, cleaned each round, and re-clipped it. BAR men loaded their magazines, bayonets and knives were sharpened, rations and gear packed, every item checked. The three fire teams of the new 13-man squad operated as an entity. In effect the squad leader only had to direct three men, the team leaders. Team leaders led by example: whatever they did, as directed by the squad leader, their teams would do. When he got up and moved forward his team would follow. When he fired they would fire in the same direction. Each fire team had a corporal team leader, an automatic rifleman, an assistant automatic rifleman, and a rifleman. All but the BAR man had grenade launchers. The squad concept took into account that under heavy fire small groups of men managed to advance forward, so squads were organized into self-contained teams to accommodate this. Each division was assigned a geometric symbol in which a three- or four-digit number indicated the unit down to company level. The numbering system varied between divisions. Here Company I, 1st Battalion, 24th Marines is identified. Besides marking clothing, unit equipment and crates were also so marked. One Marine wears a camouflage-painted helmet liner and another the 1941 utility cover. (Howard Gerrard © Osprey Publishing) and destinations), plans for future operations, or the effect of enemy actions. They were also urged not to discuss the names of casualties for fear of family members receiving word before military authorities notified them of details. Most of all they were warned not to give out their location other than "somewhere in the Pacific." Mail was censored by officers. They were also told to keep their mouths shut and not talk about these aspects to anyone. An official directive cautioned, "If you come home during the war your lips must remain sealed and your written hand must be guided by self-imposed censorship. This takes guts. Have you got them or do you want your buddies and your country to pay the price for your showing off? You've faced the battle front; it's little enough to ask you to face this home front."

On July 1, 1942, US servicemen of all branches of service received a considerable boost in pay. Prior to that date a private was paid $31 a month. They now drew $50 ($1.67 per day) on pay day – "eagle s**ts" – the month's last Friday. Pay was also based on time in service, with a 3 percent increase given every three years to a maximum of 50 percent of base pay. After one year's service, a $35-a-year clothing allowance was paid in quarterly installments of $8.75 to replace worn-out items. Those so fortunate as to qualify as an Expert Rifleman received another $5.

Overseas a Marine's finances improved somewhat. He received an additional 20 percent over his base pay for Sea or Foreign Shore Pay – "overseas pay." For a private this was $10 a month. Awards of the Medal of Honor, Distinguished Service Medal, Distinguished Flying Cross, or Navy Cross earned a man $2 per month. When engaged in combat Marines were not paid until they returned to base. This system resulted in numerous crap and poker games, with Japanese souvenirs also offered as bets. There was no specific combat pay during the war. Servicemen did not pay Federal Income Tax or Social Security. While their souls belonged to the Corps, Marines did retain certain rights. These included the right to vote in national elections, and all but three states (Delaware, Kentucky, and New Mexico) permitted absentee voting in local elections. Most Marines, however, did not bother to vote.

A Marine could elect to allot an automatic pay deduction to his wife or parents. For wives and unemployed parents or a widowed parent the government would match the deduction. The Servicemen's Dependents' Allowance of July 23, 1942, allowed men in grades 4–7, the four lowest grades, to make automatic pay deductions up to $27.50 for certain relatives (unemployed parents, siblings) or dependents (wife, children). A Marine's wife with no children received $50 a month, a wife with one child $62, wife with two children $72, and wife with three children $82. Out of his remaining pay the Marine paid $6.40 for National Serviceman's Life Insurance and roughly $5 for

Rear-area tent camps were built of shelter-halves rigged as fly tents and cots with mosquito nets provided. Note the US Marine Corps towel right and above the standing man, a white towel with white letters on a red strip. (USMC)

laundry. After shoe polish, cigarettes, toothpaste, stationery, postage stamps, other necessities, and the occasional soft drink, beer, candy bar or visit to the base theater, there was not much money left for liberty. This explained why many simply stayed on base at the slop chute or visited the off-base United Service Organization (USO) Club for free entertainment and snacks.

Since the Marine Corps was classed as a component of the Navy Department, it relied on the Navy for some of its logistical and material support. Much of the equipment, some weapons, and most general supplies were used by the Navy. Some equipment was Army issue and only a small percentage was unique to the Corps. All medical personnel supporting the Corps were of the Navy Medical Corps (physicians and surgeons), Dental Corps, Medical Service Corps (medical administrative officers, pharmacists, technologists, etc.), and Hospital Corps (hospital warrant officers and enlisted medical Corpsmen). Apart from providing most of the personnel for FMF medical units, naval personnel operated base hospitals, dispensaries, and dental clinics. A Marine division contained almost 1,100 Navy medical personnel. The medical battalion was assigned almost 600 personnel, but about four-fifths were Marine service troops. An infantry regiment headquarters and service company had 24 Navy medical personnel, and 44 within a battalion.

Navy chaplains ministered to the Corps and the Judge Advocate General's Office provided lawyers, although there were some Marine lawyers. Another naval element was the Naval Construction Battalion (NCB – "Seabees") assigned to divisions until the fall of 1944. This battalion was manned by over 800 specialized construction personnel. An NCB would remain attached to divisions for combat operations.

Sailors assigned to Marine units wore Marine uniforms with Navy rank and undertook tactical training provided by the Corps. Navy hospital Corpsmen were detailed from battalion to each rifle platoon. The Corpsmen were considered the integral part of each platoon and were universally known as "Doc" or "Bones." Most Marines did not realize their Corpsman was often a conscientious objector.

COMBAT CASE STUDY – THE ATTACK ON ROI-NAMUR

By the time of the Iwo Jima action in 1945, the USMC had gained huge amounts of combat experience, and had tasted both defeat and a string of hard-won victories. The following case study explores a major USMC action of 1943, and it illustrates many

The 24th Marines fighting on Namur in 1943 found the island totally devastated by naval and aerial bombardment, to the point that it was almost impossible in many areas to identify landmarks. The key buildings were simply shattered and roads covered with debris. (USMC)

of the lessons that US forces would take with them to Iwo Jima. It also shows how US Marines fought at the small-unit level.

A lot of Marines had hoped for a Christmas leave in 1943. It would be the first time home for many of them since joining the Corps. "Scuttlebutt," or rumors, however, were spreading fast about deploying. They were given a short liberty and began ferrying loaded trucks to the port of San Diego where details were formed to combat-load transports, LSDs (Landing Ship, Dock), and LSTs (Landing Ship, Tank). Amtracs and tanks were railroaded south to the port. The slow LSDs and LSTs with the artillery and amtracs departed on January 6 and 7, 1944, followed by transports on the 13th. The 4th MarDiv was about to make history by being the first US division in the Pacific to be committed directly to combat from the States, and would cover the longest distance of any amphibious assault, 4,300 miles (6,920km; surpassed only by the British Falklands expedition in 1982).

Once America had disappeared below the horizon, the troops were informed of their objective, the twin islands of Roi-Namur on the north end of Kwajalein Atoll, located inside the Marshall Islands. They would also conduct the first

Namur Blockhouse Assault. Flamethrowers had seen limited use in the Solomons, but the old M1 "Zippo" suffered from problems. They came into somewhat wider use on Tarawa and the bazooka made its first appearance there. These weapons would see wider use at Roi-Namur, but it would not be until the summer of 1944 that they came into wide general use. (Howard Gerrard © Osprey Publishing)

assault on territory held by the Japanese before the war. These two small islands were linked by a sandbar and causeway. Roi possessed a Japanese Navy airfield and Namur was crowded with support facilities and quarters. Operation *Flintlock* was in motion.

The Marines aboard their transports were getting used to their new world. Few had been to sea for a prolonged period. The exercises had seen them aboard ship no more than a night or two. With the focus on exercises there had been no need to fall into shipboard routine. Now quarters were tight, with troops bunked in three- to five-tier racks. Their sea bags were in the hold and the slung 782 gear and weapons made conditions even more cramped. The hot, stifling air below decks was stale, so troops spent their days on deck. Many slept on deck, as the steel ships absorbed heat all day and did not cool. Training continued with lectures in map reading, first aid, use of weapons, etc. A lot of time was spent practicing weapons crew drill, firearms disassembly and assembly, loading ammunition belts and magazines, sharpening knives and bayonets, and occasional weapons firing at floating barrels. There were daily calisthenics and regular weapons cleaning to prevent the firearms rusting in the salt air. Much time was spent in chow lines. With three big meals a day and limited exercise, some men skipped certain meals and the endless lines. The food was simple, sometimes monotonous. There were lifeboat and fire drills. Some men stood watch scanning for periscopes, torpedo wakes, and aircraft on the horizon.

Soon briefings were being held among the officers and then presented to the troops. Among the many briefings the Marines were told how to perform if captured: If captured, you are required to give only three facts: name, grade, serial number. Don't talk, don't try to fake stories and use every effort to destroy all papers. When you are going into an area where capture is possible, carry only essential papers and plan to destroy them. Do not carry personal letters; they tell much about you, and the envelope has your unit on it. Be sensible, use your head.

They knew the reality though. No Marine had been taken prisoner since the fall of the Philippines. The enemy took no prisoners, nor were the Marines inclined to.

Marines were taught the importance of live prisoners, but they were few and far between. Marine tactical intelligence collection efforts had been sloppy in the early days. Marines were now strongly encouraged to turn in captured maps, diaries, documents, and equipment.

Roi-Namur was defended by over 3,500 Imperial Navy guard troops, air service personnel, and laborers. Accurate and objective island maps were scarce. Those provided for operations were made from aerial photographs. The division D-2 (intelligence) produced sketch maps of island objectives and these were given to each Marine to study. These showed roads, trails, obstacles, key terrain features, and known fortifications and obstacles. They were not to be taken ashore.

Rubber-molded terrain models of the objective island were prepared by divisional engineers. These 3-D maps depicted natural and manmade features and key points were tagged with their actual or code names. The models were passed from unit to unit and the troops had ample time to memorize the terrain. They were also provided with recent aerial and submarine periscope photos of the coast. Platoons and companies discussed their movements on the terrain board. Leaders had to know the actions of the next higher element in case they had to take command, and even individual Marines would be familiar with their higher and adjacent units' missions.

A representative unit was 1st Squad, 2nd Platoon, Company C, 1st Battalion, 24th Marines. Company C – Charlie Company (lettered companies were commonly referred to by their phonetic alphabet name) – was usually shown as C/24 Marines. The battalion designation was not included as the initiated knew that A–D belonged to 1st Battalion, E–H to 2nd Battalion, and I–M (no "J") to 3rd Battalion. Companies D, H, and M were weapons companies with .30-cal. M1917A1 water-cooled HMGs and 81mm M1 mortars. Battalions were called, for example, "One/Twenty-Four Marines," not "1st of the 24th" as was Army practice.

Wounded Marines were taken to battalion aid stations, then to the regimental aid station. Sometimes, especially in static situations, small company aid stations were established. Here slit trenches have been dug for protection from small-arms and mortar fire. (USMC)

Since 1930 the term "regiment" has not been required to be included in the designation, nor was a functional designation used. The regiment was simply the 24th Marines – it was incorrect to call it the "24th Marine Infantry Regiment." (While seemingly plural, regiments are habitually addressed in the singular pronoun context as "it" rather than "they.") The regiment was the Marine's tribe, and he identified with the regiment even more closely than his division.

The 1st Squad consisted of 12 men, a "buck" sergeant (the lowest rank of sergeant) squad leader, a corporal assistant squad leader, two automatic riflemen and their assistants, and six riflemen. All hands were armed with the M1 rifle, with the exception of the automatic riflemen with BARs. One man had an M7 grenade launcher. The platoon headquarters consisted of the platoon leader, a 2nd lieutenant, platoon sergeant (both his duty position and rank title), a sergeant platoon guide, demolition corporal, and three messengers. One messenger would be detailed to the company headquarters and a Corpsman (pharmacist mate 2nd or 3rd class, grade 4 or 3) would be attached from the battalion medical section.

Marines carried three types of rations in combat. K-rations, the most widely issued, consisted of breakfast, dinner, and supper meals in individual pocket-size cartons. It was a lean meal, but provided over 3,000 calories in all three meals. A D-ration was a 4oz (113g) vitamin-enriched chocolate bar, a special "tropical chocolate" resistant to melting. C-rations were issued with three meals in a single carton; three cans of meat products and three cans with crackers, instant coffee, and cocoa. C-rations were heavy and bulky and were usually consumed by support troops. Marines would heat the K-ration meat unit, a small can, using heat tablets if the situation allowed, but more often they were eaten cold. They were monotonous, greasy, and not very filling. D-ration bars supplemented the Ks and provided a back-up if out of Ks. A problem encountered in combat was that stressed Marines pumped up with adrenaline in a hot, humid climate, and with limited opportunities to eat, often ate only one or two rations a day. This, coupled with dehydration and lack of sleep, weakened them and increased the chance of combat fatigue and heat exhaustion.

ASSAULT ON ROI-NAMUR

D-1 (January 30, 1944) was a flurry of activity throughout Task Force 53 as it approached the north corner of Kwajalein Atoll and Roi-Namur. The Army's 7th Infantry Division would assault Kwajalein Island some 40 miles (64km) to the south. Carrier aircraft began pounding the still unseen islands. USAAF bombers had been blasting the islands for months. Equipment was being readied, amtracs and landing craft prepared. Officers and NCOs gave pep talks, chaplains made their rounds, and Marines wrote letters home. They knew and were reminded that not all would reembark. The landing force was acutely aware of 2nd MarDiv's ordeal on Tarawa two months before.

The attack force took up station outside the huge lagoon before dawn on D-Day. A number of tiny outlying islands first had to be secured before the main February 1 assault. Artillery landed on these small islands to provide fire support. Reveille was early and the troops had been up for hours before the 0712hrs sunrise. They received the traditional breakfast of steak and eggs. The guns of 29 battleships, cruisers, and destroyers commenced firing on the tiny islands before sunrise and carrier strikes rolled in. The endless gun flashes lit up the sea and the Marines could see smoke and dust-obscured flashes on their target islands.

Rain squalls drifted through overcast skies. The winds were 20mph (32km/h) and the sea was rougher than expected. Marines lined the railings to watch Regimental

As Marines pushed inland on Roi-Namur, company and battalion mortars were set up to provide immediate fire support. Here an 81mm M1 mortar squad pumps out high-explosive and white phosphorus rounds. (USMC)

Combat Team 25 (RCT25) in its all-day fight to clear the outlying islets. While resistance was minimal, the operation quickly ran into difficulties. The rough seas forced amtracs back to half speed, sea spray drowned radios, and it became quickly apparent that the amtrac crews of the new battalion were poorly trained – the rehearsals in California had been inadequate. The six islets, however, were all secured by 1716hrs. RCT25 was reassigned as the Division Reserve for the next day's main assault. RCT23 would seize Roi and RCT24 Namur.

W-Hour was set at 1000hrs on February 1, but problems were developing even before dawn. (Note that H-Hour normally identified the time an assault would commence, but to prevent confusion other letters were used to designate the assault times for different islands in the same area.) The amtrac battalion that would land RCT24 had been used for the outlying island assaults, and suffered from mechanical failures, damage, and inability to refuel from LSTs. Many amtracs were simply lost and sitting out the night on islets, and little over half the necessary amtracs were assembled for the operation. From their transports the Marines were boated to LSTs inside the lagoon aboard LCVPs (Landing Craft, Vehicle, Personnel). They boarded their amtracs inside the LSTs rather then doing so on open water. Charlie Company was in the reserve battalion and would follow the 2nd and 3rd Battalions on to Namur. The nervous Marines were quietly grateful to be in the reserve. There was excitement and tension in the air, though. The Marines of 1st Squad remained aboard LCVPs, as they were the reserve of the reserve battalion.

The palm- and brush-covered island was shrouded in dust and smoke, with shell bursts erupting continuously. To the left barren Roi was likewise obscured. Destroyers were slamming rounds into the 800 x 890-yard (731 x 813m) island and Landing Craft, Infantry (LCI; Gunboat) vessels were rippling out loose barrages of rockets. From the left the regimental weapons company and three battalion weapons companies pre-positioned on tiny Abraham islet poured machine-gun, antitank gun, and mortar fire onto Namur. Low in the water, the Marines could see little of the amtracs ahead of them through the drifting smoke and mist. Word was passed that companies had been rearranged, and amtracs taken from the battalion reserve companies were given to the assault companies, which were short of the vehicles.

W-Hour was delayed until 1200hrs, but finally the red Baker flag was lowered on the control craft and the amtracs began their run in, with 1st Battalion following. The LCIs were firing streams of tracers into the smoke cloud shrouding the island. Men peering over the sides were speculating if there would be any Japanese troops left. Non-coms were telling them not to worry, there would be plenty left to kill. The naval bombardment had only had mediocre success in the past. The men of Charlie Company could not see the actual landing, but before long amtracs were churning past them on their way back to the LSTs.

Expecting to find the narrow beaches littered with dead Marines, Charlie Company rushed out when the ramps were dropped directly on to Beach Green 2, the men hardly experiencing wet feet. The din of firing and explosions was continuous, the acid smoke gagging. While there were no casualties evident, there was a great deal of confusion. Men from the assault battalions' reserve companies were scattered about the beach, officers were trying to get their bearings, and beach party personnel collected ammunition boxes and water cans that had been tossed over the sides of amtracs as reserve stocks as they came ashore. The word was that companies had intermingled or were in the wrong places. Resistance had been light, but this did not sound like the case farther inland. Amphibious tanks were still on the beach, having been halted by the seawall, antitank ditches, and rubble covering the island from the many shattered buildings. The same was true for the amtracs, which were supposed to have disembarked their troops 100 yards (91m) inland. Baker Company had been attached to 3rd Battalion and was already fighting its way inland.

The O-1 Line (Objective 1 Line, the line the Marines hoped to secure the first day) had just been reached by most units. Then, as Charlie Company was forming up to move inland, an indescribable detonation rocked the island at 1300hrs. A Company

Japanese prisoners were rare. Not only did most fight to the death or take their own lives, Marines were only too happy to help them on their way. Most prisoners taken on islands were actually Korean or Okinawan laborers. Prisoners were stripped down to loincloths because of the danger of concealed grenades. (USMC)

F Marine had unknowingly thrown a satchel charge into a torpedo storage bunker. The resulting explosion killed 20 Marines and wounded 100 across the island, and left a 100ft (30m) diameter crater. Company F lost a third of its strength. A massive cloud of black smoke and coral dust rushed across the island and towered over 1,000ft (305m) above the island. Chunks of concrete, coral rocks, and palm trunks rained across the island and lagoon, hitting some men. Firing actually paused for a few minutes. The blast so disrupted 2/24 that it was unable to continue the attack. This rattled the troops, but the company moved out into the shroud of smoke, to be attached to 2/24 and placed in the line between Fox and Echo Companies. The island was unrecognizable. Even large buildings counted on as landmarks were gone and the 6ft (1.8m) high brush further limited visibility. The grid-like system of roads was so covered by debris that it was unidentifiable. Marine dead began to be encountered and wounded were trickling back on litters or walking on their own. The land was also littered with dead Japanese – because of lessons learned at Tarawa, the naval gunfire was so effective that an estimated 50–75 percent of the defenders were killed before the landing. The scenes were sickening, but the boys pressed on, not wanting to show any uneasiness: they had to demonstrate their toughness among peers. Firing increased, appearing to come from all directions, and tension increased.

More tanks landed in the late afternoon and moved inland to support the assault. Progress was made inland on the left in the 3/24 zone, which was less affected by the blast. Most units managed to push beyond the O-1 Line, although reaching this line did not mean they would halt for the day. At 1930hrs the regiment was ordered to dig in for the night; sunset was at 1945hrs. This was a common mistake. The Marines had pushed ahead to clear as much ground as fast as possible, but it gave them little daylight to establish their night defense, reconnoiter the ground before them, redistribute ammunition, and receive supplies. The men on Namur did not know that Roi, mostly covered by an airfield, had been secured three hours earlier.

Marines and their buddies quickly scraped out foxholes behind a pile of rubble and made sure where the adjacent holes were. Once night fell a Marine could not leave his hole under any circumstances for fear of being shot by his own men. In theory the Marines would take turns sleeping, but this being their first night in combat, sleep was impossible. It was a long night filled with fear and weariness. There were rifle cracks and bursts of machine-gun fire, with American red tracers going outward and Japanese pink and pale blue tracers incoming. US troops considered the Japanese tracers wimpy, but they would still kill. Destroyers fired star shells all through the night, casting the rubble and brush before them in an eerie yellow glow, criss-crossed with constantly drifting shadows. Every rubble pile and bush would look like a creeping enemy – some in fact were enemy soldiers trying to infiltrate, typically shouting "Hey, Joe!" or "Corpsman!" in an attempt to get the Marines to reveal their positions by firing.

As the sun rose the Marines hurriedly ate their K-rations. A weak counterattack hit the line on the island's west portion and was beaten back with the assistance of tanks. Ammunition, water, and more rations were distributed. The Marines were constantly told not to drink any water found on the island, only to fill their canteens from the 5-gallon (19-liter) cans brought forward. They were briefed by their squad leader and at 0900hrs the US attack commenced. Tank support did not arrive on time, however, being held up by the battered terrain, and the attack was delayed an hour. Three-quarters of the island had been taken the day before, so the remaining distance to the north shore was crossed by 1215hrs. Two hours later the island was declared secure.

It was a good first operation for the 4th MarDiv. One commander declared the clearing of the islands to be a "pip." The Marines had the advantage of a great many lessons learned by other units on the earlier South Pacific operations to make their job easier.

A battalion beach aid station on Namur. Aid stations landed right behind the assault waves. Casualties on the beach were collected and the flow of casualties from the front began immediately. (USMC)

Fire discipline had been lax and control measures poor in some instances, mainly owing to the light resistance and relieved Marines pushing ahead too fast and far. The operation had cost the division 287 dead and missing and 617 wounded. They killed at least 3,570 Japanese and took 90 prisoner. They had gotten off lightly. Most troops barely saw over 24 hours of action. It was a good way to become bloodied, though. The Marines learned enough to fine tune their procedures and correct deficiencies without having to make such adjustments while embroiled in intense combat over a prolonged period.

There was still mopping up to do. Even with their hatred of the Japanese this was an unpleasant task. They were told to take prisoners, although the operation was over and they would provide little useful information. It was known that the officers would never surrender (there were rare exceptions). Intelligence always hoped that signalmen or other knowledge specialists might be captured. The few prisoners were mostly Korean laborers. The Marines generally equated the mop-up with a rabbit hunt. Lines of troops would sweep the island in succession, searching destroyed pillboxes, rubble buildings, and holes. "Searching" usually entailed shouting for anyone in there to come out; if there was no answer or an answering shot a grenade or demo change was chucked in. No one considered a live prisoner worth a single Marine. The few prisoners were ordered to *Ha-daka-ni-nare* ("Take off your clothes!"), stripped down to loincloths, and marched to the rear. There was a valid fear of their hiding grenades on themselves.

In mid February the 4th MarDiv set sail for Hawaii. The morning before, Japanese flying boats had bombed Roi, destroying fuel and ammunition dumps and inflicting 330 casualties, mostly Seabees. Most of the Marines were on Namur or already aboard ship.

Mop-up went on for days and even weeks after an island was declared secure ("secure" meaning that organized resistance had ceased). These Marines are searching for signs of Japanese infiltrators. In the background is a Japanese Daihatsu landing barge and a stranded Sherman M4 tank with fording vents. (USMC)

REST AND RECOVERY

The 4th MarDiv transports reached Maui (between Oahu and the island of Hawaii) a week and a half later and occupied a new camp at Kahului Harbor, which became their camp after each operation. The complete facilities of a division camp were erected to include the typical amenities. The area was beautiful and the locals hospitable. The main complaints were the incessant rain, mud, and high winds. All forms of entertainment were available, including movie theaters, playhouses, and a large organized sports program that fostered competition between unit teams, with baseball being the most popular sport. Training continued of course. There were 47 training areas and numerous ranges.

Tactical exercises, CP exercises, range firing, compass courses, landing exercises, and forced marches were frequent. The crater of Haleamkala volcano, the world's largest extinct volcano, served as a superb obstacle course. Division schools provided a jungle training center and village, cave, infiltration, and fortified-area fighting courses. The latter had 22 pillboxes and emplacements concealed among trees, brush, and bamboo. All elements of the division were able to perfect their skills and conduct joint training. The lessons learned on Roi-Namur were worked into training and staff planning.

New men to replace casualties and the new billets resulting from the reorganization were assigned from replacement battalions from the United States. Because of fresh personnel and the need to conduct extensive unit training under the new organization, and sometimes train with new equipment, a problem was encountered with veterans. They had already conducted extensive training, been in combat, and felt they knew their duties. They resented having to undertake what they now considered as boring training for the benefit of new hands. Another problem on Maui was the sometimes monotonous diet: fried Spam, stewed tomatoes, and sliced pineapple for breakfast and baked Spam, breaded tomatoes, and diced pineapple for supper.

The division underwent further reorganization in February and March. The new Table of Organization affected all elements of the division. The engineer regiment was to have been deactivated with the return of the Seabee battalion to the Navy, and the engineer and pioneer battalions would become separate units. However, the 2nd, 3rd, and 4th MarDivs preparing for the Marianas campaign had already developed their tactical plans, so the regiments were temporarily retained. The infantry battalions lost their weapons companies, resulting in Companies D, H, and M being disbanded. The rifle companies, however, retained their original lettering. The weapons companies' machine guns were incorporated into the rifle companies and the 81mm mortar platoon assigned to the battalion headquarters company. The rifle company's weapons platoon was redesignated a machine-gun platoon and armed with six M1919A4 LMGs (a section of two machine guns was to be attached to each rifle platoon), plus it had six M1917A1 HMGs as substitutes. The 60mm mortar section was reassigned to the company headquarters.

The rifle platoon headquarters did not change, but the rifle squads underwent a drastic change. There were now 13 men, a squad leader and three four-man fire teams. A great deal of time was spent practicing three-fire-team movement formations, and assault techniques, with teams alternating covering fire and maneuver.

On May 29, 1944, the 4th MarDiv departed Maui for Saipan. The 2nd and 4th MarDiv landed on the lower west coast on June 15.

CASUALTIES

In the face of blistering Japanese defenses on many of the Pacific islands, large numbers of Marines ended their war as dead or wounded. Those who were wounded, and who had the strength to do so, yelled "Sailor, Sailor" to call for the Corpsman. Marines had learned not to shout "Corpsman," as this alerted the enemy that a Corpsman would soon appear. For the same reason, Corpsmen did not wear red cross armbands or a red cross on their helmets. They carried carbines or pistols to protect their patients and themselves.

Medical units in the combat zone stabilized the wounded and kept them alive long enough to make it to surgery. When "Doc" arrived he would rip or cut open the victim's clothing, then sprinkle sulfa power on the wounds (to prevent infection) and place field dressings on the larger injuries. The medic would then drag the man to cover, assure him that he would be okay, and disappear in search of other wounded. A litter team would pick the wounded Marine up and lug him to the battalion aid station. If necessary, he was given a morphine syrette and eight sulfa tablets with a canteen cup of water (the tablets were never to be taken without water), but if his wounds were minor he was pretty much ignored. Eventually a Corpsman checked his casualty tag and loaded him into a "Duck" amphibious truck, which was driven across the beach and through the water to a transport. Correspondents often commented on how quiet and steady wounded US troops were as their litters were loaded into landing craft bound for an assault transport. Hoisted aboard, the wounded man's litter was set on deck before he was carried into the sickbay. En route it was typical for sailors to ask the wounded Marine if he had any Japanese souvenirs, as such items would have a good trade value on board the ship and back at home.

Transports were equipped with operating rooms, sickbay wards, and a complete medical staff. Once treated, the more seriously wounded were transferred to hospital ships for return to Hawaii or nearer island bases for further treatment. The chances of surviving serious wounds were twice as high in World War II as in World War I. Penicillin (from 1944), sulfa drugs, sufficient supplies of plasma and whole blood, and effective surgery were responsible for this. If the Marine recovered enough, he would rejoin his regiment, but not necessarily his original platoon or company.

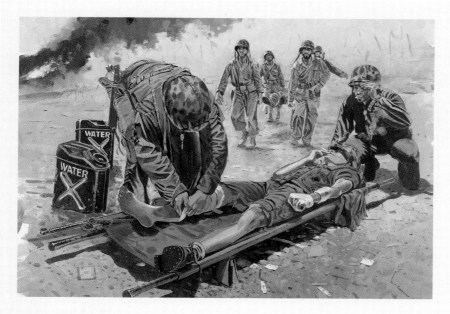

SAIPAN AID STATION
Before the war two men were specified for litter carriers, but the realities of combat made it apparent that four were necessary to move a casualty to safety quickly under fire over rough terrain in order for him not succumb to exhaustion caused by the environment and combat. Litter bearers were provided by the division band and from service units, often volunteers. This corpsman, a pharmacist's mate 2nd class, carried the unit's three medical pouches containing large and small field dressing, gauze rolls and pads, adhesive tape, tourniquets, iodine swabs, petrolatum, sulfa powder and tablets, morphine syrettes, casualty tags, scissors, forceps, safety pins, and other items. The corpsman also carries a .30-cal. M1 carbine, and a machete-like hospital corps knife. Five-gallon (19-liter) water cans were identified from fuel cans by white-painted crosses or "WATER" stenciled on the upper sides. (Howard Gerrard © Osprey Publishing)

Casualties went beyond those downed by enemy fire. Combat fatigue took a high toll. The prolonged stress, sleep deprivation, poor and irregular food, the enervating heat and humidity, dehydration, and physical and mental exhaustion brought many out of the line. Some required extensive treatment as they had pushed themselves to the limit. Most needed a hot meal, water, and a few hours' sleep to put them back in the line. Almost all combat troops suffered from combat fatigue at one time or another. Malaria, dysentery, dengue fever, and "undiagnosed fevers" were all problems. Most island campaigns suffered under massive clouds of flies owing to the numerous unburied bodies and this resulted in many illnesses, especially diarrhea (known as "GIs" or "sh**s"). Flies and mosquitoes were so bad that torpedo-bombers would fly over islands spraying DDT in the midst of combat. Accidental casualties were also frequent and not included in combat casualty figures. These included dead and injured from work and vehicle accidents, falls, drowning, fires, electrocution, etc.

Major efforts were made to account for casualties as soon as possible. This was difficult because of the cross-attachment of elements between units and the chaotic fighting. If a Marine was killed, wounded, or missing, his next of kin were notified by telegram. Over the subsequent months letters of condolence might be received from the War Finance Committee (which would dedicate a combat aircraft in his name), from senators and congressmen, and an engraved Purple Heart was sent by Headquarters, Marine Corps. If the Marine was killed, a killed in action (KIA) certificate was sent, along with any campaign and unit award decorations. After the war families were notified that they had the option of requesting that their Marine's remains be returned home for burial in a Veteran's Administration Cemetery (at no cost) or a private plot. If they opted to let him remain in an overseas cemetery with his buddies, a sentiment held by many, they could not later change their minds. If a Marine was reported missing he continued to accrue pay for one year, less allotments to relatives and savings accounts. If no further information became available he would be assumed dead and all pay was stopped.

For the living the Marines had intended to implement a rotation system, but because of the expansion of units and higher than expected losses it was two years or much longer before the Marines rotated home. In 1945 a point system was instituted to rotate men home (initially 85 points were required, but the number was later lowered as the demobilization pace increased). The system was based on one point for each month of service up to September 1945, an additional point for each month overseas, five points for each battle star and combat decoration, and up to 12 points for dependents.

On return to the United States the "nearly civilians" were given a $250 discharge bonus, any back pay, and an Honorable Discharge Emblem ("Ruptured Duck") for the uniform to wear home, which they could wear for up to 30 days. They would also receive a percentage of pay for wounds or service-connected disability.

The Servicemen's Readjustment Act of 1944, better known as the "GI Bill of Rights," was instituted to assist veterans financially. This included veteran education and job training support; home, farm, or business loans; unemployment pay; and job-finding assistance. It was responsible for hundreds of thousands of men obtaining college degrees. The Selective Service Act ensured that honorably discharged servicemen could apply for their former jobs, and former employers must restore them to their former position or one of like seniority, status, and pay.

Another after-the-battle event – award ceremonies. Here Marines are decorated with the Purple Heart. (USMC)

JAPANESE INFANTRYMAN

Every army in World War II possessed its own elite, unique, and curious units. Rangers, commandos, paratroopers, mountain troops, Marines, and others fall into these categories along with the notorious, such as the Waffen-SS. No country, however, had an army that presented such an enigma and was as perplexing to Westerners as the Imperial Japanese Army (*Dai Nippon Teikoku Rikugun*, or simply *Kogun*). The army had borne this title since 1925 when it was changed from *Nihongun* or *Kokugan* – Japan's Army or the Nation's Army. This change had wide-ranging effects on the army's psychological and legal authority. Whatever it did, it now did for the Emperor.

Much is not understood of this army and much more is misinterpreted. It was extremely brutal to its enemies and the populaces of occupied areas. It was not much easier on itself. Dedicated to the Emperor, its soldiers of all ranks adhered to a stern code of honor requiring them to die for the glory of the Emperor and the Empire. It really was an army that would fight to the death.

The Japanese Army, while armed with relatively modern weapons, had only recently emerged from a medieval, feudal past where it fought with swords, spears, bows, and arrows. It was never quite able to leave that past behind. Already immersed in a de facto war in China, Japan (*Nippon*) largely ignored its many shortcomings and embarked on a war of conquest against more industrially capable nations, firmly believing that a superior spirit would prevail over material resources. It would establish its place in the world by carving out the Greater East Asia Co-prosperity Sphere (*Dai Toa Kyoei-Ken*). World War II, what Japan called the Greater East Asia War (*Dai Toa Senso Senkum*), did indeed change the map.

Here we will provide a basic study of what made the Japanese soldier (*hetai*) different from the soldiers of other armies and offer some explanations as to why.

Across the sea,

Corpses in the water;

Across the mountains,

Corpses heaped upon the field;

I shall die for the Emperor,

I shall never look back.

It was the grim fatalism of the *Uni Yukaba* (Across the Sea) that conveyed to the conscript what was expected of him as he entered a strange new world. Japanese society was extremely class-oriented and the Imperial Army was no different, except that the division of classes was not related to what the soldier had experienced in his former life. A recruit, regardless of his previous station in the civilian world – whether an uneducated peasant from the rice paddies or a wealthy merchant's son – found himself to be the lowest of the low once he donned the Emperor's uniform. The classes superior to him were senior soldiers, NCOs, and officers. Each subsequent rank was superior to the one below, not in the Western sense of customary military authority, but implying an ability to abuse inferior ranks in almost any manner. Such power acted as a means of defining and maintaining authority – total control through submission.

The China Incident (*Shina Jihen*), engineered by the Japanese to start a war with China, had begun on July 7, 1937, with the Marco Polo Bridge Incident in Shanghai. A de facto war had been ongoing since 1931 when Japan took control of Manchuria and established the puppet state of Manchukuo in 1932. In 1938 the Soviets moved troops into Outer Mongolia in response to Japan's build-up in Manchukuo. Border battles were fought with the Soviets in 1938–39. A neutrality pact was instituted between Japan and the USSR in 1941, but the Japanese continued to maintain significant forces in the form of the Kwantung Army defending Manchuria. The USSR and Japan would not clash until the Soviets invaded days before Japan formally surrendered on September 2, 1945. Japan occupied French Indochina in July 1941, placing itself in position to launch the Southern Operation, the conquest of Burma, Malaya, the Philippines, the Dutch East Indies, and Commonwealth possessions. War against the Western colonial powers would commence at 0215 hours, December 8, 1941, Tokyo time.

CONSCRIPTION

All Japanese males from 17 to 40 were liable for military service, a fact of life since 1873. At age 17 young men registered at their local police station giving their domicile of origin (*honseki*), that is, their parents' home, where they probably still resided. If an

A typical infantryman early in the Greater East Asia War. Here a young soldier (*hetai*) wears standard Meiji Type 30 (1897) infantry equipment, the Type 98 (1938) uniform, and carries a 7.7mm Type 99 (1939) rifle. (US Army)

individual moved away, he was required to report his present domicile (*genjushu*). The Home Islands were divided into 14 divisional districts (*shikan*) plus two in Korea and one on Formosa. Each divisional district was divided into two to five regimental conscription districts (*rentaiku*). The regimental district in which the individual's honseki lay would be his reporting station when called to the Emperor's service by the Military Administration Bureau (*Heimu Kyoku*). Even Japanese living in Manchuria and China were obligated and took their examinations at local military headquarters.

Deferments were few, mainly going to students who may have postponed their service up to age 26 depending on the type of schooling, and those who could prove their service would cause a family hardship. The deferment was extendable at two-year intervals. Criminals were exempt as were the physically and mentally disabled. Men could volunteer between the ages of 17 and 20 and there was a pre-conscription apprentice training program for young men to learn technical skills. From 1938 Koreans could volunteer, as could Formosans from 1942. Those living overseas could postpone their examination one year at a time, unless they returned to Japan for 90 days or more. This included colonists living in the Japanese Mandated Islands (Marianas, Marshalls, Carolines).

Recruits undergo stretching exercises before beginning the day's rigors. As always, an NCO watches their every move. Constant direct supervision was the order of the day. Even "free time" was supervised. A soldier's conduct and performance were constantly monitored and corrections made quickly and usually harshly in order to ensure the lesson was remembered. (Courtesy Akira Takizawa)

Two recruits, wearing *kendo* (wooden sword fighting) protective outfits, practice bayonet-fighting techniques with wooden rifles with padded ends. The instructor, an acting sergeant, holds his own significantly larger wooden rifle with which to "reinforce" teaching points. Perfection was sought after in training and even the most minor infractions, omissions, and errors were corrected swiftly and often brutally. (Courtesy Akira Takizawa)

The young man who would turn 20 between August 1 and December 2 reported for examination and testing between April 16 and July 31 before his birthday. If his birthday was after December 2, he reported between April 16 and July 31 after his birthday. In 1943 the reporting age was lowered to 19. From 1944 Koreans could be conscripted and from 1945 Formosans. Both had been recruited, or press-ganged, into Japanese service since 1942 as unarmed laborers receiving no military training. (Korea and Formosa had been Japanese possessions since 1910 and 1895, respectively.)

Those available for active service (*genekihei*) were divided into two categories, Class A – 5ft (1.52m) tall and in good physical condition, and Class B-1 – 4ft 11in (1.5m) and of slightly less able physical condition (mainly minor sight or hearing difficulties). Class B-2 and B-3 conscripts were the same as B-1, but with poorer sight and hearing. They were assigned to the Conscript Reserve (*Hojuhei*) and could be called up for reserve training not to exceed 180 days over the next 17 years and 4 months. Eye, ear, and teeth problems were common because of an often vitamin-deficient diet. During the war many of these reservists were called to active service. Those rated as Class C due to poor physical condition, between 4ft 9in and 4ft 11in (1.45 and 1.5m), and not suffering from a disabling ailment, were assigned to the Second National Army until age 40. Class D, those less than 4ft 9in (1.45m) or suffering from certain ailments that could not be improved, were exempt. Class F was for those with temporary ailments, who were re-examined annually.

Soldiers completing their active service were assigned to the First Reserve (*Yobieki*) for 17 years and 4 months. They could be called up for a maximum of five 35-day periods or for fewer periods if such call-ups had been extended up to 50 days. Most First Reserve soldiers had been recalled to service between 1939 and 1941 for duty in China, Manchuria, and the upcoming Pacific War (*Taiheiyo Senso*). After completing that duty they were assigned to the First National Army until age 40. Class C personnel and those of Classes A and B who were not needed for active service were assigned to the Second National Army. The two National Armies (*Kokuminhei*) were not actual formations, merely categories of trained and untrained reservists, respectively.

In October 1942 student deferments were canceled, except for students in certain medical and scientific fields. Highly skilled factory technicians were also exempt. In December 1943 the conscription age was lowered to 19, and to 18 in June 1944, when the term of active service was extended to three years – although this was not specified to be for the war's duration, it was. Men were now liable for service until age 45. Japanese residing in occupied areas (Philippines, Dutch East Indies, French Indochina, etc.) who had been allowed to delay their entry examinations also became liable for service.

The prospective soldier received a postcard that ordered him to report for examination and assigned him a reporting date and location. There were over 10,000 military affairs clerks located throughout Japan's prefectures (*ken*) managing the army and navy conscription system (*chohei seido*). Each clerk was responsible not only for maintaining the records of 200–300 possible conscripts, but also the various categories of reservists residing in their regimental district, being familiar with the individual's work and family situations, and reporting changes in address and status. The conscription notices were delivered to the police station from the regimental district headquarters and a policeman or the military affairs clerk would take them to the mayor. They would be opened in his presence and delivered, often at night. If the conscript was residing elsewhere, the notice was turned over to a parent and he or she was legally liable for its delivery. The mayor and clerk were reprimanded if the subject failed to report.

Clerks and other officials were busy in the late summer and fall of 1937 when call-ups were sent after the beginning of the China Incident. Call-ups for the coming Pacific War began in July 1941, with notices delivered in great secrecy and conscripts told to report at night without the usual family fanfare. Levels of volunteers rose significantly in the first few months of the Pacific War, but quickly dropped off. By 1944 even Class C and D individuals were being called up and 17- and 18-year-olds were being strongly "encouraged" to volunteer. Mayors, assemblymen, other local government officials, and military affairs clerks were exempted from service. By the war's end they too were being called up, with the exception of the clerks, without whom the army and navy could not be maintained.

The red notification card, called the Red Paper (*Akagami*), ordered the recruit to report to his training depot on a given date. In the few days before he was to report, his family began work on the "belt of a thousand stitches" (*sen'ninbari*). This was a white cloth belt several inches in width that could be wound around the waist. The women would journey around their village or neighborhood asking everyone they met to sew in a stitch for good fortune. The stitches of thick black yarn could be formed in straight lines or a pattern such as a tiger (representing ferocity). A five-sen coin with a hole in the center was sometimes sewn on, because the number was higher than four (*shi*), which also means death. It was believed the belt might cause bullets to miss. Small wooden panels (*ema*) with best wishes were placed in the local Shinto shrine in the recruit's memory. The conscript was often presented with a small rising sun flag (*Hinomaru*) inscribed with good wishes and the names of family and friends. Even poor families did their best to prepare a memorable farewell feast. On the day of departure, banners were hung offering prayers and congratulations, and marching

Companies were assigned a number of specialist soldiers, including buglers. Bugles were relied on to communicate commands to units deployed tactically. Here three buglers demonstrate their skills to other buglers. (Courtesy Akira Takizawa)

parties (*sokokai*) trooped through the neighborhood. A small rising sun flag was flown over the homes of men called to the colors and their families set a place for them at meals. As the recruits boarded a train under the care of an NCO, family and friends bid farewell, shouting "Tenno heika banzai!" ("May the Emperor live ten thousand years!"). They departed to serve their Emperor to the solemn notes of the *Kimigayo*, the national anthem. As the war wore on such sendoffs became more subdued.

The attitude of the individual soldier towards his service varied over time. As the China Incident wore on, more recruits and reservists were called to serve the Emperor and it was known that service in China came with a high degree of risk. To some extent the country was already experiencing war weariness before the Pearl Harbor attack. By 1943 it was recognized that the Empire was suffering high casualty rates and the mortal implications of service grew through the remainder of the war.

Regardless, a young man called to serve the Emperor usually experienced a degree of excitement and pending adventure, as well as apprehension. He expected to be sent overseas, an exciting prospect in spite of his perilous future, especially since he had seldom traveled further than the horizon beyond his home town. A less willing recruit was simply resigned to his fate, especially among the lower classes. He had no alternatives, no chance of avoiding conscription through family influence or opportunities for posting to less hazardous technical units, NCO schools, or officer training. He knew that military life was hard, that he would experience tough discipline, and he vaguely knew of the brutality and unbending discipline, but to serve the Emperor and to bring honor on his family he was willing to make sacrifices.

TRAINING

Since 1930 Japanese children were required to complete at least six years' education in primary schools. Those fortunate enough to receive further education attended middle and high school for five years. From age eight (3rd grade) boys received minimal military training from teachers. In middle and high schools and universities, active military officers provided training. This training was only two to four hours a week with possibly a four- to six-day annual field exercise. Youth schools offered military training to those who had completed only six years' education and were now employed in the workforce. During the war middle and high schools were required to expand their military training so as to produce cadets, while universities were essentially transformed into reserve military academies.

Japanese society had already prepared future soldiers for military life in that it required obedience to and respect for elders, a degree of regimentation with endless

Soldiers were expected to maintain their own clothing and equipment, and units possessed workshops for this purpose. Here soldiers make minor repairs to their marching shoes. Unit cobblers and tailors were assigned for more sophisticated repairs. (Courtesy Akira Takizawa)

government rules and regulations strictly enforced by the police and local authorities, the demand for individual conformity, crowded living and working environments, and spartan conditions.

Before the war, recruit training lasted three to six months. Recruits were assigned to a depot division (*rusu shidan*), of which one was assigned to each divisional conscription district. Besides recruit training they equipped and provided refresher training to recalled reservists, dispatched replacements to field units, organized new field units, and arranged for the return of casualties and the ashes of the dead. When new infantry divisions and non-divisional units were raised the depot division provided drafts of recruits, not always trained, and cadres of officers and NCOs drawn from other units.

Once assigned to his replacement training regiment, the recruit was issued his uniform and equipment. Under peacetime conditions he underwent recruit training from January to May. One of his earliest experiences was the first of many readings of the Imperial Receipt to Soldiers and Sailors (issued by Emperor Mutsuhito on January 4, 1884) by an officer. This stipulated his duties, responsibilities, and what was expected of him in the Emperor's service. There was no military oath in the Western sense, just complete obedience to the Imperial Receipt.

Whether receiving his training in a replacement or field unit, the recruit was assigned to a training unit (*naumu han*) within his company. This consisted of 20–30 recruits under the charge of a corporal or sergeant and was organized into two sections

LIGHT MACHINE-GUN TRAINING

The section's LMG had a four-man crew, although it was often manned by three. The crew were armed with pistols, but in practice they more likely carried rifles. There were some problems with Japanese LMGs. Their rapid extraction sometimes caused stoppages. To overcome this the Type 96 (1936) LMG required that its cartridges be oiled before loading in the magazine, which was accomplished by an oiler built into the magazine loader. A special reduced-charge round was issued. Standard load 6.5mm rifle rounds could be used, but with an increased chance of stoppage. The 7.7mm Type 99 (1939) was an improved Type 96. The gunner carried only one 30-round magazine in a case plus the tools and spare parts case. The second gunner carried two magazines in a carrier, the magazine loader, and an ammunition bag with 150 rounds. The third gunner carried two ammunition bags and the spare barrel. The crew leader (not pictured) carried the telescope sight in a leather case. LMGs had been at the core of Japanese small-unit tactics since 1922. They based LMG application on the French concept of a single LMG being assigned to each section, and in fact called the sub-unit an LMG section rather than rifle section, emphasizing that the weapon provided the section's base of fire. The portable shield could be penetrated by rifle fire at close range, but provided some protection at over 328ft (100m). The shields were seldom used, however, because of their weight and bulk. (Michael Welpy © Osprey Publishing) (*buntai*), analogous to a US squad. There was no set number of *han* in a company; it depended on the company's strength and available NCOs. The *han* trained, messed, and quartered together. It was not until a rifle company (*chutai*) was deployed to the field that it was reorganized into three rifle platoons (*shotai*) of, usually, three LMG sections and a grenade discharger section with a lieutenant commanding. During training it was seldom that the soldier saw officers, only during the frequent readings of the Imperial Receipt to Soldiers and Sailors and inspections. The Five Principles of Battle Ethics – loyalty, courtesy, courage, truthfulness, and frugality – were taught as well. These were extracted from the Field Service Code (*Senjinkun*) published on January 3, 1941. Training was repetitious and by rote memory with swift punishment for inattention, negligence, and errors.

Complete subservience and obedience to all superiors was demanded. While officers endured the same hardships in the field as their men, they did not directly participate in any group effort or work. Their philosophy was that they gathered the efforts of the group and directed them in a unified endeavor.

Most regular officers were graduates of the vast system of military preparatory schools and academies. At age 14 to 15 junior cadets would enter a preparatory school.

Soldiers detailed from their sections march back to the barracks with their section's cooked meals in insulated containers. A strict accounting is being kept on the chalkboard. The duty NCO overseeing the detail is wearing a red and white weekly duty armband. (Courtesy Akira Takizawa)

In theory it was open to all who could pass the rigid exams, but the family had to pay the considerable food cost and this kept the lower classes out. Enlisted men under 22 and NCOs under 25 could apply for an academy, but most officer cadets were from upper-class families and applied between 16 and 18. Reserve officers were selected from conscripts with at least two years of high school and who had passed an exam, which they studied for on their own during their first three months of conscript training. After another three months a second exam divided them into officer and NCO candidates. Infantry officer candidates undertook 6–11 months' training at one of seven reserve officer schools. After that they served with a field unit on probation for four months and were then placed in the reserves or retained on active service if required. Most line officers in infantry units were products of this training.

Enlisted men were selected for NCO training after three months' basic training or later in their service. This was a voluntary move and they were expected to become career NCOs. They continued their unit training for another nine months, but were given additional responsibilities, instruction, and study. Infantry NCO candidates attended one of three one-year NCO schools (*Kyodo Gakko*) in Japan or one in Manchuria (the training period was shortened during the war). Technical specialists destined for duties such as signals, ordnance, medical, veterinary, intendance (administrative), supply, and so forth were assigned to infantry units and trained in divisional courses or formal branch service schools.

Recruit training initially focused on the care and use of uniform and equipment, rank identification, courtesies to superiors, and individual and section drill with endless marching. The recruit learned the procedures and responsibilities of guard duty. While not a formal part of the recruit's schooling, he also learned the intricacies of soldier hierarchy and his place as the lowest of the low. The primary goal of training, including the graduated abuses inflicted by all above him, was immediate and unquestioned obedience to orders. Without this the army could not have functioned as it did. Every mistake, every omission, any lack of vigilance and attention was swiftly and harshly dealt with by those above. The infantryman was trained through a gradual toughening process with increasingly longer forced marches and endurance tests. Short rations and severe water conservation were typical. Recruits returning from forced marches were ordered to upend their canteens. Those whose canteens emptied first were beaten and reprimanded as weak-willed. Surprisingly, when considering the degree of toughness expected of soldiers, they did not spend any more than five days in the field at a time for fear of affecting their health. In February a five-day "snow march" was conducted where the soldiers learned to live in cold weather conditions.

While soldiers kept diaries and wrote letters home, the abuses and harsh conditions were seldom mentioned. Such talk was not permitted and the hard surroundings were simply a fact of life.

A major part of training was marksmanship and maintenance of the rifle. The amount of ammunition allotted to target practice dwindled during the war. Individual accuracy was not a major concern though, as massed rifle and machine-gun fire was the preferred method of combat. While there were exceptions, individually speaking Japanese soldiers were only fair marksmen. Bayonet fighting was regarded as essential and was psychologically linked to Japan's past sword-wielding warriors. The rudiments of section tactics were taught, but without the benefit of integrated supporting weapons.

As the war went on, even in China before the Pacific War began, deployed units were increasingly sent untrained recruits to be trained by the field unit. From 1937 units began to receive recruits and recalled reservists (*hojuhei*) every few months rather than on an annual cycle. If small numbers were received they were simply integrated into platoons. If a unit received a large number of untrained or partly trained recruits they might be organized into training companies and trained by NCOs detached from line companies. Individual and small-unit training could be erratic for units in China and Manchuria. The recruits might be committed to combat or engaged in security operations, and while they gained experience, their training was neither complete nor efficient.

A 5cm grenade discharger crew wearing tube packs prepare to launch a projectile from a covered position. (US Army)

Once assigned to a unit, individuals were selected to man LMGs and grenade dischargers. Others were assigned to battalion machine-gun, regimental infantry gun, or antitank companies. Here they learned to operate and maintain their new weapons and function as a crew. They were assigned a crew number and trained in a specific duty – gunner, loader, ammunition carrier, etc. They undoubtedly learned how to handle other crew duties, but had little opportunity to perform them. It is not completely true that if a machine-gunner was killed the other crewmen were incapable of operating the weapon; they knew how to, but their restraint was more a matter of motivation or fear of violating a rule, as it was not their place to assume such a responsibility if not ordered to do so by a superior. The deeply instilled sense of harmony, that is, not deviating from what was required or expected, and fear of affronting a superior, was as much a part of this rigid mindset as any lack of training.

Those with civilian skills or who demonstrated the ability to perform special tasks were selected from within a company to be specialist soldiers (*tokugyo hei*). NCOs or others skilled in the tasks trained the novices. Specialists were promoted after completing a year's service and demonstrating their skill. They included armorers, cobblers, tailors, buglers, barbers, cooks, and medical orderlies. These specialists were exempt from general work details and guard duty. The company was an extended family and in garrison was fairly well self-contained in regards to routine services.

After three months of training, unit officers conducted the first-quarter inspection (*ikki ken-etsu*). This was of several days' duration and consisted of barracks and field inspections plus tests in which soldiers demonstrated their skills from drill to reciting the Imperial Receipt to Soldiers and Sailors and the Five Principles of Battle Ethics.

Unit training progressed through a year-long schedule beginning with individual and section training and culminating in regimental or divisional autumn maneuvers. January to May was spent on training and integrating recruits, section tactics, rifle and bayonet training, and cold weather conditioning. June and July meant more rifle and bayonet practice, platoon and company tactics, crew-served weapons training, 18½-mile (30km) marches every day, and constructing field fortifications. August saw a continuation of company training as well as battalion exercises, tactical firing, more bayonet drill, swimming, and 25-mile (40km) marches. Marches were increasingly longer and faster, with full equipment, often conducted over rugged terrain and in harsh weather. Battalion and regimental exercises were conducted in October and November with live-fire exercises and the large unit maneuvers.

Unit training was demanding and unending. Physical and mental toughening by exposure to the elements under progressively harsh conditions was the standard.

Officers fully participated in the training alongside their men. While discipline was unforgiving, units developed a close-knit loyalty and soldiers were imbued with a great deal of unit pride. December saw the discharge of those completing their active service, plus the maintenance of equipment and facilities, and preparation for the next training year and its influx of replacements. After six months' service the recruits were eligible for promotion to private 1st class (*itto-hei*). After a year they and company specialists could be promoted to superior private (*joto-hei*).

Training deteriorated through the war as lower-quality personnel were drafted, qualified instructors dwindled, and training resources and facilities proved inadequate for the growing army. Previously only small numbers of young men from the teeming inner cities were conscripted, as they tended to be more unruly, less subservient, and unused to the hardships of field life. They were now drafted in large numbers to provide the necessary manpower, but proved troublesome and were poorly adapted to jungle warfare. The myth that the Japanese soldier was a natural jungle fighter was just that; the Japanese had conducted no such training and the terrain and climate in Japan and China did not provide the right training environment. They were initially successful because they were tough, conditioned to hardship, disciplined, and had total faith in their will.

Radio operator students learning the Japanese equivalent to Morse Code. Even comparatively short-range radios used code rather than voice. The Japanese used the *Kana* or *Katakana* phonetic alphabet, a system of 50 characters for each of the sounds of the Japanese language. (US Army)

APPEARANCE

Japan's first military uniforms were purchased from France in the 1870s. While the wartime uniforms were still European in style, the Japanese soon introduced distinctive features. Three different models of uniform were worn during the war. Each consisted of a tunic, trousers, overcoat, and raincoat. All three models were made in both wool and cotton versions for cold and warm climates/seasons. It was not uncommon for a soldier to have been issued all three models of uniform during the course of his service. Earlier models remained in use and existing stocks continued to be issued. In this way older models were worn throughout the war and were commonly mixed within units. There were also special tropical uniforms and work uniforms. All of these uniforms were of similar design, but with differences in collars, pocket layouts, cut details, and the quality of materials used. Uniform colors varied greatly from greenish tan to dark olive-drab or green. The official color was a warm olive green; Japan went from dark blue to olive-drab uniforms in 1912. Buttons could be made of brass, bronze-plated steel, green-painted steel, green or brown plastic, brown Bakelite, or painted wood depending on when produced.

Wool tunics (*guni*) were partly lined with white or off-white cotton cloth, as were the inside of the wool trousers from the knees up. Five-button tunics had a small pocket in the left inside front of the skirt for a field dressing. Wool tunics had a second internal pocket inside the left breast. The tunic, overcoat, and raincoat had an integral buttoned retaining loop on the left side of the waist to hold the bayonet frog in place and help support the leather service belt's weight. The trousers (*gunko*), instead of having a normal belt, had three belt loops positioned well below the waistband, one on each side and one on the back, through which ran a doubled tie-tape with the single tape free ends to be tied at the front over the buttoned fly. Tie-tapes secured the trouser cuffs. Trousers had only two internal side pockets.

The Showa Type 5 (1930) tunic had a standing collar and internal breast pockets with scallop-shaped button flaps, not unlike the black or blue student uniforms with which the soldier was familiar. Rank insignia were tabs on the shoulder seams secured by two small loops. The soldier may also have received the Type 98 (1938) uniform with a stand-and-fall collar on which rank insignia tabs were sewn. Type 5 uniforms remained in use throughout the war, but most soldiers would not have worn the old colored branch swallowtail flashes, which were worn on the collars with brass unit numbers or special insignia devices or the 1¼ x 3½ (3 x 9cm) rank shoulder tabs. These were deleted from older uniforms when the Type 98 was introduced and instead the ¾ x 1¾in (20 x 45mm) Type 98 collar rank was worn. The Type 98 retained

PRIVATE 2ND CLASS INFANTRYMAN

A young recruit no doubt felt both proud and strange in his new uniform and equipment (1). This soldier wears the Type 98 (1938) wool winter uniform with the Type 92 (1932) helmet, Meiji Type 30 (1897) leather equipment, and is armed with a 6.5mm Meiji Type 38 (1905) rifle. The back view (2) shows his backpack, blanket bedroll with the shelter-half rolled on top, haversack over his right hip, canteen atop it, broken-down shovel, Meiji Type 30 (1897) bayonet, Type 99 (1939) gasmask case, and reserve ammunition box. Pieces of kit displayed separately are: steel helmet with cloth cover displaying the means of securing the tie-tape (3a); the helmet's suspension system (3b); shovel (4a); shovel and handle stowed in the carrying case (4b); Type 95 (1935) gasmask (5a); Type 99 (1939) gasmask (5b); Type 99 gasmask case with cleaning cloth, anti-freeze bottle, and anti-fog disks (5c); decontamination powder (5d); marching shoes displaying the heel cleat and hobnails (6); puttees (7); old-type backpack with leather straps (8); tube pack (9); shelter-half with two-piece pole and tent stakes (10). (Michael Welpy © Osprey Publishing)

Type 5 breast pockets, but added internal skirt pockets with buttonless flaps. Soldiers may or may not have later been issued a Type 3 (1943) uniform. This was essentially of the same cut as the Type 98, but of simplified design and made with lower quality and substitute materials. With it were introduced ¾ x 1in (20 x 40mm) rank insignia with the stars moved toward the backing's leading edge. These uniforms were used for service, field, and off-duty wear.

Wool overcoats (*gaito*) were unfamiliar garments to many Japanese soldiers. These were unlined, single-breasted with five buttons, possessed relatively small stand-and-fall collars and internal waist pockets with buttonless flaps, and lacked waist belts. Lined detachable hoods large enough to be worn over the helmet could be fitted. Type 98 collar rank was worn on all overcoats. The raincoats were similar in design to the overcoats, but were double-breasted with two rows of five buttons and made of tightly woven cotton. Detachable hoods were provided. When the Type 3 uniform was adopted, the Type 98 raincoat was retained. Few enlisted men were issued raincoats.

All Japanese soldiers would have appreciated the tropical uniforms they received before departing for the South Seas. These were introduced well before the war, for wear in the South Seas Mandated Islands. Early issues were tan cotton, but medium to dark green became more common. They had open collars, buttoned side vent flaps below the armpits, pleated patch pockets with flaps, and patch skirt pockets without flaps, although later models had Type 98 internal skirt pockets with buttonless flaps. Trousers could be full length, three-quarter length, or loose-fitting breeches style. Knee-length shorts were also available for informal wear with the tropical lightweight cotton shirt, which had only three front buttons, three-quarter-length sleeves, and patch breast pockets with small squared flaps. This was often worn as an outer garment and might have had rank insignia sewn on the collar or sometimes above the right breast pocket. It was common for officers to wear lightweight white or off-white

The brown leather Meiji Type 30 (1897) infantry equipment (*kojin sobi*) consisted of the service belt, two 30-round cartridge boxes, a 60-round reserve cartridge box with oilcan, and a bayonet frog. While substitute materials replaced leather during the war, the basic equipment design remained unchanged. (US Army)

tropical shirts as an outer garment with the green tropical trousers. When officers wore a green tropical tunic the shirt's collar would be worn exposed over the tunic collar.

Olive-drab or white cotton work uniforms were cut similar to the Type 5 and had plastic buttons of the uniform color. It was common to see soldiers on work details wearing white tunics with regular olive-drab trousers. Field caps (*ryakubo*) were made in both wool and cotton and adopted in 1938. They had a short semi-rigid visor, a brown leather or artificial leather adjustable chinstrap, normally worn above the visor, and a tie-cord in the back slit for adjusting size. The crown had a characteristic shallow front-to-back crease and there were two or three vent eyelets in each side. A yellow five-point star was embroidered on a pentagon-shaped or circular cloth backing sewn to the cap's front. A tan four-flap Havelock was sometimes worn on the cap for neck protection from the sun, attached by small hooks fitting in thread loops around the outside of the cap band.

Camouflage garments were locally produced in the Solomon Islands and packed in bales for forward shipment. They were made of a shaggy, reddish-brown fiber that grows at the base of the fronds of coconut palms. Sheets of this fiber were sewn together as a rainproof and camouflage garment. When used for camouflage it and the helmet net would be additionally embellished with local vegetation. Japanese fishermen and farmers in the Home Islands made similar garments from palm fibers and reeds or rushes. (US Army)

A soldier was typically issued one winter, one summer, and one work uniform plus an overcoat. A spare uniform was not carried in the field. In the tropics a regular tropical field uniform was issued along with another with a short-sleeve shirt and shorts. Overall most soldiers found a great deal of latitude in regards to uniform regulations in the tropics.

The Type 92 (1932) steel helmet (officially *tetsubo* – steel cap) was a simple chrome molybdenum steel dome with a short rim protruding equally all round. It was originally referred to as a steel helmet (*tetsukabuto*). A star was soldered to the front and the helmet (and star) painted olive-drab. It was sometimes whitewashed in winter. A tan, olive-drab or green two-layer, fiber-insulated linen cover was available with a yellow star sewn on the front. The leather suspension system was held in place by tie-cords. An elaborately laced tie-tape system secured the helmet under the chin. Bullets and fragments easily penetrated the low-grade steel.

While most Japanese habitually wore sandals, the army issued light-brown horsehide Type 5 marching shoes (*henjoka*). Many experienced difficulties adapting to the heavy, confining ankle boots. The leather soles were hobnailed and a J-shaped steel cleat was nailed to the heel protecting the outer and back edges. From 1943 rubber-soled shoes were issued with molded circular grips. Shoes were also made of pigskin as an economy measure. Many soldiers preferred the lightweight ankle-high black canvas shoes with rubber soles known as *jikatabi* or *tabi*. These either had a conventional round toe or a split-toe, with the big toe being separate. Shoe sizes were indicated by a *mon* number (an old 1in/2.5cm diameter coin), for example, "9.5" or "10." Olive-drab wool or cotton puttees (*makikyahan*), for winter or summer wear, were wound around the lower legs from the ankles, covering the top of the shoes to below the knees. A tie-tape was sewn to one end. Long tie-tapes were wrapped across the shins in an X-pattern and short tie-tapes were wound around the top. Homemade rigid woven rice straw (*waraji*) or wooden (*geta*) sandals were often worn in barracks or on bivouac.

The flannel-lined light cotton undershirt (*juban*) was off-white or light green. It had a four-button front opening and was collarless. It had patch breast pockets with rectangular buttoned flaps and was long-sleeved with button cuffs. The soldier's breechcloth (*fundoshi*) was a white cotton rectangular section of cloth, wrapped around the groin and waist and secured in place by a tie-string on one end. Light green cotton or white wool long underdrawers (*koshita*) were worn in warm and cold weather, respectively. Tie-strings were attached to the waistband and cuffs. Socks were white and of the straight tube type. Heavy knit white cotton gloves were issued.

INDIVIDUAL CLOTHING AND EQUIPMENT

Each soldier was issued a white cotton work uniform (1). The wool service tunic (2) was lined with white cotton. The large inside pocket is for the soldier's Pay Record Book (2a) and the smaller for the field dressing (2b) and triangular bandage (2c). The cotton service trousers (3) display the unusual waist tie-tape. A low-cost backpack (4) was issued in 1938 for the China Incident mobilization. One of the most common backpacks (5) was issued from 1941. The rifleman's equipment (6a) included the service belt, two 30-round cartridge boxes (6b), a 60-round reserve cartridge box in the center with oil bottle (6c), and bayonet frog, and identity tag (7). Items carried in the pack included an undershirt and underdrawers (8a), two pairs of socks, with one used to carry rice in the haversack (8b), shoe brush, soap box, scissors, and toothbrush (8c), wool/cotton blanket (8d), tabi split-toed shoes (8e), and hand towel (8f). Haversacks varied in design – this was an early war issue (9). The early type 1-pint (0.5-liter) canteen was still in limited use (10a). The 2½-pint (1.2-liter) Type 94 canteen was standard issue (10b). The elaborate four-piece rice cooker (11) consisted of cover tray, side-dish, soup pot, and rice pot. (Michael Welpy © Osprey Publishing)

Unit insignia were little used. In some instances a small square or rectangular patch was sewn about the left breast pocket depicting a unit symbol. Sometimes small vertical rectangular cloth nametapes were attached above a breast pocket. The double-V branch insignia was abolished for combat arms in 1940. Regardless, it was seldom worn in the field. Even rank insignia were often removed in combat. In October 1943 some branches were authorized a thin colored strip on the bottom edge of their collar rank insignia, but this too was seldom worn.

The identity tag (*ninshikihyo*) was a 1¼ x 2in (3.2 x 5cm) aluminum or brass oval on a narrow cloth tape threaded through a small rectangular hole in each end. Since the dead were cremated there was no need for a second tag to remain with the body. Information was minimal. The Soldier's Pay Record (*Guntai Techo*) was a 3 x 5in (7.6 x 12.7cm) booklet bound in light olive-drab or tan cloth. The soldier was admonished not to lose it or face severe punishment. Information included personal and parents' names, birth date and place, permanent and residential addresses, civilian schools, civilian employment, military qualifications, assignments, pay entries, awards, punishments, uniform sizes, etc. Only unit code numbers were entered rather than actual designations. The soldier carried it in the inside left breast pocket of his wool tunic and the outer left breast pocket of his cotton and tropical tunics. Japanese soldiers were famous for keeping diaries and journals, which they took into combat. While they were cautioned not to enter information of military value, this was not well supervised and captured diaries proved beneficial to Allied intelligence.

A field dressing (*hotai*) – gauze and cotton layers with tie-tapes – was issued in an olive-drab cloth package. An olive-drab cotton triangular bandage (*sankakukin*; 20in/50cm on two edges, 32in/81.3cm on the third) was wrapped in paper and often used as a scarf. Both were carried in a pocket in the left inside of the tunic skirt.

A Japanese infantryman's hair was cut very close for sanitary reasons and to eliminate time-wasting grooming. The Japanese seldom found it necessary to shave and some did not carry shaving gear. Prolonged combat, however, found officers and men with scruffy thin chin-beards and mustaches. Mustaches were rare among enlisted men; they were more common among officers, but by no means worn by the majority.

In the field the Japanese Army prided itself on its scruffy appearance, even amongst officers, but arms and equipment were well maintained. However, the soldiers' dusty, muddy, and often stained uniforms, thread-bare collars and cuffs, patched trousers knees, mixed uniforms, unshaven faces, undershirts worn as outer garments in hot weather, and sweaty triangular neck scarves showed them to be veteran campaigners.

WEAPONS

The Japanese Army, being a force centered around the infantry, viewed its most important weapons to be those arming its infantrymen: rifle, bayonet, LMG, grenade discharger, and hand grenade. Put simply, the Imperial Japanese Army was comparatively well armed in 1930, but by 1943 it was far out-classed by the Allies.

The standard Japanese rifle and LMG round was the 6.5mm. Even with a new bullet and more powerful propellant the 6.5mm provided insufficient range, penetration, and knockdown force on Manchurian and Chinese plains. In 1938 a new 7.7mm round was adopted along with a new rifle and LMG. Japanese rifles and machine guns were noted for emitting little muzzle flash and smoke. Apart from the type of propellant, this was due to the rifles' long barrels, which resulted in most of the propellant being consumed in the bore. Divisions in Japan were the first armed with 7.7mm weapons, in mid 1939, followed by units in China, then Manchuria. Many units on the mainland still had 6.5mm weapons at the beginning of the Pacific War. As units were deployed piecemeal into the Pacific, island defense forces might be armed with both 6.5mm and 7.7mm weapons in different battalions, causing ammunition supply problems.

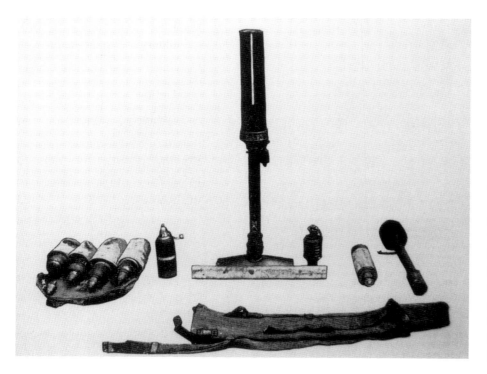

A key infantry weapon was the 5cm Type 89 (1929) heavy grenade discharger (*jutekidanto*), commonly misnamed the "knee mortar" by Allied troops. From left to right are an ammunition carrier (two carried by the gunner and the No. 2 gunner), an HE mortar round, a Type 97 (1937) hand grenade with a propellant change, a colored smoke signal round (called a "dragon" by the Japanese), and bore cleaning brush. Beneath the discharger is a canvas carrying case, which was slung over the shoulder and not carried on the leg as rumored by Allied troops (hence its nickname). (US Army)

The Arisaka 6.5mm Meiji Type 38 (1905) and 7.7mm Type 99 (1939) rifles (*shoju*) could be quite a handful for a 5ft (1.52m) tall soldier. While not as nicely finished as Western counterparts, they were as reliable and rugged as any five-shot bolt-action in use. The Type 38 rifle was 50¼in (127.6cm) long and the Type 99 rifle 50in (127cm), and both weighed just over 9lb (4kg).

Although a well-designed rifle, there was nothing exceptional about the Type 38, apart from its Mauser-type action being stronger than that of the US M1903 Springfield, of which the same could be said of the Type 99. Both rifles were provided with a simple leather, web, or rubberized canvas sling, metal muzzle cap, and sleeve-like dustcover that fitted over the bolt. Soldiers most likely discarded the dustcover, as it rattled, slowed the working of the bolt, and added a bit of weight. The Type 99 had several innovative features. These included a folding wire monopod to help support the long, heavy rifle when firing from a prone position and fold-down lead arms fitted to the rear leaf sight to aid in firing at aircraft, though it is doubtful these were of much value. Late war production Type 99s lacked the chromed bore, monopod, sling swivels, and cleaning rod, had a laminated stock with a wood butt plate, and a simple rear peep sight. They were produced with low-quality materials and today are considered unsafe to fire.

Each soldier, including those who did not carry a rifle, was issued a Meiji Type 30 (1897) bayonet (*juken*) with a 15in (38cm) blade. He knew it as the "burdock sword" (*gobo ken*), as the black-painted steel scabbard looked like a burdock (a vegetable). It had a J-shaped guard, which if deftly handled could hook the blade of an opponent's bayonet, yanking his rifle from his hands. Late war production replaced the hooked guard with a straight one and olive-drab-painted wooden scabbards were sometimes issued.

NCOs might carry the Type 95 (1935) sword (*shin-gunto*). Like the officer's finer Type 94 (1934), it was of the traditional Japanese design with a single-edged, shallow curved blade with a small oval guard and long grip. Issue officer and NCO swords were machine made, as opposed to the hand-made ancient family blades carried by a minority of officers. Overall length averaged 39in (99cm) and the blade 26½in (67cm). The grip was solid copper or aluminum cast to simulate the officer's green cord-wrapped grip. Officers sometimes wrapped their sword's grip with white cloth to protect it. A leather strap with snap-hooks attached the scabbard to the special NCO's belt. The metal scabbard (*saya*) was painted olive-drab. A brown leather NCO's tassel was attached to the sword butt (officers had colored tassels indicating their rank category).

The two most common *keikikanju* or LMGs were the Nambu 6.5mm Type 96 (1936) and 7.7mm Type 99 (1939). They were bipod mounted and fed by 30-round top-feeding magazines. Both had 2.5x telescopic sights and quick-change barrels. To emphasize the Japanese propensity for close combat, these 20lb (9kg) weapons could be fitted with a rifle bayonet. The obsolete Nambu 6.5mm Taisho Type 11 (1922) LMG was issued as a substitute in many units, even alongside the Type 96, and was used throughout the war. It had a unique feed hopper, doubling as an oil reservoir, in which six five-round rifle-charging clips were stacked. This feed mechanism tended to collect dirt and vegetation debris, causing jams. Besides a bipod, a tripod was also available. The Type 11 lacked a telescope sight and quick-change barrel.

The Nambu Taisho Type 14 (1925) pistol (*kenju*) was of poor design. The even more poorly designed Type 94 (1934) was produced only as a lower-cost alternative to the more expensive and complex Type 14; it offered no improvement over the Type 14. Both fired an underpowered 8mm cartridge and used eight- and six-round magazines, respectively. Holsters were brown leather with one or two belt loops and a leather or web shoulder strap. The Type 14 had a hard leather clamshell cover with a spare magazine carried in a pocket inside the pistol compartment, and a pocket beneath the cover to hold two ten-round cartridge packets. The Type 94 holster had a simple flap with an external magazine pocket.

The 5cm Type 89 (1929) heavy grenade discharger (*jutekidanto*) was not only an important close-combat weapon, but was provided with a full-range of colored signal flares and smoke grenades (known as "dragons"). Besides rifled HE and WP mortar rounds, the Type 89 could fire hand grenades with propellant charges fitted. The Taisho Type 10 (1921) grenade discharger (*tekidanto*) was still in wide use. Popularly called "knee mortars" by the Allies because of their curved base plates, these compact weapons could not be fired from the thigh, as rumored, without breaking a bone. Another theory for their nickname is that they were carried in a bag strapped to the thigh. This is not true – they were carried in a canvas case slung over the shoulder.

Japanese soldiers learned about a wide variety of hand grenades (*shuryudan*), which had poor lethality and reliability. The most common were the Type 97 (1937), Type 91 (1931), and Type 99 (1939) HE; as well as various WP, smoke, and tear-gas grenades. The Japanese made a great number of expedient grenades, many of which were as dangerous to the user as the intended victims. Various models of cup- and spigot-type rifle grenade launchers (*tekidank*) were issued.

INDIVIDUAL EQUIPMENT

A Japanese soldier was issued a bewildering array of belts, straps, pouches, bags, and carriers – personal equipment (*kojin sobi*). While his life was one of austerity and simplicity, this did not apply to his equipment. If it was a piece of military equipment that could possibly be of use to a soldier, it was probably issued. He quickly learned that his equipment was the property of the Emperor and it was his responsibility to care for it, especially the rifle, the sole piece of equipment marked with the Imperial Chrysanthemum symbol. The equipment was European style, with occasional unique aspects, and had not changed significantly since before the turn of the century; nor would its basic design change much during the war.

Early war issue equipment was of fairly high quality, and extensive use was made of leather along with cotton, canvas, and webbing. Horsehide leather (cowhide was too costly) items were light brown, but canvas gear varied greatly in shade from light tan to olive-drab. Metal fittings could be steel, brass, nickel, or aluminum. The marking of items varied, but might consist of the type (year) number, production date (often just the year), the manufacturer's code or logo, and sometimes a five-pointed star indicating army property. Officers' equipment was of significantly different design and higher quality in keeping with the class structure.

For riflemen the basic Meiji Type 30 (1897) equipment consisted of a one-size-fits-all 1¾in (4.5cm) wide, 3ft 3in (1m) long leather service belt (*obigawa*) fitted with two sliding loops (often discarded or lost) to secure the free end. The open-faced rectangular buckle could be brass, aluminum, or steel, the latter painted olive-green or black. The soldier was issued three leather cartridge boxes (*danyakugo*). The two rigid rectangular boxes (*kogo*) fitting on his belt's front were unusual, as they had top-opening lids hinged on the upper front and secured by metal studs on the boxes' ends that fastened through leather tabs. This means of opening helped prevent the soldier from losing ammunition if he inadvertently left the box open. On the back were two belt loops. The belt's free end could be retained by the cartridge box loops, which explains why the belt's sliding loops were often discarded. The

An early war Type 94 (1934) 2½-pint (1.2-liter) canteen. The stopper is held in place by a buckled leather strap. Later canteen stoppers were secured by a tie-tape. (Velmer Smith Collection)

boxes were divided into two compartments by a leather center divider, allowing three five-round charging clips to be held in each to give each box a capacity of 30 rounds of 6.5mm or 7.7mm ammunition. A reserve cartridge box (*zengo*) was worn centered on his belt's rear. It differed in design, being hinged in the rear and secured by a single stud and leather tab on the box's front center. On the right end were carrier straps holding a black or olive-drab metal or plastic oil bottle. The bottle had a stud on its cap to which the vertical strap was fastened to retain it. This larger box had three compartments with each holding four charging clips to total 60 rounds. In theory the soldier could not use this reserve ammunition unless ordered. The leather bayonet frog was worn on his belt's left side, and consisted of either two narrow belt loops or a single wide one. The tunic's small integral cloth support strap was looped around the belt between the frog's two belt loops (those with a wide loop had a hole in which the support strap was fitted). The scabbard was slid through the retainer on which a small buckle and strap were fitted. At the top of the scabbard was a small metal bracket and the frog's strap was passed through this and secured by the buckle.

The Type 94 (1934) 2½-pint (1.2-liter) canteen (*suito*) was of olive-drab painted aluminum with a cork or wood stopper. The stopper was fitted to a metal cap with a ring attached. A thin web strap passed through the cap's ring and both ends were fastened to the canteen carrier by small buckles to hold it in place. The carrier was made of horizontal and vertical web straps. An adjustable shoulder strap was fitted to the carrier. This strap was slung over his left shoulder and passed under the belt to be carried over the haversack on his right hip. There was an older short-necked bottle-style 1-pint (0.5-liter) canteen still in wide use, which had either a leather or web carrier.

The soldier's haversack (*zatsuno*) was a simple canvas single-compartment shallow bag with a large flap covering most of the bag's outer side for additional water-proofing. Its sides were pleated to allow it to expand when filled. A single strap or tie-tape secured the bag's opening and two more on the inside of the flap's bottom end gave further attachment. A wide adjustable strap was slung over his left shoulder and passed under the belt to be carried beneath the canteen. On the back at the top was a metal flat hook that attached to the belt to take some of the haversack's weight. The haversack allowed the soldier to carry essential items when his pack was not carried, such as on guard duty or during patrols. It was mainly intended for one day's tinned rations and up to five days of rice, sometimes carried in a spare sock. Chopsticks (*o-hashi*), a small knife (*kozuka*), sometimes a soup spoon and bowl, saké cup, and other small items might be carried.

The old-type backpack (*haino*) was a flat rectangular leather box with a wood internal frame. A single strap secured the large flap covering its entire back. Some were still being issued with the flap covered with Korean oxhide for waterproofing. All-canvas versions without frames began to be issued well before the war, and could have a large flap covering the entire back of the pack or only a short flap large enough to cover the top opening. In 1938 a new type of canvas pack was issued with a large flap, but once this was opened two horizontally opening flaps revealed the inside of the pack. Straps and edge binding were usually leather. A wartime version was made of rubberized canvas. All types of packs had pairs of buckled straps or tie-tapes on the sides and top to secure bedrolls. These packs measured 5 x 13 x 13in (12.7 x 33 x 33cm).

The backpack's integral shoulder straps were attached to the top of the pack, ran over the top of the shoulders and at the pit of the shoulders split into two narrow straps. One, with adjusting eyelets, ran back under the armpits to attach to buckles on the pack. The other had a flat metal hook, and was attached to the service belt behind the ammunition pouches to help support the belt's weight. Soldiers knew this tangle of straps as "octopus legs" (*takoashi*). The haversack and canteen straps were worn beneath the pack straps, but the gasmask case's strap was worn over the pack straps.

A Japanese soldier's pack contents were simple: spare breechcloth and undershirt, two pairs of socks, towel, toilet articles in a ditty bag (*hokobukuro*) with soap box, toothbrush, cleaning brush, scissors, and sewing kit; some carried a razor, possibly rations, and sandals. The soldier's bedroll was strapped to the outside of the pack in a "horseshoe roll" with a blanket and shelter-half rolled on top. In the winter an additional blanket might be carried along with the overcoat. The tan or olive-drab 62 x 72in (157.5 x 182.9cm) wool and cotton-blend blanket (*mofu*) had hemmed edges. Later production shoddy wool blankets were smaller, thinner, and often had raw edges. The shelter-half (*tenmaku*) was a 56 x 59in (142.2 x 149.8cm) tan or olive-drab canvas rectangle with grommets and tie-tapes or cords along the two long edges. These allowed two soldiers to fasten together their two halves to form a two-man tent. Each soldier carried a two-piece wooden tent pole and two wooden tent stakes. Additional shelter-halves could be fastened together to make larger tents, with designs provided using up to 28 shelter-halves. Such large shelters were seldom used, however. In the center of one end was a length of cord allowing the shelter-half to be suspended from the shoulders and tied under the chin as a rain cape, which was generally preferred over the raincoat. A cord loop fastened though grommets at chest-level held the front closed. When not inside a shelter, the soldier would simply roll up in his overcoat, blanket, and shelter-half as a simple sleeping bag.

SOUTH SEAS INDIVIDUAL AND SECTION EQUIPMENT

Japan had long issued lightweight tropical clothing for use in the Mandated territory of the South Seas, but it was the Pacific War that saw widespread issue of new tropical uniforms and equipment items, as well as increased use of substitute materials. The items shown here are: the cotton tropical tunic (1); long and short tropical trousers (2) – the short version reached to below the knees and was still intended to be worn with cotton puttees; Type 92 steel helmet (3) fitted with a camouflage net; a pickax with a detachable head (4); wire cutters (5); small sickle (6) – this was provided to clear fields of fire and cut camouflage materials; late war service belt (7) – the front cartridge boxes, reserve cartridge box, and bayonet frog are made of light tan rubberized canvas; Type 94 canteen (8) issued with a simplified cap-retaining cord; rice cooker (9); late war marching shoes with rubber soles and capped toes (10); homemade rice-straw sandals (11); puttees (12); rising sun flag with best wishes and names of friends and family (13); "belt of a thousand stitches," here pre-printed (in red) band sold commercially, to which family's and friends' stitches were added. (Michael Welpy © Osprey Publishing)

A section assembles its shelter-halves into a larger tent. This version required 16 shelter-halves. (Courtesy Akira Takizawa)

A Japanese infantryman was provided with a 6ft (1.8m) long tube pack (*seoibukuro*) made of olive-drab canvas lined with white cloth and sewn across the center to form two compartments. It was open at both ends with cloth strips extending beyond the ends and a pair of tie-tapes to tie it shut. A pair of larger tie-tapes was sewn to the center portion. It could be worn slung over his right shoulder and around his left hip like a horseshoe roll or carried around his waist over the equipment belt. The center tie-tape secured it in place. The pack was used to carry spare clothing and rations when traveling, similar to a Western duffel bag, but was sometimes used in the field.

One of the most important items for any Japanese soldier was the shovel (*enpi*). This was carried in a canvas case, blade down, attached to the left side of the pack with the wooden handle detached. A length of rope secured the handle to the blade. Most European entrenching tools had short fixed handles. The Japanese system allowed a longer handle, providing a more efficient tool. When assembled the handle was inserted in the spade's handle socket. The knotted end of the rope ran through a hole in the handle about one-third its length from its knobbed end. It was threaded through a hole beside the blade's socket, with several turns made around the socket, and pulled tight to hold the handle and blade together. It is often suggested that the rope's only purpose was to allow the shovel to be carried slung over the shoulder. One in three infantrymen carried a small pickax rather than an entrenching tool. This had a detachable head carried in a long canvas triangular-shaped case on the pack. Other men might carry a small sickle for clearing brush and cutting camouflage materials, or a wire cutter. Most tool handles were left as natural wood, but were sometimes painted olive-drab.

The olive-drab painted aluminum, kidney-shaped mess kit, called a rice cooker (*hangou*), was similar to German and Russian models, but was more elaborate. It consisted of four components: cover, which also served as a food tray, side-dish pan, and soup pot, which nested in a rice pot. The rice and soup pots both had wire bail handles. The rice cooker was attached to the back of the pack by a strap threaded through brackets on the cover's side and on the rice pot. A simplified model lacked the soup pot. Fur-lined canvas covers were available for the canteen and rice cooker to protect them from freezing.

The soldier's gasmask case was a simple canvas bag with a flap secured by a single stud fastener and an adjustable shoulder strap. The strap was worn over his right shoulder with the bag carried on his left side, and could be rigged with the case worn on his chest to allow faster donning. Two types of gasmask (*hiko*) were commonly issued. Both had heavy light-brown treated fabric face-pieces, removable circular eyepieces, six adjusting straps on the back of the head, a brown rubber corrugated hose, and an olive-drab-painted oval filter canister. The Type 95 (1935) had a longer 6in (15.2cm) canister with six reinforcing ribs. The Type 99 (1939) mask had a larger nose cup and an improved 4½in (11.4cm) canister with nine reinforcing ribs. American gasmask canisters could be fitted to Japanese hoses and provided better protection from choking agents than the Japanese models. When the gasmask was worn the hose ran over the left shoulder and the canister was removed from the case and fastened to the case's shoulder strap by a tie-tape.

Early equipment was of relatively good manufacture using quality materials. From 1943 this began to change with the introduction of substitute and even shoddy materials, simplified designs, and manufacturing shortcuts.

BARRACKS LIFE

Conformity, subservience to authority, and close living conditions were part of the Japanese soldier's everyday life. He quickly learned that he was at the very bottom of the military hierarchy, and all above him, including recruits who arrived earlier, could inflict their wrath on him. He was reminded he was worth only *issen gorin* (one *sen*, five *rin* – less than a penny), the cost of a Red Paper postcard. When more men were needed the Military Administration Bureau merely mailed more postcards. After all, a private 2nd class cost less than a good artillery horse.

A typical barracks with its closely spaced bunks and the central tables on which soldiers maintained their weapons and equipment, studied, and ate. The rifle rack is seen to the right. A duty NCO ensures that all is in order, even while the troops sleep. Prior to the China Incident soldiers were issued more uniforms than later, with items becoming scarcer as the war wore on. Replacements for worn-out uniforms were simply not available to some units deployed on remote islands. (Courtesy Akira Takizawa)

Barracks hierarchy went beyond mere rank. Recruits themselves had their own divisions: recruits with over three months' service (first quarter inspection), those with over six months', further subdivided into those who had been promoted to private 1st class and those who had not, recalled reservists with different lengths of previous and current service, superior privates, and acting corporals. Those selected for NCO and officer candidate training had their own place in the hierarchy. Among recruits the older soldiers behaved as if they held more status than NCOs and officers – when the NCOs and officers were not present. The older soldiers forced recruits to clean their weapons and equipment, polish shoes and leather gear, serve them meals, run errands, and often perform their minor work and clean-up assignments in the barracks. One's time in the service was an important status symbol; there was nothing else that gave more status, not even promotion. Service time was described as *menko*, a term originating during the 1904–05 Russo-Japanese War, meaning the wooden tray on which food was served. It now meant the rice cooker's side-dish pan and defined the number of meals consumed in one's service. The number of *menko* were more important than the number of stars indicating rank on one's collar.

As a form of entertainment for the old hands, recruits would perform a ritual known as the *min min semi*. A recruit mimicked the cry of the cicadae (*semi*), protesting summer heat as he clung to an 8–10in (203–254mm) diameter barracks center support, his arms and legs wrapped around the varnished post. He might cry "min min" twice before sliding to the floor, no matter how hard he gripped the slick post. He immediately jumped up and repeated the act until completely sapped of strength.

BARRACKS LIFE

Two- or three-story wooden or masonry barracks consisted of long rooms lined on both sides with closely spaced bunks, each provided with a straw-filled mattress, sheet, sawdust-filled tubular pillow, blanket, and a quilt in the winter. A narrow shelf ran along the wall on which were stacked folded clothing and a box for small items. Footwear was stowed under the bunk. At one end of the room was a shelf for buckets and cleaning supplies and beneath it hung brooms, brushes, and mops. Long wooden tables were placed end to end down the aisle with benches on either side. Rifle racks were positioned to divide section areas. It was on the tables that the soldiers cleaned weapons and equipment, studied, and ate. Latrines and baths were in separate buildings. Soldiers washed their own clothes, but unit tailors and cobblers were available for repairs. Unit garrisons were on the outskirts of towns and sometimes located within cities. Soldiers spent what little spare time they had studying and maintaining their equipment. There were moments of amusement though. Here a recruit performs the *min min semi* ritual while his han enjoys a special treat of bottled cider, tinned mandarin oranges, cherries, and pickles received from a soldiers' aid association. (Michael Welpy © Osprey Publishing)

The "flight of the warbler across the valley" (*uguisu-no tani-watari*) employed the long barracks tables placed end to end with a 3ft 3in (1m) gap between each. The recruit picked to play the warbler (*uguisus*) would duck under the table when ordered to "fly" and crawl as fast as he could on all fours to pop his head up in the "valley" between the tables. He would sing out "ho ho-kekyo," mimicking the warbler's spring song as soldiers atop the tables pelted him with shoes, sticks, and manuals. "It was all in fun, a mean fun," reflected an old soldier, "but we all dreaded when it would be our turn."

These and other antics were no more than simple entertainment for the old hands at the recruits' expense, a simplistic hazing and initiation. Corporals and higher-ranking NCOs dealt out real punishments, regardless of the following prescriptions from the Imperial Receipt:

> … Superiors should never treat their inferiors with contempt or arrogance. Except when official duty requires them to be strict and severe, superiors should treat their inferiors with consideration, making kindness their chief aim, so that all grades may unite in their service of the Emperor.

The most common abuse was the liberal use of the fist. On their first day the NCO in change of the han lined the recruits up and ordered them to stand spread-legged for balance, remove their eyeglasses, and clamp their mouths shut. He then went down the line punching each in the face. This was often a daily ritual and might be repeated many times, both for poor performance as a unit or because of the errors of a single recruit. Bamboo swagger sticks, service belts, and even rifle butts were used. NCOs had a pair of "slippers" for off-duty wear around the barracks. This was a pair of worn-out marching shoes with the sides and uppers cut out to form an open slipper, but retaining its hobnails. With these offenders were slapped in the face, leaving scars. At meal times the NCO would select recruits to recite passages of the Imperial Receipt and those making mistakes in the formal court language were denied dinner, although the victim's friends might hide their share of the evening meal and give it to him after lights out. Such punishments were officially forbidden, but officers simply ignored such activities. "It was a game," said a former soldier. "We tried not to get caught, but the sergeants were always watching, and they would catch and punish us … even when we had done nothing wrong. It was just the way of things."

The recruits sometimes inflicted punishment of their own. One who caused problems for others, resulting in group-punishment, often suffered nocturnal beatings from his han. He had dishonored the han and caused a loss of face to the unit as a whole, as the Imperial Receipt once again made clear:

> … you will finally grow selfish and sordid and sink to the last degree of baseness, so that neither loyalty nor value will avail to save you from the contempt of the world. It is not too much to say that you will thus fall into a life-long misfortune. If such an evil once makes its appearance among soldiers and sailors, it will certainly spread like an epidemic, and martial spirit and morale will instantly decline.

Some men broke under the strain and were discharged as unfit.

For minor official infractions the company commander dealt out punishment. Crimes might include minor insolence, being late for formations, damage to property, sleeping on duty, etc., and could mean one to three days' confinement in the unit detention room (*eiso*) behind the guardhouse on poor rations, and of course some unofficial beatings. For more serious crimes such as insubordination or threatening violence to an officer, and theft, gambling, and plundering, a soldier could be court-martialed and assigned to an army disciplinary unit (*rikugun kyoka tai*) maintained in each divisional district. Confinement here was for up to two years. If the sentence was longer, the offender did his first two years in the disciplinary unit and then completed his time in a national prison.

A unit on parade. The regimental color bearer, a lieutenant, was assigned on the table of organization and was not simply an additional duty. Infantry regimental colors depicted the 16-ray rising sun. It differed from the Naval Ensign on which the sun was off center, toward the staff. Unit colors had a purple fringe. The white patch in the lower right corner would bear the regimental designation in black characters. (Courtesy Akira Takizawa)

Regardless of recruit's treatment, he was typically loyal to his unit. The section was his family, the platoon and company an extended family, and the regiment his clan. The army world was an extension of traditional Japanese society, conformity, and clan loyalty. This structure was further enhanced as Japanese units were recruited on a regional basis. Divisions, designated by numbers, were often informally known by the name of their home depot's prefecture. Many of the divisions and regiments existing at the beginning of the war had long histories dating from the 1870s or the turn of the century when they fought in the Russo-Japanese War. That war was a proud moment in Japanese history, the first war in which an oriental country decisively defeated a European power.

Although some American accounts say the soldiers had no lunch, in actual fact three meals per day were served. Breakfast and dinner were eaten in the barracks. There were no mess halls. Meals were carried from the kitchen in covered pails by men sent from each han. In garrison the soldier ate comparatively well, receiving up to twice as much food as his family at home. The daily Japanese diet revolved around a basic rice, fish, and vegetable combination. The army attempted to duplicate this diet and added some meat, extra vegetables, and sweets. The additions were not because soldiers were privileged, but necessary due to their physical exertion and to counter a lifetime's bland diet with insufficient protein and vitamins.

Contrary to popular belief, the Japanese soldier did not live entirely on rice and fish. To the Japanese rice was a staple food, just as bread is to Westerners, and constituted over 50 percent of the soldier's diet. A soup or stew side dish accompanied the rice as did pickles, different from Western varieties.

Polished (white) rice was more common than the more nutritious unpolished (brown) as it could be preserved longer. Bulk uncooked rice (*kome*) was shipped in woven rice-straw or burlap bags, as were wheat, barley, flour, salt, and sugar. Being relatively stout, the bags were used as sandbags once emptied. Pre-cooked compressed cakes of rice, barley, and wheat were packed in tins, sometimes mixed with red beans. White bread was also served.

The Japanese usually seasoned cooked rice (*gohan*) with soybean sauce (*shoyu*) or fermented soybean paste (*miso*). Japanese soy sauce is much saltier and "hotter" than that found in oriental restaurants in Western countries. *Miso* was commonly used for preparing soups. Both *shoyu* and *miso* were issued in liquid and dehydrated form. Salt, vinegar, curry, ginger, and bean paste were other basic condiments. Tea (*ocha*) was the preferred beverage and was served hot if at all possible. Canned rice beer (*biru*) and bottled rice wine (*saké*) were frequently issued. Cider was another popular beverage.

BELIEF AND BELONGING

The Japanese soldier relied on two kinds of strength: the strength of individual will (*seishin*) and the national quest to expand the Empire, the Spirit of Yamato (*Yamato damashii*). "Bringing the eight corners of the world under one roof" – world hegemony or unity (*Hakko Ichi-u*) – was the ultimate goal. The destiny of the army, therefore, was the destiny of the Japanese Empire and the Emperor. A Japanese citizen was taught this in school and in the army. Whatever he did was justified, for he did it for the Emperor, a deity. From the Imperial Receipt to Soldiers and Sailors:

> If you all do your duty, and being one with Us in spirit do your utmost for the protection of the state, Our people will long enjoy the blessings of peace, and the might and dignity of Our Empire will shine in the world.

Japan knew its resources were insufficient for a protracted war against the unified Western colonial powers. It would mobilize its limited resources and plunder the

Very small numbers of Japanese were taken prisoner. The Marine Corps captured only 4,500 prisoners while killing over 200,000. Here an off-frame Japanese-American interpreter questions a rare prisoner on Guam. (USMC)

conquered territories, but the total mobilization of the national spirit (*kokuminseishin sodoin*) was what would win the war and allow the Empire to prevail against the enemies surrounding it on all sides. "One-hundred-million people, one mind" (*ichioku isshin*) was a popular slogan, though misleading as was much else – Japan's population was 72 million.

Japan was both an agrarian and industrial society dominated by a warrior class. The samurai no longer existed, but their traditions and values did. The concept of *bushido* (way of the warrior) very much guided the armed forces. *Bushido* evolved between the 9th and 12th centuries, influenced by Zen, Buddhism, Confucianism, and also by Shintoism, the official state religion since the 1880s. It stressed a martial spirit, self-sacrifice, loyalty, justice, a sense of shame if dishonored, refined comportment, purity, modesty, frugality, and honor – honor being more important than life. However, there was no stipulation for these virtues to be granted to one's enemies.

The army placed complete faith in spiritual training (*seishin kyoiku*), its strength of will over the material superiority of its enemies. While Westerners tend to dismiss

Army life saw the observance of frequent ceremonies. Here officers participate in a ceremony honoring warhorses lost in combat. Such traditions formed a bond within units and made recruits understand the sacrifices made by all who served before them. (US Army)

spiritual training, often owing to the Japanese's misplaced faith in it and resultant disasters, it was nonetheless a viable factor, within certain limitations. Belief in it was so strong, and the Japanese soldier so hardened to field conditions, that *seishin* can be attributed to many of the feats of endurance that astounded Western foes. Soldiers were expected to be tough and never demonstrate sensitivity or weakness in the face of adversity.

Regardless of the class system and the vast separation between officers and men, Japanese officers willingly shared the perils of combat with their troops. Officers literally led from the front with even senior officers directly engaged, more so than was common among their Western counterparts. Command posts were often located further forward than Western practice. Officers were expected to be physically and mentally tougher than their men.

Tactical doctrine focused on attack, surprise, rapid movements, commanders operating well forward, and relatively simple plans. Offensive actions were the norm. In the 1928 edition of *Tosui Koryo* (Principles of Strategic Command), the words defense, retreat, and surrender were expunged, as they were considered detrimental to morale and the martial spirit. The Japanese had an almost unreasonable abhorrence of defensive actions. If a Japanese officer were confronted with an unexpected, unusual or complicated situation in battle, he would find a way to attack – attack at unexpected times and points, along unanticipated routes and often with force ratios Western armies would not have attempted, all increasing the surprise factor.

Complete annihilation of the enemy (*teki*) was the primary goal; allowing the enemy to escape to fight again was unacceptable. This of course resulted in the surrender of large numbers of Allied prisoners, who did not fight to the death as the Japanese did and who could not be as easily disposed of as the Chinese. The conquering of Western colonial territories meant large numbers of civilians were interned, a situation for which the Japanese were totally unprepared. The treatment of prisoners and internees varied greatly, with little guidance provided from higher command.

Self-sacrifice was expected of any soldier. It was the Imperial Receipt on Education, issued in 1880, that established the perception of an absolute and divine Emperor, a "deity incarnate," and that "… the climax of harmony is the sacrifice of the life of a subject for the Emperor." The most perplexing aspect of the Japanese soldier to Westerners was his willingness to die in combat (known as *shiki*) for the Emperor. Shintoism elevated dying for the Emperor to a state of grace. This belief was not simply limited to officers or some elite, fanatical unit, but was common to virtually every soldier regardless of rank or position. The Field Service Code (*Senjinkun*) spelled this out: "In defense, always retain the spirit of the attack and maintain freedom of action. Never give up a position, but rather die." This spirit was not just a simple statement in a regulation; it was the result of lifelong conditioning in a culture revering honor, loyalty, and obedience to superiors above all else. To surrender or even to be captured in what the West considered honorable conditions meant failure and dishonor to the Emperor, and this brought dishonor to the soldier's family. As Captain Rikibei Inogichi explained: "We must give our lives to the Emperor and Country, this is an inborn feeling. We Japanese base our lives on obedience to the Emperor and Country. On the other hand, we wish for the best place in death, according to Bushido."

The Japanese martial spirit went beyond mere fighting to the death; it meant a willingness to sacrifice oneself in a fatal attack that might result in the death of only one enemy solider and, if necessary, committing suicide to prevent capture. Ritual suicide (*seppuku*; incorrectly called *hara-kiri* – belly-slitting) committed by officers failing in their mission was one thing, but for a private, with no superiors present, to willingly place his rifle's muzzle to his head and push the trigger with a toe, or hold a grenade to his chest and pull the pin, is another thing entirely. There was no ritual about it; no one "made" him do it. Obligation was foremost in Japanese culture, and the soldier was obligated to die for the Emperor.

Facing an enemy with few heavy weapons allowed the Japanese to employ medieval-like stone and masonry forts in some areas in China. Here a Nambu 6.5mm Taisho Type 11 (1922) light machine gun is mounted atop a rice-bag platform. Its tripod can be seen between the rifleman's legs. (US Army)

Mass suicide was also common. The *banzai* charge, ordered by a commander as a last resort, or a self-destructive *gyokysai* (lit. "breaking of the jewels") attack ordered by the Emperor, was a final hope of shattering the enemy's will with the superior *seishin* of the Japanese soldier. Such futile attacks only hastened the inevitable end, however.

Japanese soldiers were captured, however; often severely wounded or unconscious. Allied authorities reported Japanese prisoners through the International Red Cross, but Japanese authorities reported to their families that they had died in combat. The Japanese government actually paid death gratuities to the families of 40,000 men reported dead who were repatriated after the surrender. Once he found himself a prisoner, the soldier lost all sense of worth and honor. He had dishonored himself, his family, the army, the Empire, and the Emperor. He was no longer worthy, no longer alive. Viewed by the Allies as brutal, merciless, cunning, and capable of all forms of trickery, Japanese prisoners surprised their captors by their complete cooperation and willingness to provide intelligence.

What did the average Japanese soldier think of the war? Here is an excerpt from the diary of an unidentified 144th Infantry Regiment soldier tasked to seize Guam:

> Japan-America, War! It looks as though the hardships we have borne until now will be rewarded! We have received life from the Showa Reign. Men have no greater love than this. Now, prosper, Fatherland!

ON CAMPAIGN

The campaign experience of the average Japanese soldier varied tremendously during the war, depending on his theatre of deployment, his military occupation and the time period of his service. A good route to exploring the type of soldier who would eventually fight at Iwo Jima, and the general combat capability of the Japanese Army, is through the experience of a composite character. Note, however, that the following narrative is based entirely on documented events – the soldier is a composite of real individuals rather than an entire fiction – and all events and tactical procedures are faithfully rendered.

Nito-hei Taro was conscripted in January 1943. His residence was in the Nagoya Divisional District and his father was a fishing-net manufacturer. (Nagoya is located south-west of Tokyo on central Honshu, largest of the Home Islands.) He undertook training in the 3rd Depot Division's 6th Infantry Replacement Training Regiment. After only three months' training he was shipped to North China with his replacement unit. They would not serve together as a unit, but would be assigned to different battalions within the 26th Division's 11th Independent Infantry Regiment. The 11th was one of several regiments, assigned to different divisions, which received replacements from the 6th Infantry Replacement Training Regiment whose personnel were conscripted in the Nagoya Regimental District. The 26th Division had been raised in 1939 and deployed to China that same year. It was unusual in that its assigned regiments were designated "independent." The division served in Shansi Province protecting coalmines and industrial facilities. The independent regiments' battalions had only three rifle companies rather than the usual four, lacked antitank guns, and had fewer supporting weapons.

Taro was shipped aboard an army-operated troop transport from Hiroshima, one of the main ports of departure. The often stormy passage across the Yellow Sea to Tientsin lasted only a few days, but was a miserable experience. Troop quarters were crowded with seasick soldiers. Board platforms were provided for sleeping, meals were irregular and usually cold, and latrines consisted of wooden stalls hung over the ship's side.

Japanese infantry regiments (*rentai*) varied greatly in internal organization, but typically possessed three infantry battalions (*daitai* – designated I–III), a regimental gun company with six 7.5cm infantry guns, an antitank company with six 3.7cm or 4.7cm guns, and a company-sized regimental train for transporting ammunition and supplies. Battalions generally had four rifle companies, although some had only three. Rifle

A Nambu 7.7mm Type 92 (1932) heavy machine gun crew searches for targets in China. An 11-man section manned heavy machine guns with either eight or 12 assigned to infantry battalion machine-gun companies. (US Army)

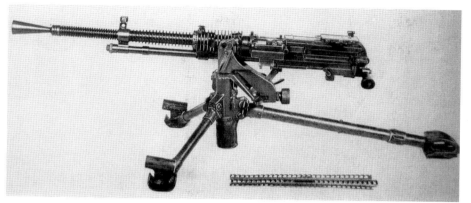

A Nambu 7.7mm Type 1 (1941) heavy machine gun. This was an improved model of the similar Type 92 (1932), which differed in that its larger cooling fins went all the way to the foresight. Fed by 30-round strips, the weapons seldom overheated because of the robust cooling system and slow rate of fire: 450–500 rounds per minute. US machine guns fired at the same rate, but overheated more easily because of a less robust cooling system. (US Army)

companies were numbered in sequence through the regiment (1–9 or 1–12). The battalion had a machine-gun company with eight or 12 7.7mm HMGs (*kikanju*), a gun platoon with two or four 7cm infantry guns, and a company-size train. Japanese units had a higher strength level at regimental and lower echelons than comparable US units, but their combat power, because of fewer crew-served weapons, was less.

The 180-man rifle companies (*chutai*) had a 19-man headquarters with a captain or lieutenant as commander (*chutaicho*), a personnel warrant officer (equivalent to an executive or administrative officer), sergeant-major in charge of personnel records (roughly equating to a 1st sergeant), supply sergeant, arms and equipment sergeant, four medical orderlies (often there was only one), an officer's orderly, bugler, and eight messengers. The three 54-man rifle platoons (*shotai*) had a two-man headquarters with a 2nd lieutenant platoon commander (*shokoricho*) and a liaison sergeant (*renrakukashi*). Roughly equating to a US platoon sergeant, the liaison sergeant's main combat duty was to ensure orders were relayed to the sections through arm signals and messengers. The three 13-man LMG sections were led by corporal section leaders (*buntaicho*), and consisted of eight riflemen and a four-man LMG crew. One rifleman usually carried a rifle-grenade launcher. Sections assigned to strengthened units had the addition of a two-man 5cm grenade discharger crew. The grenade discharger section was led by a corporal and had three two-man grenade discharger crews plus six riflemen, who also carried ammunition. The grenade discharger crews were armed with rifles. Smaller sections were common. In combat, when strength dwindled the grenade discharger section was usually absorbed into the LMG sections.

Most divisions possessed fewer than 200 trucks. Even German divisions, heavily reliant on horse transport, might have 500–600 trucks. Horsepower was a major facet in all units down to company level. Packhorses and one-horse, two-wheel carts hauled headquarters and communications equipment, aid stations, rations, horse forage, ammunition, and crew-served weapons. Most soldiers were involved to some degree in the care and rigging of packhorses, of which a regiment might have 600–800.

NORTH CHINA

To the warriors of the Yamato race, the Chinese were less than human, as equally despised as the Koreans; to the Chinese the invaders were Japanese devils (*Jihpen kuei-tzu*). This centuries-old hatred led to a medieval form of warfare, with mercy and sentiment unknown to both sides. Apart from fighting the nationalist and communist armies, the Japanese had to deal with guerrillas. They were not viewed as armed combatants, but termed "bandits" (*hizoku*), the colloquial for guerrillas. Captured bandits were not considered prisoners of war, but outlaws.

Much of Taro's China service consisted of guard duty and patrols. Guard duty was an endless and boring task necessitating long hours of diligence. Guerrilla raids and sabotage, while infrequent, were always a threat. Taro, now a private 1st class, found that while discipline remained strict, so long as he remained awake on guard duty, was never late for formations, was suitably subservient to superiors, maintained his rifle and equipment, and made a show of working hard, China service was relatively easy – except for the mind-numbing boredom and exhausting marches through mud or dust. He had gone through a brief period of hazing from the veterans, but once he had participated in a patrol he was accepted as a member of the unit. NCOs were rough with the men and not above applying the fist or boot to a slow or negligent soldier, but such punishment was infrequent and usually deserved.

Typical punishments included repeatedly apologizing to a dropped piece of equipment or standing at attention for hours in full equipment with the rifle on the right shoulder in the heat of the day, snow, or rain. A section or platoon might be punished for some group transgression by standing at attention in formation and endlessly singing *Hohei no Honryo* (The Heart of the Infantry).

Acceptance by the unit came with a price on that first patrol. The platoon was marching down a back road before dawn to establish a checkpoint on a main road. The quiet shuffling of boots was the only sound when a startlingly loud rifle shot cracked out, immediately followed by the snap of the passing bullet. Corporals shouted and men scattered off the road, deploying as skirmishers as they had practiced. Lying in the weeds Taro could hear nothing except the hard breathing of the men next to him, their rifles aimed at the faint horizon. After a few minutes there were chuckles and remarks about bored bandits.

After more minutes of silence four scouts were sent toward the rising ground from where the shot had come. Time passed and a scout returned. Taro heard him tell the lieutenant there was a small hamlet over the low ridge. The shot had been a warning to

FIGHTING "BANDITS", NORTH CHINA

Japan's basic policy in China was "burn all, destroy all, kill all," at least in regards to the "bandit extermination" campaigns. "Bandits," regardless of their actual status, were outlaws, and their capture usually led to their execution. To deal with the freezing conditions of North China, Manchuria, and Korea, the Japanese soldier was well supplied with cold-weather clothing and equipment. The fur-lined winter coat was provided with detachable sleeves, allowing it to be worn in milder conditions. Lined wool trousers were provided as well as wool knit undershirts, three-finger mittens, and winter shoes, felt boots, and fur-lined felt puttees. Fur-lined canteen and rice cooker covers were also issued, the latter because pre-cooked food was carried in the cooker and this prevented its freezing. The infantryman on the left is issued a 7.7mm Type 99 (1939) rifle, much more effective than the 6.5mm rifle with which he trained. He carries his gear in a tube pack while his corporal section leader (center) uses the 1941 backpack. Officers carried different equipment. The soldier's platoon commander (right) carries a Nambu 8mm Taisho Type 14 (1925) pistol, officer's canteen, binoculars, dispatch case, and a Type 94 (1934) sword, soon to be tested. The evidence of the bandit's illicit activities lay on the ground in the form of two Chinese 23rd Year (1933) Model hand grenades. (Michael Welpy © Osprey Publishing) alert the bandits obviously hiding there. The platoon moved fast. Three sections formed a horseshoe around the dozen mud and straw-thatched huts while one section under the liaison NCO barged into huts, rousting out the sleeping inhabitants. The surrounding of the cluster of shabby structures was conducted as a double-envelopment, an exercise they had practiced often. There was a great deal of shouting, women screaming, children crying, breaking pottery, and chickens squawking. Taro had expected a vicious firefight to break out in the bandit stronghold, but not a shot sounded.

The cordoning sections were called into the hamlet, leaving sentries posted on the outskirts, and men were spotted among the huts as others searched them. Terrified families huddled in the mud under a guard pointing a bayonet at them. Some soldiers occupied themselves collecting food and chickens. "We saw them only as creatures and not a care we gave of them," remarked a China veteran.

Taro and his comrade were overturning water barrels in which weapons and contraband may have been hidden when his section corporal pointed at him and motioned him to follow. Rounding the corner of a hut Taro found himself in the company of the lieutenant, liaison NCO, his section leader and another, a couple of lance corporals, and the two other newly assigned men. Three young Chinese men were lying on their backs in the mud, their arms and bare feet bound. Two were wearing only breechcloths and one was clad in black peasant's clothes. All bore the signs of rifle butt blows on their terrified faces.

The liaison NCO, carrying a muddy Chinese-made Mauser rifle, fell in the three new soldiers. Standing at attention, the lieutenant simply ordered, "With bayonets, execute these bandits." Taro was later stunned when he realized he had not hesitated a moment. He simply followed orders as had been drilled into him over the brutal months of conditioning.

Faint crying could be heard from behind the platoon as they marched on toward the main road. No one said a word. At the evening meal the three new men received an extra share of fresh chicken with their rice.

Such was duty in China, for which servicemen received the colorful China Incident Medal (*Sina Jihen Jugun Kisho*). Itto-hei Taro was awarded the red chevron of the Diligence Award (*Seikin Sho*) to sew on his upper right sleeve, which represented six months of good conduct and efficient service.

In the field the soldier carried one or two days' worth of tinned meat or fish rations and up to five days of rice ration. Sections often pooled their rations for collective cooking, but battalion field kitchens also provided meals. A containerized group ration with 40 meal portions was also provided. Its contents were packed in a tin container inside a wooden crate. Each portion contained: 10½oz (297g) polished rice, ½oz (14g) dehydrated miso, vitamin B paste, vitamin A and D tablets, and powdered tea (for vitamin C). Matches were included along with 20 3oz (84g) tins of heating alcohol; one tin was sufficient to heat two rice portions.

Foraging, or rather pillaging, was a common means of supplementing rations in China. Punitive patrols, dispatched as much for foraging as for tactical objectives, would loot peasants' gardens and homes, steal chickens and pigs, and hand-grenade ponds before wading in to pick up stunned fish. Comfort bags (*imon bukuro*) were provided from soldiers' aid associations. These might include soap, toothpaste, razorblades, cigarettes, matches, postcards, needles and thread, hard candy, tinned meats and vegetables, and a letter with good wishes. An unknown soldier reminisced, "Sometimes we talked of home or women, but mostly we talked about food."

The issue of the Japanese armed forces' mass employment of comfort women (*jugun ianfu*) is controversial, with Japan making little effort to compensate victims or officially apologize after the war. Up to 200,000 women were forced into

Sections often combined their rations and cooked in the field. Here rice cookers are tended over an open fire. The rice was cooked in a small number of mess kits and then distributed to all troops. (Courtesy Akira Takizawa)

institutionalized prostitution: Koreans, Chinese, Filipinos, Indonesians, Burmese, and others. The concept of army-managed comfort stations is said to have originated in Shanghai in 1932 because of 223 reported rapes by Japanese soldiers. The system grew and was an established operation in all occupied areas. Young women were recruited as entertainers, laundresses, or factory workers with promises of good pay. They were taken away from their home areas; Korean women, for example, were shipped to all corners of the occupied zones. They received only minimal pay – if any – little food, suffered poor living conditions, and were virtual prisoners servicing 20–30 soldiers a day. Specific hours were allotted for other ranks, NCOs, and officers. In some cases special comfort stations were established for officers. Many women were brutalized, murdered, or died of disease. Suicide was common. Contractors, to whom soldiers paid a minimal charge, operated the comfort stations rather than the army directly. Charges made were mostly profit for the operators, which explained the poor food and conditions the women suffered. Army doctors periodically inspected the women and the troops were issued condoms, though some refused their use. "I am going to be dead soon," some soldiers told the women, "I do not fear a disease." Some women were allowed to return home when their one- or two-year contracts expired, but many were held until the war's end. Few received any of the promised back pay and were fortunate to be given minimal travel expenses.

The Japanese soldier's ability to march long distances at a rapid rate, and the use of bicycles by some units, caught the enemy by surprise. Soldiers traveled much lighter than their Western counterparts. The author once asked a veteran of the China Incident what of his service he remembered most vividly. Looking thoughtful he shrugged and said, "We marched and we marched. And it was always hot or cold."

In the attack the company deployed from a march column and moved to a line of departure (*tenkaisen*) where it may or may not

While soldiers mostly did their own cooking in the field, during active operations regimental field kitchens cooked rice, soup, and stew for issue to the troops for breakfast and dinner. For lunch they would produce rice balls. A field kitchen like this could operate on the move, being drawn by two horses. (US Army)

have occupied assembly areas (*kaishin*), depending on the degree of coordination and preparation time allowed. Seldom did leaders conduct reconnaissance or brief the troops: the aim was to attack as quickly as possible. Platoons crossed the line of departure on order with two LMG sections forward traveling in files. The third LMG and grenade discharger sections followed. Moving in files eased control, presented a narrow target, and allowed rapid movement, especially through rough terrain and at night. When contact was made with the enemy the two lead sections swung outward, pivoting in the center to form a line. They would place heavy fire on the enemy position while the third section launched a flanking or enveloping attack to the left or right depending on enemy positions and terrain. The enveloping attack differed from the flanking attack in that it went deeper into the enemy's rear. The grenade discharger section remained behind the fixing sections and placed grenade fires on the enemy. It might also fire smoke rounds in an effort to blind the enemy. While the flanking/enveloping attack was doctrine at all echelons, it was more common for units to attack immediately from the front. The attack would close rapidly with little effort to maintain alignment. Grenades were thrown and the infantrymen rushed in with bayonets fixed.

A unit pack column crosses a makeshift footbridge during the Philippines campaign. Pack mules and horses were used extensively in China and the Philippines. (Yoshinobu Sakakura)

The company would often advance with a single platoon in the lead, preceded a few hundred yards forward by a handful of scouts. When contact was made the lead platoon would fix the enemy with fire, possibly supported by HMGs, the battalion's main fire-support weapon. Of the two following platoons, one might move forward to join the fixing platoon while the other, or both following platoons, conducted a flanking or enveloping attack. If the enemy was weak, occupied a narrow front, or the terrain was favorable, a double-envelopment might be executed. Double envelopments were risky because of separating one's forces and the possibility of the enveloping elements firing into each other.

In October summer uniforms were turned in and wool uniforms issued, with an extra blanket, a pile-lined winter coat with fur-fringed hood and cuffs, and other cold-weather clothing. Campaigning largely came to a halt, but sniping and harassing ambushes were inflicted on patrols and supply trains. There were few standup fights – as was guerrilla practice. The officers grew more frustrated and often found relief by selecting villagers to be executed in reprisal. All considered this a justifiable "punishment" of those who harbored and fed bandits.

December 1943 found an unexpected increase in communist guerilla activity. Two of the 11th Independent Infantry's battalions were dispatched further south than they had been before, along with a battalion of the 13th. Being a security division, the regiments possessed few packhorses; horses had to be borrowed from other battalions to

An advancing heavy machine gun section manhandles its Nambu 7.7mm Type 92 (1932) gun using the detachable carrying handles fitted to the tripod. The complete gun weighed 122lb (55kg). (Saburo Miyamoto)

move ammunition and supplies. Battalions from other divisions were involved in the "bandit suppression campaign." The days were spent marching over rolling hills in long columns. Nights found them camped on hilltops around roaring bonfires with pickets posted on the hillsides. Villages were cordoned, searched, and looted. Bandit suspects were rounded up and marched along with the columns. Every third day the battalion rested. Most of the prisoners were sent to a local base, but some were kept to "initiate" replacements and recalled reservists. After all had been tested in this manner, the officers and senior NCOs still held some prisoners back to test their ever-thirsty swords.

Taro's battalion soon had its chance for action. A group of 30–40 bandits had attempted to ambush a supply train late one afternoon. Fortuitously, a following company crested a hill as the bandits initiated their ambush. Surprised, the would-be ambushers withdrew to a ridge to the south. Taro's battalion, to which the supply carts were heading, was bivouacked to the east on its rest day, and immediately moved to intercept the bandits. Moving west of the ridge's south side, the bandits collided with the battalion. Unable to escape to the east because of the pursuing company, nor foolish enough to strike north across the broad open plain, they scattered into an area of maze-like ravines bordering the river blocking their way south. After dark they would abandon their weapons and brave the river's ice floes.

The battalion encircled the area and, ascertaining the bandits' plan, began randomly lobbing infantry gun rounds into the ravines. HMGs were set up to cover the ravines' outlets along the river. Probes located the ravines' inland mouths and blocked them as platoons were moved into position. Hours passed, but finally two red flares fired from a grenade discharger signaled platoons and sections to begin sweeping down ravines. There was a high chance the advancing probes would run into one another, but that was a risk the battalion commander accepted. To wait until dawn meant the bandits would escape.

All armies endorsed the night attack, but few practiced it on a regular basis. Control and coordination were next to impossible. Once contact was made any semblance of control

The Wound Badges (*Gunjin Shoi Kisho*) were instituted on August 3, 1938. The gold 1st Class was for combat wounds and the silver 2nd Class for disabling non-combat injuries or illness. The badge was worn on the left breast pocket. (Gordon Rottman)

would fall apart, elements would become lost, intermingled, and casualties would be high, with many inflicted by friendly fire. The Japanese Army routinely accepted the risks and for them the night attack was common. They were used to small units operating independently; even daylight attacks were frequently uncoordinated, and a moderate casualty count was of little concern.

Taro's section moved down a ravine, their rifles with bayonets fixed in their right hands and their left hands gripping the belt of the man in front. Moving quietly at a crawl, even though rifle shots, sharp machine-gun bursts and the bang of grenades covered their movement, the dozen men wound their way down the ravine.

Without warning, rifles cracked from the right and the section machine gun ripped loose a long shattering burst. Rifles crackled and grenades detonated with blue-white flashes. Blinded by flashes, Taro rushed to the side of the ravine from which the rifles had fired. He clambered up the slippery snow-covered slope and kneeled. A black shape rushed at him. He fired once and slashed wildly with his bayonet. The body crashed into him, bowling him over – to save his life. A grenade detonated only meters in front of him, ringing his ears as fragments whined over his prone body. Another soldier flopped down beside him with a moan. Regardless, the man staggered to his feet and rushed forward. Taro was up and moving. More rifle shots and his comrade gagged and tumbled into a shallow ravine to their front. Taro slid across the snow into a prone position and fired his four remaining rounds into the ravine. He rolled on to his back, yanked open his left cartridge box, pulled out a clip, silently thanking the lieutenant for ordering them to remove their right gloves before advancing, rolled back, and stripped the rounds into his rifle. He fired once before hearing a thump to his left. Peering in that direction he saw sparks and then a blinding blue-white flash.

At dawn the aidman and lieutenant found him. Tiny grenade fragments had peppered his left shoulder, side, and leg. The lieutenant noted the six expended cartridges in the trampled snow, the bloodstained bayonet, and the bodies of three dead bandits, one lying bayoneted behind Taro and two shot in the ravine.

In the line-of-communications hospital at Kalgan an officer presented Taro with the Wound Badge 1st Class (*Gunjin Shoi Kisho*) and a letter of merit from the battalion commander, a rare honor. It was seldom that a soldier received any formal recognition for valor. For a soldier to be awarded even the lowest decoration, the Order of the Golden Kite (*Kinshi Kunsho*), was extraordinary. He was ordered to write a letter home informing his parents of his condition. After a couple of weeks he was loaded on a train and taken to a convalescent hospital in Shanghai. There, letters from his family finally reached him.

After recovering, Itto-hei Taro found himself reassigned to another unit, also supported by his home divisional district, the 18th Infantry Regiment, 29th Division, stationed at Liaoyang, Manchuria. This was a newer division activated in August 1941 and soon sent to Manchuria as part of the Kwantung Army reserve undergoing "anti-Soviet" training. February 1944 found the 29th reorganizing as a sea operations division optimized to allow its regiments to operate more effectively on semi-detached deployments on Pacific islands. (Allied intelligence referred to this structure as a "regimental combat team" organization.) Fillers were drawn from other units to bring the division up to strength, its thousands of horses were turned in, the artillery and engineer regiments were broken up and their battalions and companies were reassigned directly to the infantry regiments. The motor transport and medical units were reduced and a sea transport regiment was assigned with organic landing barges. The 18th Infantry was more heavily armed than the other regiments, with even its own light tank company. It was a strike unit intended to conduct counter-landings or to reinforce the lighter 38th and 50th Infantry defending islands.

After a three-day train ride from Manchuria, the 29th Division was issued tropical uniforms and embarked aboard three transports at Pusan, Korea, on February 24. With the 18th Infantry aboard the Sakito Maru, the division sailed for the Mariana Islands far to the south. Indications were that the Americans would soon strike into the islands.

The Japanese were adept at camouflage and deception measures. This is a dummy fighter aircraft constructed of bamboo on Yotan Airfield, Okinawa. Such deceptive measures increased as the war went on. (US Army)

SOUTH SEAS

The trip to Saipan was an ordeal with overcrowding, short rations, no bathing water, and requiring round-the-clock wear of life vests and individual equipment. On February 29 the convoy bearing the 29th Division was two days out of Saipan, its first stop en route to Guam. Taro's company was standing watch that day. Companies rotated this duty, standing two-hour watches with all men lining the decks with all available binoculars.

Torpedoes suddenly slammed into the *Sakito Maru* and *Aki Maru*. The *Aki* was only damaged, but the *Sakito* was aflame and sinking. The USS *Trout* (SS-202) launched the attack, but was soon sunk by an escorting destroyer. Rope nets were dropped and the troops went over the sides. They drifted all night in the chilly water in life vests and on bamboo rafts intended to swim machine guns ashore. Captain Sakae Oba of the 18th Infantry (who surrendered his band of hold-outs in December 1945, a year and a half after Saipan fell) recalls hearing men singing army songs as he drifted through the night. Destroyers rescued 1,688 of the 18th Infantry's 3,080 men the next morning. The regimental commander was not among them.

Taken to Saipan, the regiment was partly rebuilt with transient personnel and others detached from various straggler units. Most of the regimental artillery and eight of its tanks were lost with the *Sakito*, as were most other weapons. Some men managed to retain rifles, belts, and bayonets as expected, but most were without and some had even shed shoes and uniforms.

Other units sent to Saipan suffered from submarine attacks and as a result there were some 4,000 unorganized stragglers, many without weapons and of little use to the defense. Time was not available to organize and equip these "useless troops" (*yuhei*). Some 600 18th Infantry survivors were organized into a new I Battalion under a captain and attached to the 43rd Division when it arrived in May. The remnants of the other two battalions were sent to Guam. 18th Infantry was positioned north of Tanapag Harbor on Saipan's east-central coast. The battalion's mission was to execute a counter-landing via landing barges behind the invading Americans on their own beachhead. Another mission would be to reinforce Tinian a few miles to the south if the Americans landed there first. The Japanese command expected the Americans to land either further to the south of or directly into Tanapag Harbor. Taro found himself promoted to superior private (*joto-hei*) and placed in charge of an understrength 2nd Company section, nine men armed only with rifles. The platoon had only a single LMG and a grenade discharger.

His platoon was assigned to a low rise overlooking the coast road. They dug one- and two-man foxholes (*kojinyo engo*) deep enough for them to fight standing up. They called these "octopus traps" (*takotsubo*) after a hole dug above the low-tide line into which an octopus would crawl, only to be trapped when the tide went out. Camouflage was left to farm boys who had a natural eye for blending it into surrounding vegetation; city dwellers were hopelessly inept at the task. During the day they dug more holes, alternate positions in the hills, and watched American planes flying high overhead, dropping their bombs and seemingly immune to the few remaining antiaircraft guns. American ships on the horizon sailed back and forth belching puffs of black smoke. At night the soldiers went down to the shore and placed fresh camouflage on the hidden landing barges. The ships began coming at night too. The bombardment seldom ceased in the first two weeks of June. Food was adequate, although its delivery was erratic. During action when soldiers could not cook, the field kitchen supplied rice balls.

The field ration was 3lb (1.5kg), but in the South Pacific it was not standardized and varied from 2½lb (1.1kg) to 3½lb (1.6kg) per day. Two types of packaged field rations were issued in brown paper bags. The "A-ration" (3,140 calories) consisted of 2lb (0.9kg) of rice and 5oz (150g) of tinned meat or fish. The "B-ration" (3,000 calories) consisted of 1½lb (0.7kg) of hard biscuits (*kanpan*) in three meal-size paper

Blasted by bombs and machine guns, 30ft (9m) long Kohatsu landing barges lay swamped along a beach. Besides Imperial Navy landing craft, the Imperial Army Shipping Engineer units operated their own landing barges. (US Army)

bags and 2oz (57g) tinned meat or fish. Both were issued with a small amount of salt and caramel or hard candy. Vitamin B supplement was provided in tablet, liquid, or paste form (in a squeeze tube).

Rations were supplemented with locally procured foods such as sweet potatoes, bananas, coconuts, taro, and papayas. On Saipan sugarcane and a fermented palm wine (*yashizake*) could be had from the Japanese colonists. Goats, pigs, dogs, and fish supplemented issue rations. Island garrisons were encouraged to plant vegetable gardens.

Two types of specially packaged combat rations were available. The "compressed ration for one-day" (*asssku koryo*) was wrapped in heavy brown crepe paper with the folds secured by glue. It measured 3¼ x 3½ x 1¾in (8.3 x 8.9 x 4.4cm) and weighed 9oz (255g). Its "main dish" was six rectangular cakes of compressed wheat or barley, four cakes of sugar, three brown cakes of dried fish, and one or two pink cakes of salted dried plums. The cakes could be eaten as they were or crumbled into water and cooked as a hot cereal.

The other combat ration was the "rice flour and side-dish ration" packed in a cellophane package secured by tie-strings on both ends. It was about 8in (20.3cm) long and 3½in (8.9cm) wide, and was sufficient for two emergency meals. It was also used to supplement the rice ration or other foods. It held four small brown paper bags each containing two dried mixed fish-and-vegetable cakes ("side-dishes") and two bags of pre-cooked rice flour. Two bags of cakes were crumbled and mixed with one bag of flour and a small amount of water. It was mixed into a dough-like paste and eaten cold. There was also a paper-wrapped "confection bar" of limited issue for emergency use. It weighed 1½oz (46g) and was made of flour, sugar, tea, milk, eggs, and butter.

After days of incessant aerial and naval bombardment, the American tidal wave struck on June 15. One defender described the US invasion fleet as "bigger than the entire Imperial Navy." Scores of amphibian tractors rolled ashore, which the Japanese called "Alligators." "They came across the beaches like locusts, spouting flames and we could not stop them." The 2nd and 4th MarDivs carved out a large beachhead on D-Day on the lower east coast, well south of Taro's position. It was impossible to move during the day with airplanes constantly overhead. Naval gunfire sometimes fell in the 18th Infantry's area, but these were usually short bursts mostly striking in the hills behind them.

On June 17 in the early morning hours a regimental-sized counterattack was launched supported by 44 tanks. This was to be the largest tank battle in the Pacific. The counterattack struck the 2nd MarDiv on the beachhead's north flank. The results were devastating – to the Japanese. Over 300 soldiers died and 31 tanks were destroyed. That same day the Japanese Army chief of staff, Hideki Tojo, sent a message

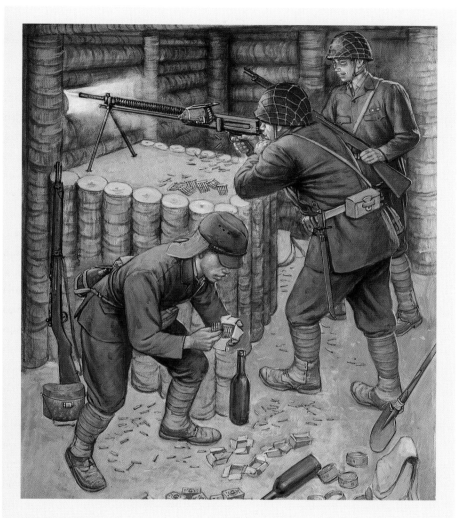

PILLBOX DEFENSE

Fighting to the death in a pillbox, a group of Japanese infantrymen operate a Nambu 6.5mm Taisho Type 11 (1922) LMG. Japanese pillboxes were stoutly constructed, often of resilient palm logs covered by thick layers of earth. The Japanese ability to blend them into the surrounding terrain and vegetation made them difficult to detect and engage. Protection from grenades and hand-delivered demolitions was paramount and might include overhead cover, a small embrasure, a ditch to catch rolling grenades, an angular entrance trench, an interior wall to block blast, and a narrow sump dug in the floor into which a grenade could be kicked. Regardless of the protective measures taken, any pillbox could be defeated by direct tank and bazooka fire, and flamethrowers. (Michael Welpy © Osprey Publishing) meant to reinforce the Saipan garrison's spirit: "Because the fate of the Japanese Empire depends on the result of your operation, inspire the spirit of the officers and men and to the very end continue to destroy the enemy gallantly and persistently and thus alleviate the anxiety of our Emperor." The division chief of staff responded, "Have received your honorable Imperial words and we are grateful for the boundless magnanimity of Imperial favor. By becoming the bulwark of the Pacific with 10,000 deaths we hope to requite the Imperial favor."

Rumors spread that the Combined Fleet was on its way to destroy the Americans and work was being rushed on an airstrip on the island's north end, as reinforcements would be flown in. Some men mentioned that no Japanese aircraft were seen battling the Americans. They were told to clear such doubts from their heads. On the afternoon of the 17th orders were received for the 18th Infantry to launch its planned counter-landing on the American beaches and attack them from the rear. They would rush ashore with grenades and demolition charges to attack artillery, command posts, and ammunition dumps. There was no coordinated plan of action: simply rush from the barge and attack. No mention was made of what they would do after that, nor was mention made of a simultaneous counterattack from inland (these were planned, but communications were so poor that orders were not received and only a few small

The interior of a machine-gun pillbox. Stoutly constructed of palm or hardwood logs, they were quite resistant to artillery fire, mainly owing to the several feet of earth heaped on the sides and tops. It usually required direct assault to neutralize them. The conditions were cramped and stifling inside and often unsanitary. (US Army)

attacks occurred). Every man was issued four grenades. Four men carried special demolition charges, four Type 99 (1939) magnetic antitank charges lashed between two small planks. Besides their normal 120 rounds of rifle ammunition, men filled their pockets and haversacks with clips. Canteens were filled, two palm leaf-wrapped rice balls, a tin of meat, and confection bars were issued. Every man had to have a bayonet and these were collected from those staying behind. Their backpacks were stacked in a ravine, the 2nd Company's assembly area behind the beach. Taro doubted he would see the few oilpaper-wrapped letters from his family he left in his pack. Removing the camouflage from their ramped Daisatsu (49ft/15m, 100–120 troops) and rampless Kohatsu (30ft/9m, 40 troops) barges, they donned kapok life vests, and boarded with bayonets fixed.

At 0400hrs on June 18, 35 barges sortied and turned south toward the Marine beaches. At 0430 the American landing craft, infantry gunboats (LCI[G]) patrolling the coast detected the barges off Flores Point north of Tanapag Harbor. Star shells lit up the night and red streams of 20mm and 40mm tracers hammered into the barges. The barges' 7.7mm machine guns, spewing out pink and pale-blue tracers, seemed a weak response. Marine 105mm shells soon began bursting among the scattering barges.

An unequaled willingness to die for the Emperor (*tennoheika no tame ni shinukoto*) meant that Japanese soldiers were rarely reluctant to sacrifice themselves in order to kill the enemy. Here a soldier dies in a hole dug in the middle of a dirt road. He would have slammed the modified 33lb (15kg) Type 96 (1936) fragmentation bomb into the belly of a tank as it drove over him. The appearance of the ground indicates that an airburst artillery round probably killed him. (US Army)

Beaching near Tanapag, the troops staggered from the riddled barges carrying the many wounded. Details were ordered back to remove the dead, who were cremated in a dawn bonfire. Other men made some effort to camouflage the 22 remaining barges. Before long American fighters strafed the beach, destroying many of the craft.

With only just over 350 effectives remaining, the next night I/18 was ordered to a limestone hill 3,280ft (1,000m) east of Garapan, the island's administrative center and largest town. The sprawling tin-roofed concrete and wood buildings had long been leveled.

Taro's unscathed section was assigned a log-and-earth pillbox on the hill's east side, a gradual slope covered with trees and scattered brush. They were given an old 6.5mm Type 11 LMG and 600 rounds of clipped cartridges in cartons. Taro assigned a soldier who had been a second gunner to man it, along with another to assist him. The platoon commander had the other men dig one-man "octopus traps" 32–64ft (10–20m) from the pillbox on both sides and to the rear. They made lifting camouflage covers to hide them in the brush, protecting the pillbox's flanks and forming a fire net (*kamo*) in front of the LMG position (*keikikanjuza*). With their bayonets they cut lower twigs from bushes to four-hands above the ground. As the Americans approached they would not realize they were walking into a kamo and the defenders could see the enemy's boots. The section was given a large sack of rice, three cases of tinned meat, and a few tins of pickled plums.

Days passed. Shells plowed the surrounding area. Many times fighters roared over with machine guns blazing. Firing to the south never ceased, and grew closer each day. At night men went out with all the canteens looking for water and food. The never-ending American parachute flares to the south lighted their way. Taro never asked permission to send them; there was no one to ask. They returned with water and sometimes rice balls or kelp-wrapped hardtack to report from defenders on the hill's west side that the Americans had halted on the edge of ruined Garapan. The sounds of fighting continued to come closer from the south and east. One day a corporal came by leaving a sack of barley cakes and tins of crabmeat and tangerines. He told them to dig a shallow pit in front of their embrasure to trap rolling grenades and falling debris from shelling so it would not block the port. During the day Taro kept a man forward as a warning sentry (*tansho*). At night he sent a two-man sentry (*nininsho*) forward.

Firing increased to the front just after dawn on July 2. A small hill (known to the Americans as Flametree Hill) to their south was shrouded in explosions and dust through the morning. Artillery began randomly falling on their hill. It intensified in the early afternoon and the barrages became more concentrated, falling on clumps of trees with some landing just behind Taro's position. Men said the Americans did not "fight with drawn sword" (*hakuheisen*), but hid behind their artillery barrages.

SOUTH SEAS AID STATION

On paper, Japanese infantry units possessed adequate medical staff, but in reality they were often severely undermanned. This captain surgeon may have been one of only two assigned to a regiment, which was authorized to have 11. The medical system was geared to traditional linear warfare with short-duration engagements. It proved woefully inadequate in the Pacific, with massive, continuous casualties inflicted by unprecedented American firepower and tropical illnesses. Many medications were found to be virtually without effect. Heavy use was made of injected drugs, issued in fragile glass ampoules without standardized packaging. Many of the drugs used had long been discarded in European and American medical practices. Great stock was held in vitamins for treating illnesses and wound recuperation, and they were even included in aidmen's medical kits. With no means of refrigeration to store whole blood, direct transfusion was necessary. Blood plasma, not requiring refrigeration, was not available. Medical instruments were nickel-plated carbon steel rather than stainless steel. While the Japanese were notorious for firing on Allied medical personnel, forcing them to shed their Geneva crosses, Japan formally adopted the internationally recognized red cross in 1886 as a "non-religious" symbol identifying medical personnel and facilities. When the end came on beleaguered islands the wounded were often given grenades, were individually shot, or simply abandoned. (Michael Welpy © Osprey Publishing)

They were not forewarned by the tansho when the Americans came. The smoke and dust drifting through the brush restricted their view. Mortar rounds suddenly thumped around them. The machine-gunner whispered that he saw movement to the right and traversed the gun. One of the riflemen to the right fired from his hole. An American machine gun immediately answered. Rifles crackled and fell silent. More movement to the front and the gunner fired a short burst. Taro gripped his arm, telling him to wait. More rifle shots sounded to the right, then the left. The gunner aimed in that direction. Seeing brown boots beneath the clipped brush, Taro ordered him to fire. He finished the hopper in three bursts. The American machine gun began firing long bursts, joined by automatic rifles. A grenade bounced to the right of the embrasure and began spewing dense white smoke, blinding them. The gunner emptied the reloaded hopper in a single long burst and the sharp cracks of Japanese rifles were heard on both sides. Fragmentation grenades detonated as the smoke grenade burned out. The No. 2 gunner was frantically slapping clips into the hopper when rifles and automatics began kicking up limestone in front of the embrasure. Orange-red flames gushed through the opening. The last sensation Taro felt was that of inhaling burning gasoline.

The experience, and the horrifying fate, of men like Taro was repeated in countless battles across the Pacific between 1943 and 1945. One of the most important tactical lessons that some (not all) Japanese commanders drew from such battles was that their greatest tactical challenge was to cope with the undeniable firepower superiority of the American forces. It was this challenge that formed the backdrop of Japanese defensive plans on Iwo Jima, where an isolated albeit large Japanese garrison would have to face the full might of US naval and land forces combat systems. Iwo Jima would consequently become one of the greatest island battles of the entire war.

The spirits of the war dead (*eirei*) are contained in white-shrouded boxes (*shiraki no hako*), in the form of ashes, but more frequently they were empty. All of this was part of a culture of sacrifice that the soldier embraced. (US Army)

EPILOGUE

The Japanese officer corps may have inherited the bushido code of the samurai, and while soldiers might be comparable to the peasants of the past within army hierarchy, they too were expected to accept the notions of bushido. All Japanese soldiers were trusted to give their lives for the Emperor. There was no greater honor than to die in combat, not only defending the Empire, but also aggressively expanding the Empire.

A rising sun flag was flown over the home of men called to the colors. When one sacrificed his life, a black streamer was added to the flag. In theory the remains of a fallen soldier were returned to his family in a white-shrouded box (*shiraki no hako*), in the form of ashes, the "spirit of the war dead" (*eirei*). In reality the dead were cremated en masse on the battlefield and ashes scooped at random into the boxes, the soldier returned united with his fallen comrades. The soldier's identity tag or a final letter written by him may have been included as "relics of the fallen." No remains or relics, of course, were returned from Pacific islands. The family received only the small wooden box – empty. The victorious Americans merely bulldozed the dead into pits or left them buried in caves and blasted pillboxes. Many Japanese soldiers sent a fingernail or hair clipping home before a battle or left these with his family when departing.

The family received a payment of 30 yen for each year the fallen soldier had served and a prorated amount for a partial year. The family would also receive the Soldier's Bereaved Family Medal (*Gunbjin Izoku Kisho*), a small silver medallion bearing the Imperial Chrysanthemum suspended from a looped cross-shaped dark purple cord tassel.

Atop a hill near the Imperial Palace is the Yasukuni Jinja, the memorial to the war dead. It houses the spirits of 2.5 million war dead dating back to 1853. Originally enshrining the spirits of those who died overthrowing the Shogunate and aiding in the restoration of the Emperor, it was created in 1869 as a symbol of national unity. This shrine has been wreathed in controversy since the end of World War II, as some interpret it as glorifying the misdeeds of the China Incident and Greater East Asia War. Among the enshrined spirits are those of executed war criminals, including Hideki Tojo.

It is believed that once a soldier is enshrined at Yasukuni (meaning "peaceful country") he becomes a national deity (*kami*), protecting the Empire as he did when he died fighting. Soldiers going into battle would sometimes shout to one another "See you at Yasukuni!" believing they would meet again as comrades in death.

Japan had 6,095,000 men in her army and navy at peak strength. She suffered approximately 2,566,000 armed forces dead of all causes including non-combat deaths (1,506,000 killed in action), plus some 810,000 missing and prisoners of war. Civilian dead numbered 672,000.

PART 3
THE BATTLE OF IWO JIMA

OPPOSING COMMANDERS

AMERICAN

On October 3, 1944, the Joint Chiefs of Staff issued a directive to Admiral Chester Nimitz, Commander in Chief Pacific (CINCPAC) to occupy the island of Iwo Jima. As with previous amphibious landings in the Marine Corps' "island hopping" campaign, he entrusted the planning and implementation of the assault, codenamed Operation *Detachment*, to his experienced trio of tacticians – Spruance, Turner, and Smith – who had masterminded almost every operation since the initial landing at Tarawa in 1943.

Nimitz was a quiet somewhat introverted Texan who never lost a sea battle. President Roosevelt had been so impressed by him that he bypassed nearly 30 more senior admirals to appoint him CINCPAC after the removal of Admiral Husband E. Kimmel following the debacle at Pearl Harbor. One of Nimitz's greatest abilities was to resolve conflicts with other senior officers. However, his long-running disputes with General Douglas MacArthur, Supreme Commander of all US Army units in the Pacific Theatre, were legendary. A man of striking contrasts, MacArthur was arrogant, conceited, egotistical, and flamboyant, and yet a superb strategist with an amazing sense of where and when to strike the enemy to greatest advantage.

Opposite:
Four Grumman Avenger torpedo-bombers unload their bombs in the area between Airfields Nos. 1 & 2. The cliffs of the Quarry overlooking the East Boat Basin can be seen in the foreground. (National Archives)

134

Nimitz and MacArthur disagreed throughout the war on the best way to defeat the Japanese, with MacArthur favoring a thrust through the Philippines and on to Formosa (Taiwan) and China. Nimitz stood by his "island hopping" theory – occupying those islands and atolls that were of strategic importance and bypassing those that had little military value or were unsuitable for amphibious landings.

Admiral Raymond A. Spruance had been Nimitz's right-hand man since his outstanding performance at the Battle of Midway in June, 1942. His quiet unassuming manner concealed a razor sharp intellect and an ability to utilize the experience and knowledge of his staff to a remarkable degree. He would continue in the role of operations commander until the final battle of the Pacific War at Okinawa.

Admiral Richmond Kelly Turner, the Joint Expeditionary Force (JEF) commander, was by contrast notorious for his short temper and foul mouth, but his amazing organization skills placed him in a unique position to mount the operation. Dovetailing the dozens of air strikes and shore bombardments, disembarking thousands of troops and landing them on the right beach in the right sequence was an awesome responsibility fraught with the seeds of potential disaster, but Turner had proved his ability time and time again.

Fleet Admiral Chester Nimitz was appointed Commander-in-Chief Pacific (CINCPAC) after the Pearl Harbor debacle. A great organizer and leader, he was by the end of 1945 the commander of the largest military force ever, overseeing 21 admirals and generals, six Marine divisions, 5,000 aircraft, and the world's largest navy. (US Navy)

Lieutenant-General Holland M. Smith, Commanding General Fleet Marine Force Pacific, "Howlin' Mad" Smith to his Marines, was on the other hand nearing the end of his active career. His aggressive tactics and uncompromising attitude had made him many enemies. In America a powerful clique of publishing barons was running a vitriolic campaign against him in favor of General MacArthur, and his recent dismissal of the Army's General Ralph Smith during the Saipan battle for "lack of aggressiveness" had not endeared him to the top brass in the Pentagon. At Iwo Jima he was content to keep a low profile in favor of Major-General Harry Schmidt, V Amphibious Corps Commander: "I think that they only asked me along in case anything happened to Harry Schmidt," he was to say after the battle.

The Iwo Jima landing would involve an unprecedented assembly of three Marine divisions: the 3rd, 4th, and 5th. Heading the 3rd Division was Major-General Graves B. Erskine, at 47 a veteran of the battles of Belleau Wood, Chateau Thierry, and St Mihiel during World War I. Later he was the chief of staff to Holland Smith during the campaigns in the Aleutians, Gilbert Islands, and the Marianas.

The 4th Division was also commanded by a World War I veteran, Major-General Clifton B. Cates, who had won the Navy Cross and two Silver Stars. At Guadalcanal

Lieutenant-General Holland M. Smith, "Howlin' Mad" to his Marines, was a volatile leader who did not suffer fools gladly. His dismissal of Army general Ralph Smith during the Saipan operation was to cause friction between the Army and the Marines for years. Seen here in two-toned helmet alongside Secretary of the Navy James Forrestal (with binoculars) and a group of Iwo Jima Marines. (National Archives)

in 1942 he had commanded the 4th Division's 1st Regiment and at Tinian became the divisional commander. In 1948 he became the Commandant of the Marine Corps.

Major-General Keller E. Rockey was another Navy Cross holder for gallantry at Chateau Thierry. He won a second Navy Cross for heroism in Nicaragua in the inter-war years and took command of the 5th Division in February 1944. Iwo Jima was to be the division's first battle, but it boasted a strong nucleus of veterans of the recently disbanded Raider Battalions and Marine Paratroopers.

Responsibility for preparing and executing Marine operations for *Detachment* fell to V Amphibious Corps Landing Force Commander Major-General Harry Schmidt. A veteran of pre-war actions in China, the Philippines, Mexico, Cuba, and Nicaragua and later the 4th Division commander during the Roi-Namur and Saipan invasions, he was 58 years old at Iwo Jima and would have the honor of fronting the largest Marine Corps force ever committed to a single battle.

"The Dutchman," Major-General Harry Schmidt, was to command V Amphibious Corps, the largest force the Marine Corps had ever put in the field. A veteran of numerous inter-war actions ranging from China to Nicaragua, he was 58 years old at the time of the battle. (USMC)

JAPANESE

In May, Lieutenant-General Tadamichi Kuribayashi had been summoned to the office of the Japanese prime minister, General Tojo, and told that he would be the commander of the garrison on Iwo Jima. Whether by accident or design the appointment proved to be a stroke of genius.

Kuribayashi, a samurai and long-serving officer with 30 years of distinguished service, had spent time in the United States as a deputy attaché and had proclaimed to his family: "the United States is the last country in the world that Japan should fight." He looked upon his appointment as both a challenge and a death sentence. "Do not plan for my return," he wrote to his wife shortly after his arrival on the island.

Kuribayashi and his staff had time to pose for a formal group photograph before the Americans arrived. None was to survive the battle. (Taro Kuribayashi)

Kuribayashi succeeded in doing what no other Japanese commander in the Pacific could do – inflict more casualties on the US Marines than his own troops suffered. Fifty-four years old at the time of the battle and quite tall for a Japanese at 5ft 9ins (1.75m), Radio Tokyo described him as having the "traditional pot belly of a Samurai warrior and the heart of a Tiger."

Lieutenant-General Holland Smith in his memoirs was lavish in his praise for the commander's ability:

His ground organization was far superior to any I had seen in France in WWI and observers say it excelled the German ground organization in WWII. The only way we could move was behind rolling artillery barrages that pulverized the area and then we went in and reduced each position with flamethrowers, grenades and demolition charges. Some of his mortar and rocket launchers were cleverly hidden. We learned about them the hard way, through sickeningly heavy casualties. Every cave, every pillbox, every bunker was an individual battle where Marines and Japanese fought hand to hand to the death.

FORCES ON IWO JIMA

AMERICAN

Against the Japanese defense force the Americans were to employ three Marine divisions, the 3rd, 4th, and 5th, totalling over 70,000 men, most of whom were seasoned veterans of earlier campaigns. Operation *Detachment* had already been postponed twice because of a shortage of support ships and landing craft due to the massive requirements of MacArthur's Philippines invasion, and it had to be completed in time to release men and materials for the upcoming Okinawa invasion scheduled for April 1, 1945

As the plans came to fruition it was time to assemble the invasion force. The 3rd Division was still on Guam having taken the island in August 1944, while the 4th and 5th Divisions were to be deployed from the Hawaiian Islands. The Navy was scheduled to provide a massive "softening up" bombardment prior to the invasion and many of the fleet's old battleships, the USS *Arkansas*, *Texas*, *Nevada*, *Idaho*, and *Tennessee*, too slow for the new Task Forces that were now prowling the Pacific, were ideal for the purpose.

On February 15 the invasion fleet left Saipan, first the LSTs carrying the first waves of troops from the 4th and 5th Divisions and the following day the troop transports with the remainder of the Marines and the plethora of tanks, supplies, artillery, and supporting units. The armada was soon spotted by Japanese naval patrol aircraft and the Iwo Jima garrison went on to immediate alert. General Kuribayashi had earlier issued his troops with a document called "The Courageous Battle Vows" which stated that each man should make it his duty to kill ten of the enemy before dying. With his defenses prepared and his men ready to fight to the death, Kuribayashi waited patiently for the approaching invader.

JAPANESE

The Japanese High Command realized the importance of Iwo Jima and as early as March 1944, began to reinforce the island. The 145th Infantry Regiment of Colonel Masuo Ikeda, originally intended to bolster the garrison on Saipan, was diverted to the island and in the period leading up to the Marine attack in 1945 the 109th Division, including the 2nd Mixed Brigade (Major-General Senda), 26th Tank Regiment (Lieutenant-Colonel [Baron] Takeichi Nishi), 17th Mixed Infantry Regiment (Major Tamachi Fujiwara), Brigade Artillery (Colonel Chosaku Kaido), and additional antiaircraft, mortar, cannon, and machine-gun battalions were drafted to the island.

The naval units, mainly antiaircraft, communications, supply, and engineering groups, were under the command of Rear-Admiral Toshinosuke Ichimaru, who also had charge of the 27th Air Flotilla. At the time of the Marine landing – February 19, 1945 – the total Japanese garrison numbered 21,060, considerably more than the American calculation of 13,000.

On the beach a Marine in pensive mood sits with his M1 rifle. (National Archives)

OPPOSING PLANS

AMERICAN

The plan of attack that was devised by V Amphibious Corps planners looked simple. The Marines would land on the 2-mile (3.2km) long stretch of beach between Mount Suribachi and the East Boat Basin on the southeast coast of the island. These beaches were divided into seven sections of 550 yards (914m) each. Under the shadow of Suribachi lay Green Beach (1st and 2nd Battalions, 28th Regiment), flanked on the right by Red Beach 1 (2nd Battalion, 27th Regiment), Red Beach 2 (1st Battalion, 27th Regiment), Yellow Beach 1 (1st Battalion, 23rd Regiment), Yellow Beach 2 (2nd Battalion, 23rd Regiment), Blue Beach 1(1st and 3rd Battalions, 25th Regiment). Blue Beach 2 lay directly under known enemy gun emplacements in the Quarry overlooking the East Boat Basin, and it was decided that both the 1st and 3rd Battalions of the 25th Regiment should land abreast on Blue Beach 1. General Cates, the 4th Division commander, said: "If I knew the name of the man on the extreme right of the right hand squad (on Blue Beach), I'd recommend him for a medal before we go in." The 28th Regiment would attack straight across the narrowest part of the island to the opposite coast to isolate and then secure Mount Suribachi. On their right, the 27th Regiment would cross the island and move to the north, while the 23rd Regiment would seize Airfield No. 1 and then thrust northward towards Airfield No. 2. The 25th Regiment, on the extreme right, would deploy to their right to neutralize the high ground around the Quarry overlooking the East Boat Basin.

JAPANESE

General Kuribayashi's first priority was to reorganize the archaic defense system that was in place when he arrived, a defense system that he recognized was completely inadequate to cope with the future US onslaught. All civilians were sent back to the mainland as their presence could serve no useful purpose and they would be a drain on the limited supplies of food and water. With the arrival of more troops and Korean laborers he instigated a massive program of underground defenses. A complex and extensive system of tunnels, caves, gun emplacements, pillboxes, and command posts was constructed in the nine months prior to the invasion. The soft pumice-like volcanic rock was easily cut with hand tools and mixed well with cement to provide excellent reinforcement. Some tunnels were 75ft (23m) under ground, most were interconnecting, and many were provided with electric or oil lighting.

Supply points, ammunition stores, and even operating theaters were included in the system and at the height of the battle many Marines reported hearing voices and movements coming from the ground beneath them. When Mount Suribachi was isolated many of the defenders escaped to the north of the island, bypassing the Marine lines through this labyrinth of tunnels.

The tunnels were constructed at an unprecedented speed. The specification called for a minimum of 30ft (9.1m) of earth overhead to resist any shell or bomb. Most were 5ft (1.5m) wide and the same high with concrete walls and ceilings and extended in all directions (one engineer in his diary said that it was possible to walk underground for 4 miles / 6.4km). Many tunnels were built on two or even three levels and in the larger chambers, airshafts of up to 50ft (15.2m) were needed to dispel the foul air. Partially underground were the concrete blockhouses and gun sites, so well constructed that weeks of naval shelling and aerial bombing failed to damage most of them; and the hundreds of pillboxes, which were of all shapes and sizes, were usually inter-connected and mutually supporting.

The complexity of the underground tunnel system can be judged from this picture of one of the existing passages. (Taro Kuribayashi)

The Japanese general had studied earlier Japanese defense methods of attempting to halt the enemy at the beachhead and had realized that they invariably failed, and he regarded the traditional banzai charge as wasteful and futile. In September at Peleliu the Japanese commander, Lieutenant-General Inoue, had abandoned these outdated tactics and concentrated on attrition, wearing down the enemy from previously planned and prepared positions in the Umurbrogol Mountains. Kuribayashi approved of these tactics. He knew that the Americans would eventually take the island but he was determined to exact a fearful toll in Marine casualties before they did.

The geography of the island virtually dictated the location of the landing sites for the invasion force. From aerial photographs and periscope shots taken by the submarine USS *Spearfish*, it was obvious that there were only two stretches of beach upon which the Marines could land. Kuribayashi had come to the same conclusion months earlier and made his plans accordingly.

Iwo Jima is some 4½ miles (7.2km) long with its axis running from southwest to northeast, tapering from 2½ miles (4km) wide in the north to a mere ½ mile (0.8km) in the south, giving a total land area of around 7½ square miles (19.4 square km). At the southern end stands Mount Suribachi, a 550ft (168m) high dormant volcano that affords commanding views over most of the island, and the beaches that stretch northward from Suribachi are the only possible sites for a landing.

On a plateau in the center of this lower part of the island the Japanese built Airfield No. 1, and further north a second plateau roughly a mile in diameter housed Airfield No. 2 and the unfinished Airfield No. 3. The ground that slopes away from this northern plateau is a mass of valleys, ridges, gorges, and rocky outcrops that provide an ideal site for defensive fighting.

Major Yoshitaka Horie, staff officer to Kuribayashi, had many discussions with his superior about the role of anti-aircraft guns. Horie was of the opinion that they would be far better employed as artillery or in an antitank role as it was obvious that the Americans would have overwhelming air superiority before and during the battle. His reasoning seems to have impressed the general, who overruled the objections of some of his staff officers and implemented some of Horie's ideas.

Horie was interviewed by a Marine officer after the war and his comments were recorded for the Marine Corps Historical Archives. He told General Kuribayashi:

> We should change our plans so that we can use most of the antiaircraft guns as artillery and retain very small parts of them as antiaircraft guns. Antiaircraft guns are good to protect the disclosed targets, especially ships, but are invaluable for the covering of land defenses.

The staff officers had different opinions.

The staff officers were inclined as follows; they said at Iwo Jima it is good to use antiaircraft guns as both artillery and antiaircraft guns. The natural features of Iwo are weaker than of Chichi Jima. If we have no antiaircraft guns, our defensive positions will be completely destroyed by the enemy's air raids... And so most of the 300 anti-aircraft guns were used in both senses as above mentioned, but later, when American forces landed on Iwo Jima, those antiaircraft guns were put to silence in one or two days and we have the evidence that most antiaircraft guns were not valuable but 7.5cm antiaircraft guns, prepared as antitank guns, were very valuable.

Horie, in his curious English, went on to describe the initial Japanese reaction to the landings:

With Mount Suribachi in the foreground, the invasion beaches can be seen on the right of the picture, stretching northwards to the East Boat Basin. Isolating the volcano was the number one priority for the Marines and involved crossing the half-mile neck of the island as rapidly as possible. (US Navy)

Japanese defense sectors and US landing beaches. Note how the Mount Surbachi area was confined in the south of the island – capturing this was just the beginning of the campaign to secure Iwo Jima.

On the February 19, American forces landed on the first airfield under cover of their keen bombardments of aircraft and warships. Although their landing direction, strength and fighting methods were same as our judgment, we could not take any countermeasures towards them, and 135 pillboxes we had at the first airfield were trodden down and occupied in only two days after their landing.

We shot them bitterly with the artillery we had at Motoyama and Mount Suribachi, but they were immediately destroyed by the enemy's counter-firing. At that time we had opportunity to make offensive attacks against the enemy but we knew well that if we do so we will suffer many damages from American bombardments of aircraft and vessels, therefore our officers and men waited the enemy coming closer to their own positions.

THE BATTLE

D-DAY: "A NIGHTMARE IN HELL"

As a prelude to the landings, Major-General Harry Schmidt, V Amphibious Corps commander, had requested ten continuous days of shelling by battleships and cruisers of Rear-Admiral William Blandy's Amphibious Support Force (Task Force 52). Admiral Hill rejected the request on the grounds that there would be insufficient time to re-arm his ships before D-Day. Schmidt persisted and asked for nine days. This was also turned down and he was offered a mere three days of softening up before his Marines went ashore. Spruance's comment – "I know that your people will get away with it" – was to sound hollow as the battle progressed. "Howlin' Mad" Smith was to be scathing in his criticism of the Navy's support during many of the amphibious landings throughout the Pacific campaign: "I could not forget the sight of dead Marines in the lagoon or lying on the beaches of Tarawa, men who died assaulting defenses which should have been taken out by naval gunfire," he was to write after the war.

The first day of the bombardment was a disappointment. Poor weather hampered the gunners and the results were inconclusive. Day two was to be a disaster. The cruiser USS *Pensacola* ventured too close to the shore and was engaged by enemy shore batteries. Six hits in rapid succession killed 17 of the crew and caused substantial damage. Later in the day 12 gunboats (LCIs) approached to within 1,000 yards (914m) of the shore as part of the support screen for over 100 "frogmen," underwater demolition teams. With distances worked out to the nearest yard from months of practice, all 12 vessels were hit by Japanese batteries and scurried away at best speed. The destroyer USS *Leutze*, which raced to their assistance, was also hit with the loss of seven crewmen.

The final day of the bombardment was again blighted by poor weather, with rainsqualls and cloud foiling the gunners. Blandy optimistically signalled Turner: "I believe that landings can be accomplished tomorrow." Schmidt complained: "We only got about 13 hours worth of fire support during the 34 hours of available daylight."

By contrast, D-Day, Monday February 19, 1945, dawned clear and sunny with unlimited visibility. During the night Admiral Marc Mitscher's Task Force 58, a vast armada of 16 carriers, 8 battleships, and 15 cruisers, fresh from highly successful attacks against the Japanese mainland, arrived off Iwo Jima accompanied by Admiral Spruance in his flagship USS *Indianapolis*. Again Holland Smith was bitter, considering these raids against Japan to be an unnecessary diversion from the more important business of occupying Iwo Jima.

As the battleships and cruisers pounded the island and swarms of carrier-based aircraft mounted air strikes, the disembarkation of thousands of Marines from troopships and LVTs (Landing Vehicle, Tanks) was gathering momentum. To spearhead the attack 68 LVT(A)s – armored amphibious tractors mounting a 75mm howitzer and three machine guns – were to venture 50 yards (46m) onto the beachhead to cover the

Landing craft circle before departing for the beaches. (National Archives)

first wave of Marines, but the first of a number of planning "foul-ups" was to frustrate their deployment. Along the whole of the landing beach the Marines, LVTs, tanks, and other vehicles were to encounter 15ft (4.6m) high terraces of soft black volcanic ash. The troops sank up to their ankles, the vehicles to their hubcaps, and the LVTs and Sherman tanks ground to a halt within yards of the shore. The planners had described the beach conditions in glowing terms: "troops should have no difficulty in getting off the beach at any point," "the isthmus provides excellent landing beaches," and "an easy approach inland," read the pre-invasion reports.

In keeping with Kuribayashi's strategy, Japanese resistance had been relatively subdued; he wanted the Americans to land substantial numbers of men onto the beaches before unleashing his well-rehearsed and coordinated bombardment. Many American naval officers were under the illusion that their rolling barrage over the landing zone was responsible for the limited response.

A steady stream of small-arms and machine-gun fire whined across the beaches and the occasional crump of a mortar shell sent sand flying, but the most formidable enemy was the sand itself – Marines were trained to move rapidly forward; here they could only plod. The weight and amount of equipment was a terrific hindrance and various items were discarded. First to go was the gas mask, always regarded as unnecessary, and many of the Marines decided to dump their packs and retrieve them later; the most important pieces of equipment at that moment were weapons and ammunition.

Abandoned landing craft on the invasion beaches. (National Archives)

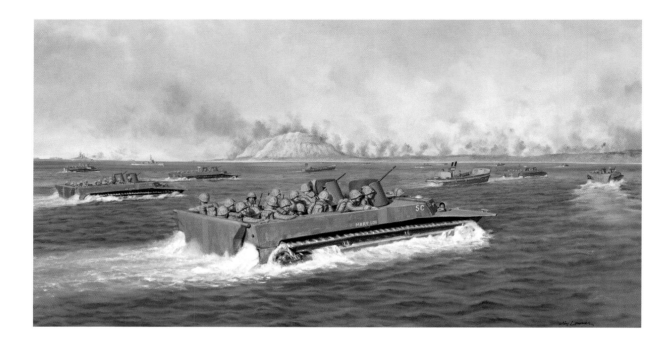

A seven-knot breeze and a calm sea provided the Marines with ideal conditions for the invasion. Admiral Raymond Spruance had arrived during the night with Admiral Mitscher's mighty Task Force 58, and the island was surrounded by over 485 ships of various types to support General Schmidt's Marines. At dawn the battleships and cruisers commenced their final bombardment of Mount Suribachi and the seven invasion beaches as the Amtracs headed for the shore. (Jim Laurier © Osprey Publishing)

As the first waves of Marines struggled to move forward, successive waves arrived at intervals of around five minutes and the situation rapidly deteriorated. Kuribayashi had intended to allow the invaders to move towards Airfield No. 1 before commencing his artillery and mortar barrages. The congestion on the beaches was an added bonus and a little after 1000hrs the full fury of the Japanese defenses was unleashed. From well-concealed positions ranging from the base of Mount Suribachi to the East Boat Basin, a torrent of artillery, mortar, and machine-gun fire rained down on the crowded beaches. Frantic messages flashed back to the control ship *Eldorado*: "troops 200 yards (183m) inland pinned down," "catching all hell from the Quarry," "machine-gun and artillery fire heaviest ever seen."

By 1040hrs Harry Hill had 6,000 men ashore and the bulldozers that had arrived in the early waves were hacking away at the terraces. Some tanks were breaking through to solid ground and troops were finally escaping the horror of the beaches where Kuribayashi's artillery and mortars were wreaking havoc. Robert Sherrod, a noted war correspondent for *Time-Life*, aptly described the scene as "a nightmare in hell."

At the extreme left of the beachhead, Green Beach, the terrain was somewhat less difficult where the volcanic ash gave way to rocks and stone at the base of Mount Suribachi. Here Colonel Harry Liversedge's 28th Regiment began its dash across the half-mile isthmus below the volcano in an attempt to isolate this vital position.

On Suribachi, Colonel Kanehiko Atsuchi with over 2,000 men in his independent command manned a mass of artillery and mortars that were dug in around the lower slopes, and above them there were dozens of caves and tunnels all the way to the summit.

The 1st Battalion, ignoring this threat to their left flank, pressed on towards the far shore but soon encountered Captain Osada's 312th Independent Infantry Battalion and fierce fighting erupted around a series of bunkers and pillboxes. Some were destroyed and others bypassed in the mad dash to cross the island. Dead were abandoned where they lay and the wounded left in the care of the Navy Corpsmen, the heroic medical teams that accompanied all Marine operations. At 1035hrs six men of B Company, 1st Battalion reached the west coast, soon to be joined by the remnants of C Company and Suribachi was isolated, albeit precariously. On Red Beaches 1 and 2, the 27th Regiment under Colonel Thomas Wornham was having great difficulty in moving forward. The Japanese artillery bracketed the crowded beach and casualties mounted by the minute. To their right on Yellow 1 and 2, the 23rd Regiment under Colonel Walter Wensinger had come face to face with a mass of blockhouses and pillboxes manned by Major Matsushita's 10th Independent Antitank Battalion and Captain Awatsu's 309th Infantry Battalion. Battling against shredding machine-gun fire, Sergeant Darren Cole, armed only with grenades and a pistol, single-

War dogs, usually Dobermans or German Shepherds, were used extensively in the Pacific War, carrying messages and locating hidden enemy troops. They provided a very valuable service; sadly they were all destroyed at the end of the battle as it was regarded that they could not be retrained for civilian life. Here a Doberman keeps guard while his handler snatches some sleep. (National Archives)

handedly silenced five pillboxes before being killed by a hand grenade and became the first of the Marine Corps 27 Medal of Honor recipients during the battle.

At the extreme right, Blue Beach 1, Colonel John Lanigan's 25th Regiment moved straight ahead to avoid the obvious danger presented by the high ground at the Quarry on their right flank, making a two-pronged attack with the 1st Battalion pressing inland as the 3rd Battalion swung right to assault cliffs at the base of the Quarry.

Second Lieutenant Benjamin Roselle, part of a six-man naval gunfire team, was to suffer a horrendous D-Day. Reaching the second row of terraces, they were pinned down by heavy artillery fire. As they attempted to move forward, the radio operator went down and Roselle strapped his equipment to his back and moved on. Within a minute a mortar shell exploded among the group. Others were able to move but the lieutenant could not, his left foot and ankle hung from his leg, held on by a ribbon of flesh. Pinned down and with no hope of advancing, he rode out the storm of mortar shells that were blasting the area. Within minutes a second round landed near him and fragments tore into his other leg. For nearly an hour he wondered where the next shell would land. He was soon to find out as a shell burst almost on top of him, wounding him for the third time in the shoulder. Almost at once another explosion bounced him several feet into the air and hot shards ripped into both thighs. Remarkably, he wondered what time it was and as he lifted his arm to look at his watch a mortar shell exploded only feet away and blasted the watch from his wrist and tore a large jagged hole in his forearm: "I was beginning to know what it must be like to be crucified," he was to say later. Eventually recovered by a medical team, he was taken to an offshore LST hospital ship where his fractured arm was set and his foot amputated.

A few tanks of the 4th Tank Battalion had succeeded in getting ashore on Blue 1 at around 1020hrs. A tank-dozer scooped a passage through the first terrace and the remainder passed through in single file, only halting when they reached a large minefield.

At 1400hrs the 3rd Battalion under their commander "Jumpin' Joe" Chambers began scaling the cliffs around the Quarry. The enemy resistance was fanatical and the Marines were soon down to 150 men from the original 900 who had landed at 0900hrs.

At the base of Mount Suribachi the 28th Regiment was consolidating its positions. Lieutenant Keith Wells' 3rd Platoon was ordered to cross the isthmus to reinforce the 1st Platoon whose position was in danger of being overrun. Under heavy fire from their left, the four squads sprinted forward, coming across many dead and wounded Marines who had to be left behind until the base of the volcano had been secured.

By afternoon a few Sherman tanks that had penetrated the beachhead were moving up to provide valuable assistance by destroying many Japanese pillboxes with their 75mm guns, and by evening Suribachi was securely isolated from the rest of the island. The grim task of occupying this formidable bastion would have to wait until later.

In the center, the 27th and 25th Regiments were gradually extricating themselves from the Red and Yellow beaches and moving towards Airfield No. 1. The Seabees (Naval Construction Battalions), largely recruited from the civilian construction industry and manned by volunteers usually in their 40s or early 50s, were performing miracles on the beaches. Landing with the early waves of assault troops they attacked the terraces with their bulldozers, carving passages through which the tanks, artillery, and transport could pass and cleared the masses of bogged down landing craft and vehicles that cluttered the shoreline. There was a joke: "Protect your Seabees. One of them could be your dad." Turner had had to halt the landings around 1300hrs as there was nowhere to get more Marines ashore, but the heroic efforts of the Seabees, who suffered heavy casualties on D-Day, allowed the flow of men and materials to resume after two hours. Even so, in virtually every shell hole there lay at least one dead Marine and at the foot of the terraces scores of wounded lay among the exploding shells and mortars, waiting for evacuation by the landing craft that were running the gauntlet of the terrific barrage.

Instead of the straightforward exit from the beaches that the Marines had been led to expect, they came upon terraces of black volcanic ash, some of them up to 15ft (4.5m) high and there were long delays in getting troops, tanks, and artillery inland. (National Archives)

General Kuribayashi had intended to let the Marines clear the beaches and head for Airfield No. 1 before unleashing his well-rehearsed artillery barrage. However, as the troops became bogged down behind the terraces of volcanic ash, and with further waves of Amtracs arriving every five minutes, he seized the opportunity to rake the beaches from end to end with devastating artillery and mortar fire that caused very heavy casualties. (Jim Laurier © Osprey Publishing)

By 1130hrs some Marines had reached the southern end of Airfield No. 1 which was sited on a plateau whose perimeter rose steeply on the eastern side. The Japanese mounted a fierce defense, hundreds being killed and the remainder pouring across the runway or disappearing into the pipes of the drainage system. At one point over a hundred Japanese charged down the runway to be met by a hail of machine-gun and rifle fire.

As evening approached, the Marines held a line running from the base of Mount Suribachi across the southern perimeter of Airfield No. 1 and ending at the foot of the Quarry. The 0-1 line, the D-Day objective, had not been reached but it was always an unrealistic goal. Perhaps if Admiral Nimitz had prised some of his deskbound planners away from their comfortable offices in Hawaii and given them a spell with the assault troops they may have come up with more realistic projections.

The Marines habitually sought to consolidate their positions during the night while the Japanese, on the other hand, were adept at night-time infiltration and favored

darkness for their famous banzai charges. Throughout the night destroyers fired flares to illuminate the frontlines. As they descended on parachutes they cast an eerie glow over the scene. The Japanese kept up their mortar and artillery fire, while at sea a shuttle service of landing craft brought in supplies and evacuated the wounded.

Aboard the command ship *Eldorado*, Smith studied the day's reports. Progress had not been as good as he had hoped and the casualty figures made grim reading: "I don't know who he is, but the Japanese General running this show is one smart bastard," he announced to a group of war correspondents.

D+1 – D+5: "INFLICT MUCH DAMAGE TO THE ENEMY"

D+1

A 4ft (1.2m) high surf on the beaches and a bitterly cold wind did little to raise the spirits of either the Marines or their commanders on Tuesday, D+1. Having isolated Mount Suribachi, the 28th Regiment were faced with the unenviable task of capturing it, while to the north the remainder of the invasion force was poised to mount a concerted attack to secure Airfields 1 and 2.

With daylight came the carrier planes, pounding the volcano with bombs and napalm while destroyers shelled the gun positions directly to the front of the 28th

Section Chief Marine Private 1st Class R. F. Callahan calls in 155mm artillery fire against a Japanese position. (USMC)

Regiment. Attacking on a broad front with artillery support, the Marines could only gain 75 yards (69m) of ground by 1200hrs in the face of fierce resistance from Colonel Atsuchi's defenders. Tanks had joined the battle at around 1100hrs following long delays in refueling and added valuable support, but the Japanese had a huge advantage in their prepared positions on the higher ground. Looking ahead, Lieutnant Wells said: "I saw little or nothing to shield us from the enemy's fire power; my men would be open targets all the way."

Colonel Atsuchi radioed General Kuribayashi that the American bombardments from both artillery and offshore naval units were very fierce and suggested that he and his men should attempt a banzai charge. The general had expected the garrison on Mount Suribachi to maintain control for at least ten days and did not even bother to reply, but suspected that Atsuchi was beginning to waver.

Little progress was made in the afternoon and the Marines dug in and awaited reinforcements and additional tanks for an all-out assault the following day. The Japanese were determined that there should be no respite for the enemy and commenced a barrage all along the frontline. "The shells continued walking up our lines, exploding only a few feet away. All I could think about was the great loss of men. What made it even more horrifying, it stopped soon after passing through us and

As landing craft continue to arrive on the beachhead, troops can be seen advancing towards Airfield No. 1 while scores of others still crowd the beaches under a barrage of artillery fire. (National Archives)

started back again," said Wells. During the night, Japanese troops began to gather near the eastern slopes of the volcano but the destroyer USS *Henry A. Wiley* blasted them under the glare of searchlights, and the anticipated night-time counterattack was nipped in the bud.

To the north, the other three regiments began their offensive at around 0830hrs, with the right flank anchored at the Quarry and the left swinging north in an attempt to straighten the line. The Marines encountered strong opposition from the mass of bunkers, pillboxes, and landmines that had been so carefully prepared. Mid afternoon saw the arrival of the brand new battleship USS *Washington*, which blasted the cliffs around the Quarry with its massive 16in guns causing a landslide that blocked dozens of enemy caves.

By 1200hrs the majority of Airfield No. 1 was in American hands, a bitter blow to Kuribayashi who had not anticipated such a rapid advance, and the Marines now had an almost straight frontline across the island, although the D-Day 0-1 objective still eluded them. General Schmidt decided to commit the 21st Regiment of the 3rd Division, an indication that the top brass did not consider that progress had been swift enough. (The Joint Chiefs of Staff had hoped to keep the whole of the 3rd Division intact for the upcoming invasion of Okinawa.) However, the high seas and congested beaches frustrated the landings and after six hours in their landing craft the regiment was ordered back to their transports.

As the second day drew to a close the Marines had control of almost a quarter of the island, but the cost had been very heavy. Kuribayashi's orders that "Each man should think of his defense position as his graveyard, fight until the last and inflict much damage to the enemy" were bearing fruit. Heavy rain began to fall in the afternoon and continued throughout the night, filling foxholes with water and collapsing their sides. The old hands among the Marines shivered and wished themselves back among the hot sands of the atolls that they had so recently liberated.

D+2

Wednesday's plan looked straightforward – the 28th Regiment would begin its final assault on Mount Suribachi and the remainder would move north on a broad front: in the west, the 26th and 27th Regiments, in the center the 23rd and in the east the 24th, but simple plans seldom develop smoothly. The bad weather of the previous day had deteriorated even further as a howling gale tore through the island and rain clouds scurried overhead. Six-foot waves crashed down onto the beaches, forcing Admiral Turner to close them down again.

On the fourth day of the battle the 21st Regiment was faced with a stubborn complex of bunkers and antitank guns adjoining Airfield No. 2. Major Houser called upon 21-year-old Corporal Hershel Williams, the last of his flamethrowers, to go ahead escorted by riflemen. Williams moved from one position to another, burning out bunkers and strongpoints until the way ahead had been cleared. He was the first 3rd Division Marine on Iwo Jima to be awarded the Medal of Honor. (Jim Laurier © Osprey Publishing)

For an 18-year-old Marine in his first battle, Iwo Jima was a trying experience for "Chuck" Tatum, a member of a machine-gun squad with the 27th Regiment:

Dawn on D+2 greeted us with a cold rain and we were still next to Airfield No. 1. I worked this out to be a grand total of 1,000 yards [914m] advance from the beach in two days – we wouldn't be arrested for speeding! The terrain we were in was flat from the edge of the runway to the western shoreline, probably the only flat ground in Iwo. The dark overcast sky filled with rain, soaked us, and transformed the volcanic soil into a gooey sticky mess. Vehicles and men struggled to move and finally bogged down. On the landing beaches to our right chaos continued as increasing winds and seas smashed derelict, broached landing craft. Beaches remained closed to all but emergency traffic and wounded lay patiently in hastily prepared shelters while Corpsmen did what they could to save lives. At 0800hrs the frontal attack northward was renewed. The 5th Division objective was the left flank of the island, the entire area between the runways and the beaches. As we had the day before, we mopped up bypassed positions and consolidated the gains made.

Supported by a blistering artillery barrage, fire from Navy cruisers and destroyers, and napalm and machine-gun fire from over 40 carrier planes, the 28th Regiment launched its assault on Mount Suribachi at 0845hrs. The gunfire denuded the ground before them, revealing chains of blockhouses and connecting trenches with little or no cover between the two frontlines. There was the additional hazard of rows of barbed wire that the Marines had placed in front of their own lines during the night to prevent enemy infiltration. It had been assumed that the morning's advance would be spearheaded by tanks that would flatten all before them, but again they were delayed by fueling problems.

The 3rd Platoon in the center met heavy opposition, but the late arrival of tanks and halftrack 75mm guns helped their progress. By evening the regiment had formed a semi-circle around the north side of the volcano and moved forward 650 yards (594m) on the left, 500 yards (457m) in the center and 1,000 yards (914m) on the right – good progress under the circumstances. "We had nothing to protect us but the clothes on our back," said Wells who was in the thick of the fighting, reducing enemy bunkers with hand grenades and receiving severe wounds to his legs. "I could feel myself running out of energy, my wounds were beginning to take their toll. I had not eaten, drunk water, or defecated in two and a half days."

The beaches were already beginning to become congested with swamped jeeps, trucks, and tanks as this group of Marines await their chance to move out. (National Archives)

To the north, 68 Navy planes blasted the Japanese lines with bombs and rockets, and at 0740hrs a massive barrage of artillery and naval gunfire added its weight as the 4th and 5th MarDivs moved against a complex of well-hidden enemy positions and casualties soon began to mount. Near the west coast, Sherman tanks led an advance of over 1,000 yards (914m) by the 26th and 27th Regiments and the D-Day 0-1 line was finally reached. On the east side of the island, the 4th Division could only take 50 yards (46m) of ground in the rugged terrain around the Quarry despite being reinforced by an extra company. Fighting among the cliffs and caves in the Quarry area was a hazardous business and involved heavy casualties. Captain "Jumpin' Joe" McCarthy, commanding officer of G Company, 2nd Battalion, of the 24th Regiment states: "We landed with 257 men and received 90 replacements. Of that total of 347 only 35 men were able to walk off the island when the fighting was over." McCarthy's men were under terrific fire all morning and were suffering heavy losses and in the afternoon he assigned an assault squad to clean out the pillboxes that had kept his advance to a standstill.

One of the group was Pfc Pete Santoro, who recalls:

> I took it on myself to go to my left as the others moved right, and below me was the entrance to a tunnel. I saw two Japs with rifles crawling out on their hands and knees. I shot them both in the back I'm sorry to say as I don't know how to say turn around in Japanese. Captain McCarthy came around the other side and shot them again and I said I got them already. As we went to take more high ground I found the entrance to another tunnel. I fired a rifle grenade but it fell short so I fired my last one. As I started to move in I was shot in the back. It felt like I was hit with a sledgehammer. I couldn't move my legs. I crawled out to two of our men who asked if I had been hit by a shotgun. The Jap had hit my M1 ammunition clip and my shells had shattered and penetrated all over my back.

Santoro was eventually taken to the hospital ship *Solace* and after treatment returned to the beach.

It was here that he disposed of a Japanese sniper who had been taking potshots at airmen from Airfield No. 1, and from there he returned to his unit much to the surprise of McCarthy who put him in charge of the ammunition dump. On March 9, a mortar round exploded close by and Santoro was severely concussed. Returning again to the *Solace*, he swore that he would not be returning to that island.

General Schmidt again disembarked the 21st Regiment of the 3rd Division and they came ashore on Yellow Beach. The Japanese continued their disruptive fire

A machine-gun crew sit among a pile of spent ammunition somewhere just south of Mount Suribachi. (National Archives)

throughout the night and between 150 and 200 troops gathered at the end of the runway of Airfield No. 2 and rushed the lines of the 23rd Regiment at 2330hrs. A combination of artillery and naval gunfire annihilated them before they could reach the Marines.

The ships of the Navy task force supporting the landings were to become the targets of one of the early *kamikaze* attacks of the war. As the light began to fade, 50 Japanese aircraft approached from the northwest. They were from the 2nd Milate Special Attack Unit based at Katori Airbase and had refuelled at Hachijo Jima 125 miles (201km) south of Tokyo. They were picked up by the radar of the USS *Saratoga*, a veteran carrier of the Pacific War, and six fighters were sent to intercept. They shot down two Zeros (Mitsubishi AGM fighters), but the remaining Zeros plowed on through the low-lying cloud, two of them trailing smoke, and slammed into the side of the carrier, turning the hangers into an inferno. Another solitary attacker smashed into the flight deck leaving a gaping hole 100 yards (91m) from the bow. Damage control teams worked wonders and within one hour the fires were under control and the *Saratoga* was able to recover a few of her planes. The others were taken aboard the escort carriers USS *Wake Island* and USS *Natoma Bay*.

Another aircraft, a "Betty" twin-engine bomber (Mitsubishi G4M), tore into the escort carrier USS *Bismarck Sea*. The decks were full of aircraft and the ensuing

Near the base of Mount Suribachi, Marines destroy an enemy position with demolition charges. The dash across the base of Suribachi was accomplished in good time, the capture of the volcano taking days longer. (USMC)

explosion caused uncontrollable fires. Abandon ship was sounded and 800 men went over the side. Within a few minutes a huge explosion ripped off the entire stern of the carrier and she rolled over and sank. Three other ships were also damaged: the escort carrier USS *Lurga Point* was showered with flaming debris as four aircraft were blasted out of the sky; the minesweeper *Keokuk* was damaged when a "Jill" dive-bomber (Nakajima B6N) hit her deck; and LST 477 loaded with Sherman tanks received a glancing blow.

The *Saratoga*, with destroyer escort, returned to Pearl Harbor, but by the time the damage was repaired the war was over. The *kamikazes* had done their work well: 358 men killed, one carrier sunk, and another severely damaged. It was a grim preview of the mayhem they would later cause during the invasion of Okinawa in April.

D+3

There was no let-up in the weather on Wednesday as Marines of the 28th Regiment, drenched to the skin and bent by the wind, prepared to renew the attack on Suribachi. Fresh supplies of ammunition had been brought to the front during the night, but the Shermans were mired in mud and the Navy declined to supply air support in the appalling weather. It was to be up to the foot soldier with rifle, flamethrower, grenade, and demolition charge to win the day.

Colonel Atsuchi still had 800–900 men left and they had no intention of allowing the Americans an easy victory. Major Youamata announced: "We are surrounded by enemy craft of all sizes, shapes and descriptions, enemy shells have smashed at our installations and defenses, their planes bomb and strafe yet we remain strong and defiant. The Americans are beginning to climb the first terraces towards our defenses. Now they shall taste our steel and lead."

Throughout the day the Marines attacked the Japanese positions on the lower slopes of Mount Suribachi. There was little room for maneuver and it was impossible to use support fire from artillery and tanks to maximum advantage because of the close proximity of the lines. By afternoon, patrols from Companies G and E had worked their way around the base of the volcano and it was surrounded. The bitter fighting on the northern slopes had reduced the Japanese garrison to a few hundred men and many were infiltrating the Marine lines through the maze of tunnels and joining Kuribayashi's forces in the north. Others moved upwards towards the summit. The final assault would have to wait until the following day.

The sweep to the north continued with Harry Schmidt placing the newly landed 3rd Division reinforcements, the 21st Regiment, in the center of the line between the 4th and 5th Divisions around Airfield No. 2. Here Colonel Ikeda with his 145th Regiment had the strongest section of the Japanese defenses. Lack of sleep and hot food, heavy casualties, and terrible weather were affecting the fighting efficiency of the men who had landed on D-Day and many of the hard-pressed units were replaced. The new 3rd Division men had a baptism of fire as they stormed the heavily defended ground south of the airfield and the day's gains amounted to a mere 250 yards (229m) – F Company of the 2nd Battalion was so badly mauled that they only lasted one day.

On the eastern flank near the Quarry, "Jumpin' Joe" Chambers had rocket-firing trucks brought forward to pound the enemy hideouts, resulting in dozens of Japanese fleeing to the lower ground where they were decimated by machine-gun fire. Chambers was himself badly wounded in the afternoon and evacuated to a hospital ship.

Colonel Kenehiko Atsuchi had established a formidable defense sector on Mount Suribachi. At the base a network of cave defenses, mortar, artillery and machine-gun positions thwarted the advance of the 28th Marines for four days, while further up the volcano, numerous emplacements were to hamper the Marines right up to February 23, when the flag was raised on the summit.

By D+1, the 28th Marines had established a secure line across the island and were supported by heavy 4.1in artillery fire from the 13th Marines to their rear. General Kuribayashi knew that severing Mount Suribachi from the northern plateau had done little to damage his overall defense system, and had decided that the volcano should be a semi-independent sector capable of continuing the battle without his assistance.

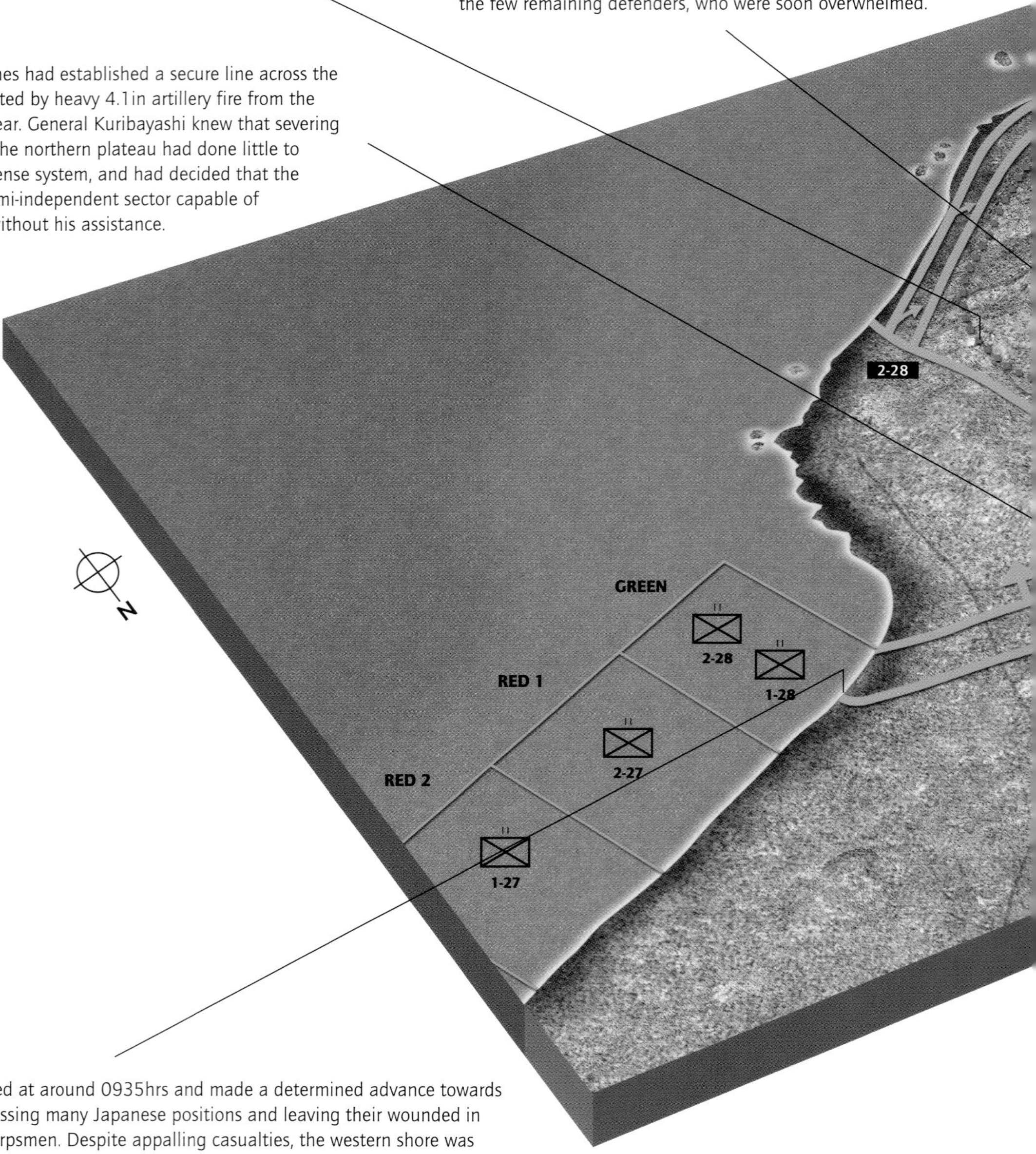

The only route to the top of Mount Suribachi lay up the north face in the 2nd Battalion's zone. At 0900hrs on D+4, Colonel Johnson sent out two patrols from Companies D and F to reconnoiter suitable routes and little resistance was forthcoming. A 40-man detachment followed them and the rim of the volcano was reached at about 1015hrs, where a short fierce skirmish developed with the few remaining defenders, who were soon overwhelmed.

2-28

GREEN

2-28

1-28

RED 1

2-27

RED 2

1-27

The 28th Marines landed at around 0935hrs and made a determined advance towards the western coast, bypassing many Japanese positions and leaving their wounded in the care of the Navy Corpsmen. Despite appalling casualties, the western shore was reached by 1035hrs. At 1039hrs, General Rockey ordered the 3rd Battalion, who had been held in reserve, to land in support of the 1st and 2nd.

Associated Press photographer Joe Rosenthal followed the 40-man detachment to the summit of Mount Suribachi, and found that a 54in x 28in (1.4m x 0.7m) flag had been raised at 1020hrs. While he was there a second flag 8ft x 4ft 8in (2.4m x 1.4m) was being hoisted to replace the smaller one – his shot of this event was to become the most famous and widely reproduced photograph of World War 2.

Heavy fighting was maintained on D+3 in the center of the regimental zone, where 3-28 forced its way to the base of Suribachi, while to the east and west patrols from Companies G and E struggled over extremely rugged terrain to link up near Tobiishi Point, completely encircling the volcano.

The Japanese attempted two infiltrations during the night of February 21/22, but they were repulsed with heavy losses. Marines from the 81mm (3.2in) Mortar Platoon killed some 60 Japanese at the front of the 2-28 position during one of these attacks, and a further 28 were killed when they attempted to move northward along the western beach.

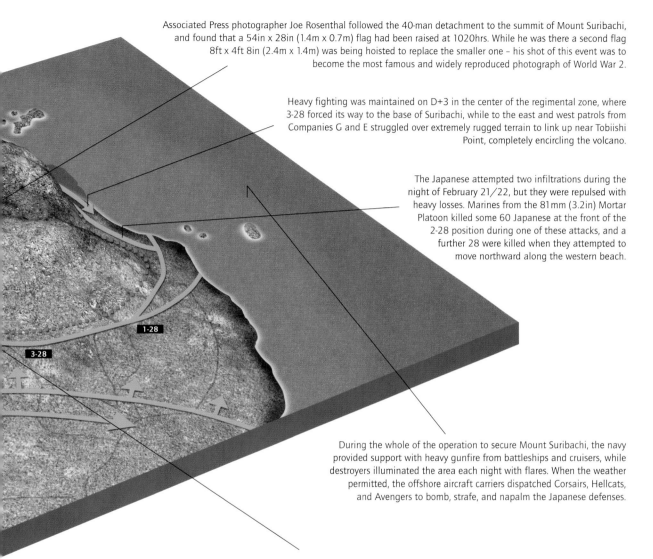

1-28

3-28

During the whole of the operation to secure Mount Suribachi, the navy provided support with heavy gunfire from battleships and cruisers, while destroyers illuminated the area each night with flares. When the weather permitted, the offshore aircraft carriers dispatched Corsairs, Hellcats, and Avengers to bomb, strafe, and napalm the Japanese defenses.

D+2 saw the Marines surrounding the base of Mount Suribachi from coast to coast. In the west was 1st Battalion, in the center the 3rd Battalion, and in the east the 2nd Battalion. Tanks did not participate in the early phases of this assault because they were unable to refuel and rearm in time as their maintenance section had not yet come ashore.

ASSAULT ON MOUNT SURIBACHI D-DAY – D+4

The 28th Marines landed on Green Beach and advanced across the 700yd (640m) wide isthmus at the base of Mount Suribachi. Despite fierce opposition and very heavy casualties, they had isolated the volcano and its defenders by 1035hrs. General Kuribayashi had anticipated that Suribachi would be cut off early in the battle, but was very disappointed that Colonel Atsuchi's garrison held out for only four days.

The Japanese mounted a series of strong counterattacks throughout the day which were repulsed by heavy artillery fire, and as the weather deteriorated further with icy rain and low mists preventing the Navy from providing gunfire and air support, the fighting died down. Casualties still crowded the beaches as the rough seas prevented LSTs from evacuating the wounded, and behind the lines near Airfield No. 1, the 4th Division cemetery was inaugurated. Up till now the dead had been left in rows under their ponchos, "stacked like cordwood" as one Marine described it.

Holland Smith aboard the USS *Auburn* was counting the cost. Three days of battle and the regimental returns listed 2,517 casualties for the 4th Division and 2,057 for the 5th: 4,574 dead and wounded and the 0-1 line had just been reached. Little did he know that as his Marines approached the hills, ravines, canyons, gullies, and cliffs of the north the worst was yet to come.

D+4

February 23 was the day that the 28th Regiment captured Mount Suribachi. General Kuribayashi had not expected this strategically important feature to fall so early in the battle and when the survivors who had infiltrated the American lines arrived in the north they were severely reprimanded.

With much improved weather, Lieutenant-Colonel Chandler Johnson gave the order to occupy and secure the summit and Marines from the 3rd Platoon started out at 0800hrs. A 40-man patrol led by Lieutenant Hal Schrier labored up the northern slopes, laden with weapons and ammunition. The going became increasingly difficult, but the opposition was surprisingly light. At 1000hrs they reached the rim of the crater and engaged a number of the enemy who attacked them with hand grenades. At 1020hrs the Stars and Stripes were raised on a length of pipe and *Leatherneck* photographer Lou Lowery recorded the moment. Throughout the southern half of the island the shout was "the flag is up" and troops cheered and vessels sounded their sirens. Around 1200hrs, a larger flag was raised to replace the smaller one and the event was photographed by Associated Press cameraman Joe Rosenthal, and this became the most famous picture of World War II. (For a full account of the flag raisings on Mount Suribachi, see Appendix 3.)

With about one third of Iwo Jima in American hands and a great improvement in the weather, General Harry Schmidt and General Cates came ashore to set up their HQs (General Rockey had come ashore the previous day), and the three met to discuss the situation. It was decided that the 3rd Division would maintain the center with the 5th Division in the west and the 4th in the east. The Navy would

The most famous photograph of World War II. Associated Press cameraman Joe Rosenthal's superb shot of Marines raising the flag on the summit of Mount Suribachi on February 23, 1945. (US Navy)

continue to add support with gunfire and carrier aircraft, and the tanks of all three divisions would come under a single command, Lieutenant-Colonel William Collins of the 5th Division.

D+4 was largely a day of consolidation and replenishment, although fighting continued south of Airfield No. 2 and north of the Quarry. Schmidt was planning a major offensive for the following day in an attempt to break the stalemate.

D+5

True to his word, Harry Schmidt provided a tremendous barrage all along the frontline. From the west the battleship USS *Idaho* blasted the area north of the airfield with her 14in guns as the cruiser USS *Pensacola*, repaired after her D-Day battering, joined in from the east coast. Masses of aircraft added bombs and rockets, and the Marine artillery and mortars expended huge amounts of ammunition.

The attack was spearheaded by the 21st Regiment deployed in the area between the two airfields. Massed tanks were scheduled to precede the infantry but Colonel Ikeda had anticipated this move, and the taxiways of both airfields were heavily mined and covered by antitank guns. The first two tanks were disabled by mines and the remainder ground to a halt. Deprived of their armor, the Marines had no alternative but to clear the mass of bunkers and pillboxes the hard way, with small arms, grenades, and flamethrowers. In what looked more like an episode from World War I, the

Marines charged the high ground and the Japanese retaliated by leaving their positions and engaging the Americans in hand-to-hand fighting. In a frenzied mêlée of clubbing, stabbing, kicking, and punching, arms and legs were broken, swords slashed, bodies fell, and blood spurted until over 50 of the enemy lay dead and the Marines occupied the higher ground.

With only four hours of daylight remaining, the Marines, exhausted and desperately short of ammunition, were determined to hold on to their gains. As the light faded the redoubtable Seabees came forward with tractors and trailers loaded with ammunition, food, and water and the troops settled in for the night. Warrant Office George Green remembers the incident well:

> The Seabees had loaded trailers with supplies and ammunition and brought them to the limit of Airfield No. 1, only 200 yards [183m] from the battlefront. As darkness fell the entrenched Marines stared in wonder as a tractor trundled towards them towing a trailer with ammunition, water, and containers of hot food preceded by two men on foot carrying flashlights to show the way. How they did it I don't know. After dark we heard the tractor coming, and sure enough there's a guy driving the thing in pitch-black night. To this day I don't know how he knew where he was going. To me that guy had guts.

Marine artillery was vital in the support of the frontline troops. Most of the Marine advances were accompanied by massive bombardments from both offshore naval units and forward artillery. (National Archives)

On the right flank, the 24th Regiment of the 4th Division was battling for "Charlie Dog Ridge," an escarpment south of the main runway of Airfield No. 2. Backed up by howitzers and mortars they blasted and burned their way to the top sustaining heavy casualties. At 1700hrs Col Walter Jordan ordered the men to dig in for the night. By Iwo Jima standards the overall gains for the day had been impressive, but so too had the casualty figures. Between D+1 and D+5, 1,034 men had died, 3,741 were wounded, 5 were missing and 558 were suffering from battle fatigue. Less than half of the island had been secured and the battle had a further 30 days to run.

D+6 – D+11: INTO THE MEATGRINDER

D+6

Having secured a front across the island that approximated to the 0-1 line, Harry Schmidt was intent on pressing northward across the plateau and the unfinished Airfield No. 3 to the north coast to split the enemy in two. Other factors also influenced the commander's choice. The west coast of the island had accessible beaches, which were desperately needed to unload the vast amount of equipment and supplies still stacked in the armada of transports. With Okinawa only two months away these ships were urgently needed elsewhere, but at the moment the Japanese still commanded the heights north-west of Airfield No. 2 from which they could shell the western coast with impunity.

Even though the southern end of the island was still within range of many of the Japanese guns, the area around Airfield No. 1 was being turned into a gigantic construction site. Over 2,000 Seabees were extending the runways to make them capable of handling the giant B29 Superfortress bombers, P51 Mustang fighters, and P61 Black Widow night-fighters. Off the shores of Mount Suribachi, a base was being established for the Catalina and Coronado flying boats engaged in rescue operations between the Marianas and Japan. Elsewhere a "city" of Nissan huts, tents, workshops, and supply dumps was replacing what only days earlier had been a bloody battlefield.

The thrust to the north began on D+6, Sunday February 25 – no day of rest for the Marines. As the 3rd Battalion moved against high ground at the end of the main runway of Airfield No. 2, 26 Shermans rumbled out to spearhead the attack and ran into a fusillade of artillery, antitank gun, and mortar fire. Three of the leading tanks burst into flames and were abandoned. The strongest point in the Japanese defenses was "Hill Peter," a 360ft (110m) high prominence just off the runway. This was stormed repeatedly but by 1430hrs the Marines had only gained 200 yards (183m). The

Flamethrowers were invaluable on Iwo Jima, where the enemy had to be prised out of every cave, pillbox, and bunker by groups of Marines. A flamethrower was always accompanied by a number of riflemen to protect him against snipers. (US Navy)

2nd and 1st Battalions had slightly better luck and were north of the airfield, although "Hill Peter" remained in enemy hands. Nine Shermans had been knocked out and Marine casualties stood at nearly 400 dead and wounded.

The 5th Division on the left were already 400 yards (366m) ahead of the 3rd Division lines and were ordered to stay where they were, but on the right the 4th Division faced a complex of four formidable defense positions that became known collectively as the "Meatgrinder." The first was Hill 382 (named from its elevation above sea level), with its slopes peppered with countless pillboxes and caves. Four hundred yards to the south lay a shallow depression called the "Amphitheater," and immediately to the east was "Turkey Knob," a hill surmounted by a massive blockhouse. The fourth obstacle was the ruins of the village of Minami, long reduced to rubble by naval gunfire and now studded with machine gun emplacements. This collective killing ground was defended by Major-General Senda and his 2nd Mixed Brigade, which included the men of Baron Nishi's 26th Tank Regiment, now largely devoid of tanks but still full of fight.

The 23rd and 24th Regiments, some 3,800 men of the 4th Division, little knowing that this was the island's most impregnable fortress, prepared to take on the Meatgrinder and at 0800hrs the now customary naval barrage and armada of carrier planes preceded the assault on Hill 382. One platoon battled its way to the summit only to be surrounded when the Japanese mounted a massive counterattack. Vicious hand-to-hand fighting ensued as the survivors withdrew under cover of smoke. Ten

The Sherman tanks had great difficulty coming ashore until the bulldozers could clear a way for them through the soft sand. Here "Cairo," fitted with wooden planks as protection against magnetic mines, has shed a track. (National Archives)

of the wounded were recovered after dark by gallant volunteers, and day one in the Meatgrinder was a complete stalemate. About 100 yards (91m) had been gained at the cost of nearly 500 casualties.

D+7

Monday February 26, dawned bright but chilly. The Marines could not believe that they had only been on the island for a week; it seemed like months. "Hill Peter" remained defiant and at 0800hrs the 9th Regiment advanced with tank support. One flamethrower tank got behind the enemy lines and incinerated a number of the enemy who were escaping through a tunnel, but the day's gains were insignificant.

To the west the 5th Division set their sights on Hill 362A, 600 yards (549m) south of the village of Nishi and surrounded by pillboxes and caves. Tanks from the 5th Tank Battalion ground through the rocks and boulders to give support but the complex proved impregnable. A little to the right, the tanks smashed through the enemy defenses to a depth of 100 yards (91m), and the 27th Regiment advanced up the west coast assisted by gunfire from the Amphibious Battalions from offshore. Day two of the battle for Hill 382 in the Meatgrinder saw the 24th Regiment replaced by the 25th Regiment. The initial attack looked promising with a gain of over 100 yards (91m) until heavy machine-gun fire from Turkey Knob brought the advance to a halt.

The 23rd Regiment to the left worked its way through a minefield beside the perimeter track of the airfield and advanced towards a ruined radio station at the foot of the hill. A massive fusillade of mortar and machine-gun fire from nearby Turkey Knob and Hill 382 brought the Marines to a grinding halt as 17 men lay dead and 26 were wounded. Under cover of smoke grenades, stretcher-bearers evacuated the survivors. It was during this engagement that Private Douglas Jacobson silenced 16 enemy positions using a bazooka single-handedly. The 19-year-old had killed 75 of the enemy in less than 30 minutes and earned himself the Medal of Honor.

D+8

"Hill Peter" still stood out like a sore thumb at the front of the 3rd Division line and at 0800hrs two battalions of the 9th Regiment, Lieutenant-Colonel Randall's 1st and Lieutenant-Colonel Cushman's 2nd, moved forward to secure the complex. Inching forward against murderous machine-gun and mortar fire, the 1st reached the top of the hill but was pinned down by fire from bypassed positions at their rear. In the early afternoon another concerted effort was launched and elements of both battalions relieved the beleaguered Marines.

The opening up of the beaches on the west side of the island was vital. Little could be landed on the east coast until the masses of vehicles and equipment were cleared. (National Archives)

To the east the 4th Division appeared to be bogged down before the seemingly impregnable Meatgrinder. General Cates committed five battalions to the area, two against Hill 382 and three against Turkey Knob, and all day the battle seesawed up and down the slopes of the hill. Rocket-launching trucks blasted the hill with over 500 rockets before having to scurry away under a torrent of enemy mortar fire, and at one point a small group of Marines actually reached the summit until shortage of ammunition and vicious counterattacks forced them to fall back. At the foot of the hill the Marines finally completed an encircling maneuver after bitter hand-to-hand fighting, and the last hours of daylight were spent in consolidating their precarious gains.

As the battle moved further north the tanks found it more and more difficult to operate among the gullies and boulder-strewn terrain. Tankdozers – Shermans fitted with bulldozer blades – were constantly in action clearing paths through the rubble and scrubland but the battle was developing into a horrific man-to-man slog in which casualties escalated by the day and prisoners were a novelty. The only grim consolation for the Marines was that their casualties could be replaced.

During the night, Japanese aircraft made a desperate attempt to get supplies to their garrison. In the only attempt that was made during the battle to support their troops, the aircraft succeeded in dropping a few parachutes containing medical supplies and ammunition. Three of the planes were shot down by carrier-based night-fighters. General Kuribayashi was moved to say: "I pay many respects to these brave aviators. It is difficult to express how the fighting youth of Iwo Jima who stood before their death felt when they saw these brave flyers."

D+9

The last day of February was to be a good one for the 3rd Division in the center of the island. Although this was the day that Harry Schmidt had predicted as the end of the battle, his orders for the day were for the 3rd to press forward towards the north coast. Relieving the battered 9th, the 21st Regiment moved out at 0900hrs and, under a huge naval and artillery barrage that appeared to have stunned the enemy, made good progress. At one point they were confronted by some of the few remaining "Ha-Go" tanks of Baron Nishi's 26th Regiment, but these flimsy vehicles were wiped out by bazookas and marauding aircraft, leaving "the Baron" with only three serviceable tanks on the island. The Japanese soon recovered and by the afternoon resistance had stiffened to such an extent that a second massive artillery barrage was called in and by 1300hrs the troops were again on the move. This time the momentum was maintained as the Marines stormed their way into the ruins of the village of Motoyama, once the largest settlement on Iwo Jima. The machine-gunners and snipers who had taken over the ruins were soon ousted and Colonel Duplantis' 3rd Battalion swept on to occupy the high ground overlooking the unfinished Airfield No. 3.

As the 3rd Battalion advanced, the 1st and 2nd Battalions were busy dealing with the mass of overrun enemy positions and in an afternoon of grim fighting the flamethrowers and demolition teams secured the flanks. The flamethrower was the most practical weapon for clearing the enemy from caves, pillboxes, and bunkers. Horrific in its effect, it saved the lives of countless Marines who would otherwise have had to prise the enemy out in hand-to-hand fighting with an opponent who did not consider surrender an option. Pfc Hank Chamberlain describes an attack that was typical:

As tanks assembled near Airfield No. 2, Marines of G Company, 24th Regiment, relax before renewing the attack on enemy pillboxes in the area. (USMC)

I was cover for a flamethrower near a row of caves. A grenade came flying out towards us and we dived behind an outcrop of rocks to our left and the grenade exploded harmlessly. The flamethrower was now alongside the cave entrance and sidestepped in front of it and let off a long blast. A single Jap came tearing out. He was a mass of flames from head to foot and his shrieks were indescribable. Both Buckey and I had emptied our guns into the cave and we reloaded as fast as we could. The Jap was now writhing on the ground with his arms flaying the air. We put him out of his agony with enough bullets to kill a dozen men.

Over on the 5th Division front, the Marines were still confronted with Hill 362A – the top dotted with antitank guns and mortars, the slopes bristling with machine guns, and the base lined with bunkers and pillboxes. Two battalions of the 27th Regiment, supported by tanks, assaulted the hill with demolition charges and flamethrowers, but little progress was made and at 1200hrs six rocket-firing trucks added salvos of 4.5in rockets. Some men reached the top but were driven back by determined enemy troops. The only gains of the day were made by the 1st Battalion who pushed back strong opposition to gain 300 yards (274m) near the base.

The impasse at the Meatgrinder continued as the 4th Division continued to batter Hill 382 and Turkey Knob. Attempts to encircle these positions were frustrated, and as smoke shells covered the withdrawal of forward troops, the operation was closed down for the day at 1645hrs.

Near the beach, rows of dead lie under their ponchos: burial parties check identification and personal possessions. (National Archives)

The most memorable event of the day came at 1400hrs when a Japanese shell landed in a large ammunition dump near Airfield No. 1, and the whole of southern Iwo Jima erupted in a spectacular display of pyrotechnics. Shells exploded with a deafening bang, bullets popped and crackled, and huge clouds of smoke rolled out to sea. Miraculously there were no casualties, but the 5th Division lost almost a quarter of its stocks.

D+10

After a night overlooking Airfield No. 3, the 21st Regiment of the 3rd Division moved forward against surprisingly light resistance and by 1200hrs were across the main runway. Tanks rolled forward to stiffen the attack and all went well until the forward troops reached Hills 362B and 362C, two more heavily defended bastions barring the way to the coast, and the advance ran out of steam.

On the west coast, the 28th Regiment, the conquerors of Mount Suribachi, was now bolstering the 5th Division front as all three battalions were pitted against the complex of strongpoints north of Hill 362A. The day started with shelling by a

Bogged-down tank, amtracs blown over by shellfire – a view on the beaches taken some days after the landing. (National Archives)

battleship and three cruisers, and as the dust settled the 1st and 2nd Battalions stormed the slopes and reached the summit. The Japanese had abandoned the site through a labyrinth of caves and taken up new positions on Nishi Ridge, a ragged cliffline 200 yards (183m) further north.

For the 4th Division, Hill 382 was the key to the impasse. Until it was taken the whole of the eastern side of Iwo Jima would be firmly in enemy hands, and in the pre-dawn darkness the 24th Regiment moved up to replace the 23rd. In a day of unremitting savagery, the battle flowed back and forth. An early advance by the 1st and 2nd Battalions was stalled by a hail of mortar fire. The Japanese then took to their caves as a barrage from naval guns, artillery, and carrier planes swept the area. As the 1st Battalion resumed the attack the enemy emerged from the depths and resumed their machine-gun, mortar, and small-arms fire from the high ground. By afternoon it was obvious that there was yet another stalemate.

The US generals were becoming increasingly concerned about the combat efficiency of their units. It was not unusual to see command pass from captain to lieutenant to sergeant and in some cases to a Pfc. A confidential report of the 3rd Battalion, 25th Regiment, makes note of the situation at the front around this time:

> Special note must here be made of the mental condition and morale of our troops. We have been in the assault for a period of ten days during which we have shown a gain of approx. 800 yards (732m). Initially, we had relieved troops whose position on the ground was far short of the position they showed themselves to occupy on the map. Throughout the assault we have suffered heavy casualties. One company commander and two platoon leaders have been killed in action. While it was true we did not move from D+11 to D+17, nevertheless throughout that period of time enemy mortar fire of various calibers fell in our zone of action inflicting many casualties. On D+8, without warning a strafing and napalm strike was made behind and within our lines although our front line panels were clearly displayed. On D+11, a TBF [Avenger Torpedo Bomber] accidentally dropped a lone bomb behind our lines. On D+12, without warning in any way, a rocket barrage, apparently from a rocket jeep, fell directly on our flank platoon. All of this contributed to make our troops "jittery." It is common knowledge that we were relieving a unit which had been unable to accomplish its mission.

General Erskine was scathing in his criticism of the quality of the replacements: "They get killed the day they go into battle," he said. The problem was the use of "battle replacements" as opposed to "organic replacements." The author and Iwo Jima veteran John Lane reflected soberly on this issue:

Lieutenant-Colonel (Baron) Nishi, commander of the 26th Tank Regiment, had won a gold medal in the equestrian event at the 1932 Olympic Games in Los Angeles, and was a member of a very influential family. Around D+20, in Cushman's Pocket, the Baron and his command were resisting strongly from a complex of caves against the 5th MarDiv. Partially blinded, the Baron and his men held out for longer than most until the Pocket fell silent. Some say that he was killed leading a raid, others that he committed *hara-kiri*. (Jim Laurier © Osprey Publishing)

Battle replacements were recruits who had gone through Parris Island in the summer of 1944, where they had fired for qualification once. In early September they were formed into an Infantry Training Unit at Camp Lejeune where they went through "musketry range" once, threw one live grenade, fired one rifle grenade and went through one live fire exercise. Designated the 30th Replacement Draft in October, they went to Camp Pendleton and straight on to Maui in Hawaii where they worked on mess duties or working parties with no additional training. The day after Christmas Day they began boarding for Iwo Jima. Those who survived went back to Maui and began receiving the training that might have helped them before the operation.

The situation was typified by one replacement who was placed with a machine-gun unit. When asked if he had any questions he replied, "Yes, how do you fire this thing?"

D+11

The pressure continued on Hill 382 and Turkey Knob. The 1st Battalion of the 25th Regiment made pre-dawn infiltrations but were driven back by mortar shells raining down from the heights above. Sherman tanks and "Zippos" (flamethrower tanks)

pounded the blockhouse on the top of Turkey Knob and the "Zippos" expended over 1,000 gallons (3,785 liters) of fuel on the caves, but the Japanese simply retired to the depths of their tunnels and sat out the inferno. Meanwhile the 26th Regiment, in some of the fiercest fighting of the day, secured a foothold on the summit of Hill 382. Casualties were horrendous, one unit losing five officers in rapid succession – two fatally wounded, two seriously wounded, and the other losing his leg below the knee.

In the center, hopes of a dash to the north coast were fading. Although the sea was only 1,500 yards (1,372m) away, the 3rd Division had yet to deal with Hills 362B and C. Four thousand men headed out in a two-pronged assault, one group headed for Hill 362B while the other deployed around Airfield No. 3. The approach to the hill was a flat area overlooked by artillery and offering virtually no cover. Tanks were brought forward and under their cover an advance of 500 yards (457m) was made to the base of the hill.

On the right the 2nd Battalion moved towards the east of the airfield but made little progress as they came face to face with Baron Nishi's lines. Without his tanks the Baron was resigned to dying on the frontline with the remains of his command. The glory days when he had won an Olympic medal on his horse Uranus and socialized with Los Angeles society and Hollywood stars were only a memory.

Colonel Chandler Johnson's 28th Regiment on the west coast were determined to secure Nishi Ridge. Advancing along the left side of Hill 363A they came under heavy fire, but pushed on to the ravine between the hill and the ridge where they had a clear area from which the Shermans could blast the cliff face. Johnson, well known for being up front with his men, fell victim to what was probably a misplaced American round which blew him to pieces.

D+12 – D+19: DEADLOCK

D+12

Casualty figures were reaching epidemic proportions. By D+12 the Marine figure stood at 16,000, of whom more than 3,000 were dead. The Japanese numbers were staggering. Of the 21,000 troops in General Kuribayashi's command on D-Day, a mere 7,000 remained. The battle was dragging on far longer than the forecast of the chiefs of staff, deteriorating into an inexorable slog from gully to gully, ridge to ridge, and cave to cave.

The 5th Division kept up the pressure on the west coast as the 26th Regiment attacked Hill 362B (previously located in the 3rd Division sector but now re-allocated to the 5th), and the 28th Regiment confronted Nishi Ridge. In a grim day's fighting during which they suffered severe casualties, the 26th finally stormed to the top of Hill 362B, although the enemy still occupied much of the surrounding area. But the best news of the day came with the capture of Nishi Ridge by the 28th Regiment, an achievement that pleased General Rockey, who had envisaged a prolonged struggle for this strategically important location.

The 3rd Division again pitted themselves against the Meatgrinder. Colonel Jordan's 24th Regiment renewed their assault on Hill 382 as Colonel Wensinger's 23rd tackled Turkey Knob, the Amphitheater, and Minami Village. Shermans of the 4th Tank Battalion had been assigned to both units, but the increasingly rocky terrain was taking its toll as a large proportion of the tanks ground to a halt before impenetrable mounds of rocks and boulders. Engineers braved heavy enemy fire in an attempt to clear a path, but with little success. As the 24th Regiment advanced they were confronted by a nest of concrete pillboxes but, with the help of the few tanks that had broken through, surrounded Hill 382. This was to be the only significant gain of the day as the 23rd came to a grinding halt from enfilading fire from the remaining positions.

A 155mm howitzer adds its support to the 5th Division barrage. (USMC)

Although the day had been disappointing in material gains it had been one of incredible valor, five Medals of Honor being awarded for acts of heroism that almost defy belief. Two Marines died saving the lives of their companions by throwing themselves onto hand grenades. Two Corpsmen enhanced the reputation of the Navy medics by outstanding acts of self-sacrifice. One ministered to the wounded until he had to be dragged to the rear to have his own life-threatening wounds attended to, and the other died as he refused aid so that he could continue tending wounded Marines. The fifth, Sergeant William Harrell, won his medal defending his frontline position against night-time infiltrators, suffering horrific wounds including the loss of both hands.

D+13

In deteriorating weather, icy drizzle, and leaden clouds, carrier plane sorties and naval bombardments were called off because of poor visibility. An overall weariness seemed to permeate the entire front as the Marines battled with a seemingly invisible enemy that spent most of its daylight hours in caves and tunnels, emerging at night to infiltrate the American line, more intent on foraging for food and water than killing the enemy.

The Superfortress "Dinah Might" was the first B29 to land on the island. The arrival attracted a great deal of attention, as crowds of Marines and Seabees gathered to see the huge bomber. (National Archives)

In the knowledge that the battle was swinging irrevocably in favor of the Americans, Kuribayashi radioed Tokyo: "Our strongpoints might be able to fight delaying actions for several more days. I comfort myself a little seeing my officers and men die without regret after struggling in this inch-by-inch battle against an overwhelming enemy…" The general's predictions were, if anything, on the pessimistic side, as his garrison would prolong the battle for another three weeks.

As tanks and rocket launchers pounded the Amphitheater in the east, the 3rd Division in the center was unable to make any significant progress. In the west the 5th Division continued to engage the more exposed positions with flamethrowers and grenades, but little progress could be reported over the entire front. A communiqué at 1700hrs from the command posts of Generals Rockey, Erskine, and Cates stated: "There will be no general attack tomorrow… Divisions will utilize the day for rest, refitting, and re-organization in preparation for resumption of action on March 6." It was clear that the Marines desperately needed a break after two weeks of the bloodiest fighting the Corps had ever experienced.

The highlight of the day was the arrival of "Dinah Might," the first B29 Superfortress bomber to land on Iwo Jima. With bomb bays jammed in the open position and problems with the fuel transfer valve, the aircraft had struggled back from a mission southwest of Tokyo. As she ground to a halt at the northern end of the main runway on Airfield No. 1, the Japanese directed a steady hail of artillery fire in the general direction, causing the huge plane to swing around and retire rapidly to the Mount Suribachi end of the airfield. The bloody sacrifices of the Marine Corps in securing the island were beginning to pay dividends in the lives of what were to be thousands of Air Force crewmen.

D+14

The day was one of consolidation, replenishment, and rest. Unfortunately, no one had informed the Japanese, who continued to lob artillery rounds and mortar shells into the Marine lines all day. Tank crews serviced their machines; ammunition, food, and fresh water were brought to the front; hot coffee and doughnuts arrived from the newly installed bakery in the rear, and replacements filtered through to relieve many of the exhausted troops who had slogged for 14 days in hell.

With undue optimism considering the ferocity of the Japanese resistance, the Navy began to run down its support. Admiral Spruance in his flagship USS *Indianapolis* departed for Guam, along with the 3rd Regiment of the 3rd Division, seasoned troops that Harry Schmidt would have much preferred to the green replacements from Hawaii, who were suffering such terrible casualties. However, there were some newcomers.

Army units who were to garrison Iwo Jima after the departure of the Marines began to disembark, and the first of the Mustang and Black Widow fighters took their places on the handstands of the airfield.

D+15

If the generals had hoped that the day of rest and replenishment would mean big advances on Tuesday they were to be bitterly disappointed. The Navy and Marine artillery mounted one of the heaviest bombardments of the battle and within 67 minutes the artillery fired 22,500 rounds. A battleship, a cruiser, and three destroyers added a further 450 rounds of 14in and 8in shells, while Dauntless and Corsair carrier planes strafed and dropped bombs and napalm canisters.

Between 0800hrs and 0900hrs the 4th and 5th Divisions moved forward, but resistance was as fierce as ever. The 21st and 27th Regiments on the west coast were halted by shredding machine-gun and mortar fire before they had gone more than a few yards, and support from "Zippo" flamethrower tanks had little effect. Marine Dale

As the 5th Division advanced up the west coast, many enemy gun positions were captured. Here a Marine stands guard over a Japanese coastal artillery piece. (National Archives)

Worley wrote: "They have almost blown Hill 362 off the map. There are bodies everywhere and the ground is spotted with blood. The smell is sickening."

In the center the 3rd Division made little progress. One element of the 21st Regiment, under Lieutenant Mulvey, battered its way to the top of yet another ridge and saw before them the prize that had so long eluded them – the sea. He estimated that it was less than a quarter of a mile away and called for reinforcements. A dozen men came forward but before they could reach the lieutenant six were killed and two wounded, and the group had to retire under a storm of enemy fire. In the east the best advance of the day was a mere 350 yards (320m) by the 3rd Battalion of the 24th Regiment aided by four "Zippo" flamethrower tanks.

D+16

General Erskine had, for a long while, been toying with the idea of a night attack. As a veteran of World War I he had witnessed many such actions and was aware that the Japanese knew that the Marines usually confined their fighting to daytime. His plan was to infiltrate the enemy lines for about 250 yards (229m) and capture Hill 362C, the last major obstacle between the 3rd Division and the sea.

At 0500hrs the 3rd Battalion of the 9th Regiment under the command of Lieutenant-Colonel Harold Boehm moved silently forward and for 30 minutes their luck held until an alert enemy machine-gunner opened up on their left. Pressing forward, Boehm and his men stormed to the top of the hill and radioed back to Erskine who said: "We caught the bastards asleep just as we thought we would." But the euphoria was short lived, as Boehm checked his maps and realized that he was atop Hill 331 and not 362C. In the darkness and driving rain, one Iwo Jima hill looked much like another. Calling in artillery support, Boehm and his battalion pushed forward despite heavy opposition from the front and both flanks, and by 1400hrs finally reached the correct objective.

As he was moving towards Hill 362C, the 1st and 2nd Battalions were advancing on his right flank, but soon encountered heavy resistance from their front and from bypassed positions. Lieutenant-Colonel Cushman and his 2nd Battalion had stumbled across the remains of Baron Nishi's tank regiment and soon found themselves surrounded. It was not until the next day that the remains of Cushman's battalion could be extricated with the aid of tanks. Bitter fighting was to continue in this area for another six days in what was to become known as "Cushman's Pocket."

On the 5th Division front, the 26th Regiment, approaching a ridge just north of the ruins of Nishi Village, found the enemy opposition to be almost nonexistent.

Cautiously proceeding to the summit they expected a fusillade of fire from the far side as had often happened in the past. Instead, the whole ridge disappeared in a massive explosion that could be heard for miles around. The Japanese had mined their command post and it was left to the Marines to recover the bodies of 43 of their comrades.

In a clever maneuver in the 4th Division sector, the 23rd and 24th Regiments moved to the east and then swung sharply south, edging the Japanese towards the 25th Regiment, which had assumed a defensive line. Realizing that they were trapped, General Senda and Navy Captain Inouye, with 1,500 men, elected for a banzai attack, strictly against the instructions of General Kuribayashi. At around 2400hrs a large column of men armed with grenades, small arms, swords, and bamboo spears moved south in a bizarre attempt to infiltrate the American lines, scale Mount Suribachi and raise the Japanese flag. Caught in the nightly display of flares provided by offshore destroyers, the column was decimated by artillery and machine-gun fire. The morning light was to reveal scores of bodies littering the area.

Two flamethrowers, Private Richard Klatt on the left and Private 1st Class Wildred Voegeli, demonstrate the terrifying effect of their weapons. (National Archives)

D+10 saw a massive assault on Hill 362A, which was preceded by a naval bombardment from the battleship USS *Nevada* and the cruisers USS *Pensacola* and USS *Indianapolis*. The 1st and 2nd Battalions of the 28th Marines stormed to the summit, but the enemy had withdrawn to Nishi Ridge 200yds (183m) to the north. The capture of Hill 362A broke the deadlock on the west coast, opening the way for flamethrower tanks to support the move north.

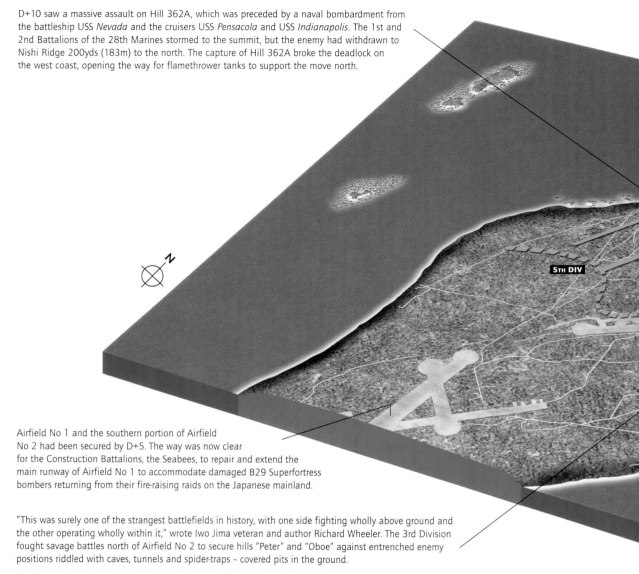

5TH DIV

Airfield No 1 and the southern portion of Airfield No 2 had been secured by D+5. The way was now clear for the Construction Battalions, the Seabees, to repair and extend the main runway of Airfield No 1 to accommodate damaged B29 Superfortress bombers returning from their fire-raising raids on the Japanese mainland.

"This was surely one of the strangest battlefields in history, with one side fighting wholly above ground and the other operating wholly within it," wrote Iwo Jima veteran and author Richard Wheeler. The 3rd Division fought savage battles north of Airfield No 2 to secure hills "Peter" and "Oboe" against entrenched enemy positions riddled with caves, tunnels and spider-traps – covered pits in the ground.

For the attack to the north, General Schmidt consolidated the tanks of all three divisions into one large group. In what was virtually an armored regiment the Marines had gathered together the largest concentration of Shermans in the Pacific zone.

THE ATTACK NORTH D+5 – D+16

Mount Suribachi, with its commanding views over most of Iwo Jima, was now secure and Major-General Harry Schmidt, the V Amphibious Corps Commander, planned to attack the Japanese on a broad front with his three divisions abreast – the 5th in the west, the 3rd in the center, and the 4th in the east. It immediately became apparent that the Marines had reached General Kuribayashi's main defense belt, and the fighting degenerated into small-unit actions of incredible savagery.

On D+15 Marine artillery expended 22,500 rounds in 67 minutes. Naval artillery lobbed 14in (356mm) and 8in (203mm) shells into known enemy strongpoints and Corsair and Dauntless fighters and bombers attacked with bombs and napalm canisters for over one hour. The pounding appeared to have little effect and only marginal progress was achieved.

In the northern sector of the 3rd Division zone all the high-ground northeast of Airfield No 3 had been seized by D+12 after harrowing close-quarter fighting, and General Erskine ordered the 9th Regiment to advance against Hill 357 in an attempt to reach the north coast and split the enemy forces through the middle of the island.

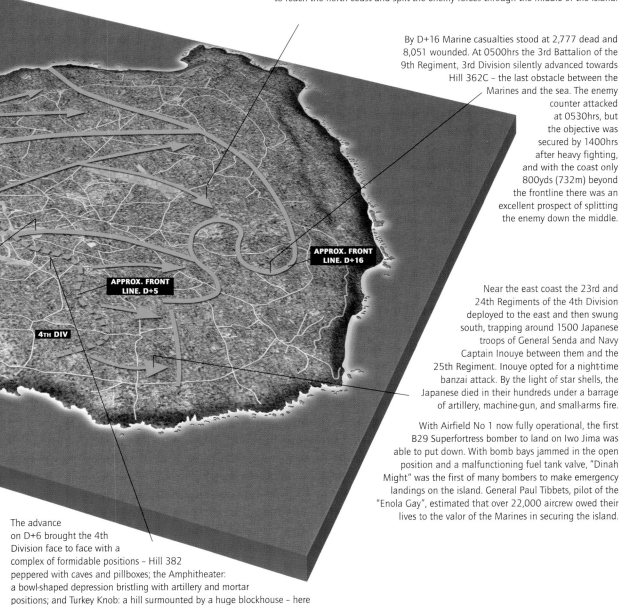

APPROX. FRONT LINE. D+16

APPROX. FRONT LINE. D+5

4TH DIV

By D+16 Marine casualties stood at 2,777 dead and 8,051 wounded. At 0500hrs the 3rd Battalion of the 9th Regiment, 3rd Division silently advanced towards Hill 362C – the last obstacle between the Marines and the sea. The enemy counter attacked at 0530hrs, but the objective was secured by 1400hrs after heavy fighting, and with the coast only 800yds (732m) beyond the frontline there was an excellent prospect of splitting the enemy down the middle.

Near the east coast the 23rd and 24th Regiments of the 4th Division deployed to the east and then swung south, trapping around 1500 Japanese troops of General Senda and Navy Captain Inouye between them and the 25th Regiment. Inouye opted for a night-time banzai attack. By the light of star shells, the Japanese died in their hundreds under a barrage of artillery, machine-gun, and small-arms fire.

With Airfield No 1 now fully operational, the first B29 Superfortress bomber to land on Iwo Jima was able to put down. With bomb bays jammed in the open position and a malfunctioning fuel tank valve, "Dinah Might" was the first of many bombers to make emergency landings on the island. General Paul Tibbets, pilot of the "Enola Gay", estimated that over 22,000 aircrew owed their lives to the valor of the Marines in securing the island.

The advance on D+6 brought the 4th Division face to face with a complex of formidable positions – Hill 382 peppered with caves and pillboxes; the Amphitheater: a bowl-shaped depression bristling with artillery and mortar positions; and Turkey Knob: a hill surmounted by a huge blockhouse – here was a killing ground that the Marines were to aptly name the "Meatgrinder".

The story of Inouye's banzai attack was revealed years later by two of his orderlies who survived and were captured. Many of his troops believed that Inouye was a superior leader who inspired his men to perform outstanding feats of bravery – others thought he was a maniac. The sight of the Stars and Stripes flying on top of Mount Suribachi had filled him with increasing rage. He is quoted as saying: "We shall destroy their banner, we shall replace it with ours in the name of the great Emperor and the great people of Japan."

Inouye was in charge of the Naval Guard Force who manned the shore guns that sank and damaged many of the US warships and landing craft, and was described as a bombastic and temperamental character, a fine swordsman, heavy drinker, and womanizer. His bizarre plan almost beggars belief. The captain was certain that the airfields would be lightly defended by service troops. He and his men would move southward, destroying B29 bombers as they passed; climb Mount Suribachi and tear down the Stars and Stripes; and replace it with the Rising Sun as an inspiration to all Japanese troops on the island.

As the battle moved further north, the terrain became increasingly difficult. Here a group examine an abandoned Japanese car among a mass of boulders and rocks. (National Archives)

General Senda radioed Kuribayashi to seek approval for the attack, but Kuribayashi was furious and declared it impractical and stupid. Senda and Inouye consulted and decided to go ahead anyway. As night fell, the Marines of the 23rd and 24th Regiments became aware of increasing activity in the enemy lines. First voices, and after about two hours, a barrage of artillery fire thundered across the front line as large numbers of Japanese troops began to infiltrate the American lines. Some, probably the officers, wielded sabres, a few had machine guns, most had rifles and grenades, and some of the sailors carried crude wooden spears or had demolition charges strapped to their chests. In the chaos that followed, the Marines fired flares and star shells to illuminate the sky as they shredded the onrushing enemy with machine-gun fire, rifles, and 60mm mortars. Some of the Japanese wore Marine helmets, others shouted "Corpsman" in English, and throughout the night bitter hand-to-hand struggles and grenade-throwing contests erupted all along the line. The morning revealed the extent of the carnage. A body count showed almost 800 Japanese dead, probably the largest number of casualties that they suffered in a single day and a justification of Kuribayashi's reluctance to sanction the attack. Marine casualties were 90 dead and 257 wounded.

D+17

March 9 saw two more Marines earn the Medal of Honor. Nineteen-year-old Pfc James LaBelle flung himself on a spluttering grenade and died saving the lives of his two companions, while in a push up the west coast towards Kitano Point, Lieutenant Jack Lummus silenced two enemy emplacements and then ran ahead of his men urging them forward. As he did he stepped on a mine and both his legs were blown off. When the dust and debris settled, his men were amazed to see him still standing on his bloody stumps waving them on. Lummus died that afternoon in the 3rd Division hospital from shock and loss of blood.

The day saw steady if unspectacular progress. Cushman's Pocket still barred the progress of the 3rd Division, and the 4th were still confronted with Turkey Knob and the Amphitheater.

D+18

The final breakthrough to the sea was achieved by a 28-man patrol led by Lieutenant Paul Connally. As the men swilled their faces in the icy water, mortar rounds began falling among them and there was a mad scramble back to the safety of the cliffs. Connally had filled his water bottle with sea water and passed it back to his CO,

Hill 382 was surrounded by minefields and it fell to the infantryman to assault the Hill with flamethrowers, satchel charges, and grenades. One platoon reached the summit only to be surrounded when the Japanese mounted a counterattack, and the survivors had to be evacuated under cover of smoke. Day one in the Meatgrinder was a complete stalemate – 100yd (91m) gained at the cost of nearly 500 casualties.

The 23rd and 24th Marines of the 4th Division, some 3,800 men, began their assault on the Meatgrinder at 0800hrs on D+6. The customary naval barrage and sorties by carrier-based bombers and fighters preceded the Marines, and Sherman tanks spearheaded the attack, but the terrain proved to be so rough that they had to divert through the 3rd Division lines and progress from the left flank: an ominous sign of the growing limitations of tank support in the appalling conditions.

By D+12, the heaviest opposition was concentrated on high ground northeast of the bypassed Hill 382, the Minami area, and in the south, where the Amphitheater and Turkey Knob were still in enemy hands, despite six days of continuous bombardment. Shermans of the 4th Tank Battalion led the day's assault, in which units of the 23rd Marines neared the blockhouse on top of Turkey Knob, but were repulsed by machine-gun and small-arms fire.

During the night of D+16, Japanese troops moved into the Marine frontline in what was thought to be an attack on the right flank. Many of the enemy infiltrated into Marine foxholes and hand-to-hand fighting continued until dawn, with 50 Japanese and 13 Marines dying in the melee. At 0502hrs a large-caliber rocket fell into the command post of the 2nd Battalion, 23rd Marines, wounding the battalion commander and most of his senior staff and killing the communications officer.

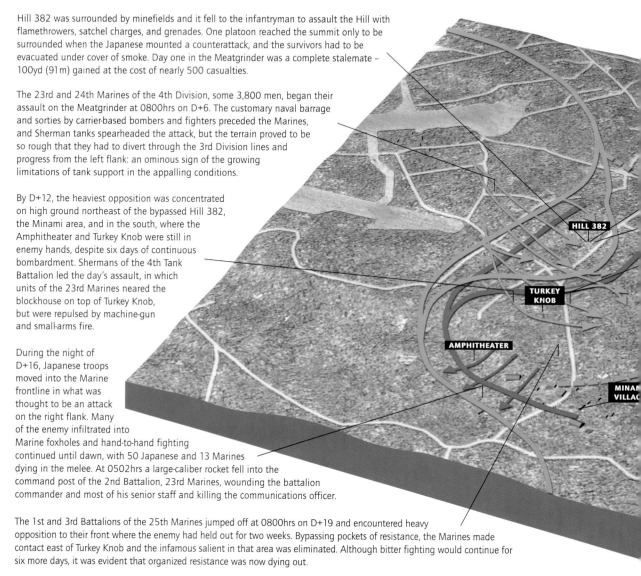

The 1st and 3rd Battalions of the 25th Marines jumped off at 0800hrs on D+19 and encountered heavy opposition to their front where the enemy had held out for two weeks. Bypassing pockets of resistance, the Marines made contact east of Turkey Knob and the infamous salient in that area was eliminated. Although bitter fighting would continue for six more days, it was evident that organized resistance was now dying out.

During the period when the 4th Division was pitted against the Meatgrinder, they were engaged in head-on assaults and fought a bloody path from Charlie Dog Ridge past Hill 382, the Amphitheater, Turkey Knob, through the ruins of Minami Village, and almost to the east coast. The right flank, the hinge, advanced only 1,000yd (914m), while the rest of the division, the door, turned upon it and attacked northeast, east, and southeast to close and sweep trapped enemy forces towards the sea.

ASSAULT ON THE MEATGRINDER D+6 – D+19

As Harry Schmidt's three divisions fought slowly northward through Iwo Jima, the 4th Division came up against a complex of four formidable defense positions to the east of Airfield No. 2, that soon became known to the Marines as the Meatgrinder. Defended by Major-General Senda's 2nd Mixed Brigade and elements of Baron Nishi's 26th Tank Regiment, Hill 382, Turkey Knob, the Amphitheater, and the ruins of Minami Village were to hold out until March 15 and be the scene of some of the bloodiest actions of the whole battle.

On D+7, General Cates alerted the 25th Marines to replace the battered 24th and three battalions attacked behind an artillery barrage. Things went well for the first 100yd (91m) before a wall of extremely heavy machine-gun fire from the Amphitheater and Turkey Knob brought the advance to a grinding halt. The 23rd Marines on the left flank worked their way through a minefield and occupied a shattered radio station below Hill 382. On this day, Pfc Douglas Jacobson silenced 16 strongpoints with his bazooka, killing 75 of the enemy and earning himself the Medal of Honor.

Moving out at dawn on D+12, Colonel Jordan's 24th Marines renewed the battle for Hill 382, while Colonel Wensinger's 23rd tackled the complex of Turkey Knob, the Amphitheater, and Minami Village. Sherman tanks assigned to both units soon ground to a halt before an impenetrable wall of boulders, and as infantry moved against Turkey Knob fire from the huge blockhouse on the summit stopped the advance in its tracks. The highlight of the day was the neutralization of Hill 382, now surrounded and of little strategic value.

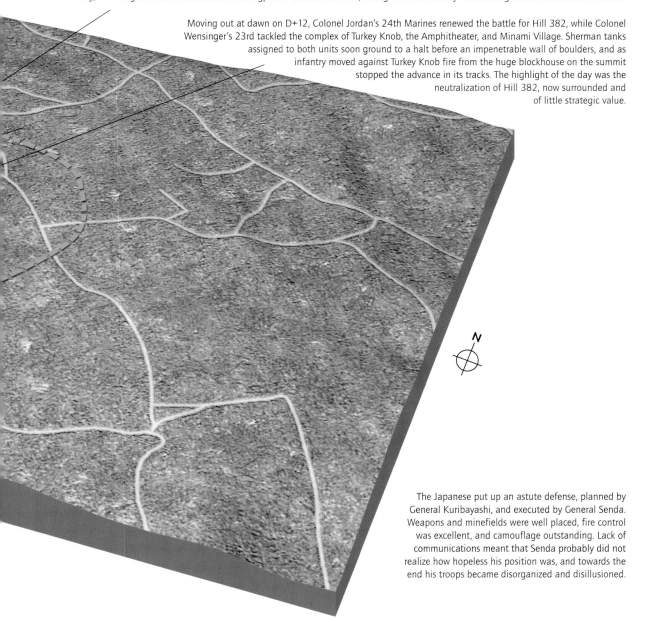

The Japanese put up an astute defense, planned by General Kuribayashi, and executed by General Senda. Weapons and minefields were well placed, fire control was excellent, and camouflage outstanding. Lack of communications meant that Senda probably did not realize how hopeless his position was, and towards the end his troops became disorganized and disillusioned.

With the battle now confined to the north of the island, the divisional cemeteries were established. The 5th Division cemetery is flanked on the left by that of the 3rd Division and on the right, the 4th Division; Mount Suribachi looms in the distance. (USMC)

Colonel Withers, who in turn sent it to General Erskine with the message "for inspection, not consumption."

That same night, as the Marines bedded down after another frustrating day that saw only minor gains on the 4th and 5th Division fronts, the drone of hundreds of aircraft was heard as they skirted the east of Iwo Jima. A total of 325 B29s from Saipan, Tinian, and Guam were heading for Tokyo for the first of General Curtis LeMay's "fire raising" raids. In a dramatic change in policy, daylight precision bombing had been abandoned in favor of "area bombing," which had been practiced by the RAF against Germany since 1941. In a spectacular raid that destroyed almost a quarter of Tokyo and killed 83,793 people, LeMay had spelled out his intentions for the future of the 20th Air Force's assault against the Japanese mainland.

D+19

It was obvious to both sides that, by March 10, the battle was reaching its climax. Cushman's Pocket was proving a tough nut to crack and the Meatgrinder and Turkey Knob were still to be taken. However, the Japanese were nearing the end of their endurance as diminishing numbers and chronic shortages of ammunition, food, and water were taking their toll. In the northwest corner of the island, General Kuribayashi prepared his final enclave, one which was significantly to be called "Death Valley" by the Marines. Located about 500 yards (457m) south of Kitano Point, it was a nightmare of rocks, caves, and gullies where the 1,500 remaining troops prepared for the end. The general informed Tokyo: "The enemy's bombardments are very severe, so fierce that I cannot express or write it here. The troops are still fighting bravely and holding their positions thoroughly."

D+20 – D+36: "GOODBYE FROM IWO"

The Japanese were now confined to three distinct areas: one was Cushman's Pocket, the second an area on the east coast between the village of Higashi and the sea, and the other was "Death Valley" on the northwest coast where General Kuribayashi and the remains of his command were entrenched. Conventional battle was abandoned as the infantry slugged it out with a desperate enemy. Tanks could only operate in the few areas where bulldozers could clear a path for them. Artillery fire was reduced dramatically as the frontlines merged, and many gunners found themselves donning combat gear. The heavy elements of the Navy departed for Guam, and the Mustangs took over from the carrier aircraft in providing ground support with bombs, rockets, and napalm.

In a cynical move to placate public alarm at the mounting casualty figures released by the War Department, Iwo Jima was declared "secure" on March 14. In a ceremony held in the shadow of Mount Suribachi, Harry Schmidt's personnel officer read the statement as an artillery barrage thundered in the north of the island, almost drowning out his words. The irony of the situation was obvious to all.

In the northwest, the 5th Division regrouped and re-armed in preparation for the final assault on Kuribayashi's headquarters in "Death Valley" (or "The Gorge" as the Marine maps also labeled it). Meanwhile the 3rd Division fought a bloody battle in Cushman's Pocket, slowly grinding down the fanatical remnants of Baron Nishi's command. The Baron, partially blinded in the fighting, held out until the end using dug-in tanks as artillery and fighting from a maze of caves until the Pocket finally fell silent. The Baron's fate is uncertain as his body was never identified and none of his staff survived.

General Senda, who had declined to take part in the mad banzai attack of D+16, was still holding out in an area east of Higashi. Prisoners estimated his strength at around 300 men, and in an attempt to reduce the carnage, General Erskine arranged for loudspeakers to broadcast to the Japanese to explain the futility of further

US gains by end of D+19. By this stage of the battle the remaining Japanese forces were confined in relatively isolated areas of the island, but the fighting remained bitter.

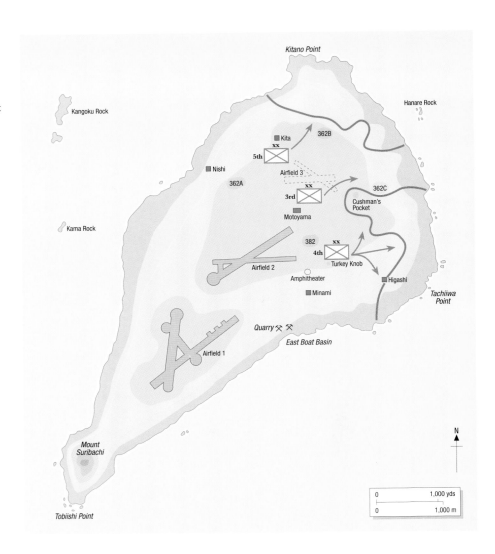

resistance. However, the equipment failed to work and his efforts were in vain. The slaughter continued four more days until the whole garrison were eliminated. The body of General Senda was never found.

With only "Death Valley" to secure, Harry Schmidt could be forgiven for thinking that the battle was all but over. He sadly misjudged Kuribayashi, and another ten days of savage fighting and 1,724 casualties lay ahead. "Death Valley" was around 700 yards (640m) long and between 300 (274m) and 500 yards (457m) wide with dozens of canyons and gullies leading off on both sides. In a cave somewhere in this labyrinth the general planned his final stand.

Colonel Liversedge's 28th Regiment moved up the coast and took up its positions on the cliffs overlooking the valley, while the remainder of the division attacked from the center and from the east. In a week of attrition, the Marines painfully squeezed the Japanese further and further back until, by March 24, the enemy had been reduced to an area of around 50 yards (46m) square. Flamethrower tanks had expended over 10,000 gallons (37,854 liters) of fuel per day burning out caves and crevices. So badly mauled was the 2nd Battalion that it ceased to exist as a fighting force, and the 1st Battalion was on its third commander in nine days. The first was decapitated, the second maimed by a mine, and the third lost his left arm to a burst of machine-gun fire.

Again General Erskine tried to persuade the enemy to give up the hopeless struggle, sending Japanese POWs and Nisei (Japanese Americans) to contact the defenders. General Kuribayashi, in radio contact with Major Horie on Chichi Jima, said: "We only laughed at this childish trick and did not set ourselves against them." On March 17, Horie had contacted the general informing him of his promotion to full general, and on the evening of March 23 received a final message: "All officers and men of Chichi Jima – goodbye from Iwo."

Prisoners were rare on Iwo Jima. A group of curious Marines stop to stare at one of the few Japanese taken alive. (National Archives)

A memorial stands near the site of General Kuribayashi's cave in "Death Valley." (Taro Kuribayashi)

In the pre-dawn darkness of March 26, the final act of the tragedy was performed. Between 200 and 300 Japanese troops from "Death Valley" and other scattered positions on the west coast silently crept through the ravines of the 5th Division sector headed for a tented area between Airfield No. 2 and the sea occupied by a mixture of Seabees, Air Force personnel, shore parties and antiaircraft gunners. Most of them were sleeping, secure in the knowledge that the battle was virtually over. In a three-pronged attack, the Japanese attackers slashed tents, stabbed sleeping men, threw grenades, and fired pistols and rifles at the hapless troops. The noise soon alerted troops from the surrounding area, and Marines from a nearby pioneer battalion, African-American troops from a shore party, and soldiers from the 147th Infantry joined battle in a frenzy of shooting, punching, kicking, and stabbing. Dawn revealed the full extent of the carnage in the ruined encampment: 44 airmen and 9 Marines lay dead with a further 119 wounded; of the attackers 262 were killed and 18 captured. Lieutenant Harry Martin of the 5th Pioneers had hurriedly organized a defense line during the attack and single-handedly killed four enemy machine-gunners before dying himself. He was to be Iwo Jima's final Medal of Honor hero, bringing the total to an incredible 27.

The circumstances of General Kuribayashi's death have always been shrouded in mystery. Over the years various sources have suggested that he died in the fighting around "Death Valley" or that he killed himself in his HQ. In a letter to the author, his son Taro offers the following version, which is probably the more authoritative:

It seems that it was after sunset on March 25 to the dawn of the 26th that surviving Imperial Japanese forces were obliged to stand still under the US onslaught and showering shells. Under such circumstances, he had his sword in his left hand and ordered the chief staff officer, Col Takaishi, who was beside him, "Send snipers to shoot"(Sgt Oyama heard the order). Oyama, who was seriously wounded in the last combat, fell unconscious, was hospitalized by the US and after having served as a POW came back and testified the dreadful account of the night to me. My father had believed it shameful to have his body discovered by the enemy even after death, so he had previously asked his two soldiers to come along with him, one in front and the other behind, with a shovel in hand. In case of his death he had wanted them to bury his body there and then. It seems that my father and the soldiers were killed by shells, and he was buried at the foot of a tree in Chidori Village, along the beach near Osaka Mountain. Afterwards Gen Smith spent a whole day looking for his body to pay respect accordingly and to perform a burial, but in vain.

What is without doubt is that Kuribayashi proved to be Japan's greatest wartime general and in Holland Smith's opinion: "Our most redoubtable adversary."

PART 4
AFTERMATH

AFTER THE BATTLE

Operation *Detachment* was planned and executed in accordance with the necessities of the time. Iwo Jima posed a major threat to the 20th Air Force's campaign against the Japanese mainland and its occupation was imperative as subsequent statistics proved. A total of 2,251 B29 Superfortress bombers made forced landings on the island during and after the battle. This represented 24,761 crewmen who would otherwise have had to ditch in the 1,300-mile (2,092km) expanse of ocean between Japan and the Marianas with a minimal chance of survival. In an interview with the author, Paul Tibbets, pilot of the Superfortress "Enola Gay," which dropped the Hiroshima bomb said:

On March 4, 1945, when the first B29 in distress landed on Iwo Jima, until the end of the war, more than 2,200 aircraft made emergency landings on Iwo. Many wounded crewmen on board would not have made the return trip to their home bases. Had it not been for the heroic valor of the Marines in securing the island and the Navy Seabees who built the runways, more than 22,000 pilots and air crew would have perished in crash landings at sea.

The capture of the Philippine Islands and the invasion of Okinawa in April accelerated the pace of the war. The 20th Air Force fire-raising raids and the dropping

of the atomic bombs on Hiroshima and Nagasaki ended it, and the island of Iwo Jima, secured at a terrible cost in Marine lives, played a major role in these events.

Since the end of the war many revisionists have condemned the dropping of the atomic bombs as acts of terrorism against helpless civilians; few have considered the alternative. Operation *Downfall*, the invasion of the Japanese mainland by the Marine Corps and the US Army, was already planned and filled the government, Army, and USMC with foreboding. Knowing the ethos of fanatical commitment to Emperor and country that was prevalent at that time, and drawing from experience gleaned at Saipan, Iwo Jima, and Okinawa, the military knew that every beach, town, village, and field would be defended to the death by both the armed forces and the civilian population.

Japan still had 2,350,000 regular troops, 250,000 garrison troops, 7,000 aircraft, 4,000,000 employees of the armed services, and 23,000,000 men, women, boys, and girls sworn to fight to the death. Adding the kamikazes and the remnants of the navy provided the ingredients for a bloodbath that would make previous battles pale into insignificance. The Joint Chiefs were expecting 70 percent casualties in the landing force and the war was projected to last until 1946 or even 1947. Troops, ships, and aircraft (Tiger Force) were already on their way from the European theater when the war ended. The authors, who have corresponded and talked to hundreds of Marine veterans, have yet to meet one who does not consider that he owes his life to the dropping of those bombs.

IWO JIMA TODAY

With the exception of Pearl Harbor on the Hawaiian island of Oahu, the majority of the Pacific World War II battlefields are remote, and difficult and expensive to visit. In the case of Iwo Jima it is almost impossible.

After the war the US Air Force maintained a base on the island for 20 years and a US Coast Guard contingent remained until 1968 to operate the Long Range Aid to Navigation (LORAN) station situated near Kitano Point in the north. This token presence vanished in 1993 when the island was turned over to the Japanese Maritime Safety Agency and Iwo Jima was returned to Japanese jurisdiction and is now a

Debris and bodies lie in the open on the beaches of Iwo Jima, giving a stark suggestion of the violence of the battle. Note the depth of the thick volcanic sand, which caused such intense problems for US mobility in the advance out of the initial beachhead. (Time & Life Pictures/Getty Images)

government installation and a national war memorial. With no visitor facilities or civilian airport, the only access for Westerners is via the annual one-day trips, organized by Marine Corps oriented tour companies, which are almost exclusively allocated to Iwo Jima veterans.

All American dead were removed prior to the handover and re-interred in either the Punchbowl Cemetery in Hawaii or returned to the United States. No such service could be provided for the Japanese dead, most of whom were either buried in mass graves or sealed in caves and tunnels during the battle. For many years groups of "bone diggers" from Japan, led by Tsuenzo Wachi, former Imperial Navy captain and one time commander on Iwo Jima, returned to recover the remains of the garrison.

The island now bears little resemblance to the wartime battlefield. The three airfields have been replaced by one huge north–south runway with adjacent hangers and living quarters. Once-familiar locations like Cushman's Pocket, Nishi Ridge, the Quarry, the Meatgrinder, and Motoyama Village have vanished under the bulldozer, and Mount Suribachi is studded with monuments. Only the landing beaches with their familiar black ash are tangible reminders, for the veterans who make their pilgrimages, of the carnage that took place here more than half a century ago.

Aerial view of Mount Suribachi from the west in March, 2000. (Taro Kuribayashi)

APPENDICES

APPENDIX NO. 1

US COMMAND AND STAFF LIST

Expeditionary Troops (TF 56)
Commanding General   LtGen Holland M. Smith

V Amphibious Corps (VACLF)
Commanding General   MajGen Harry Schmidt

3rd Marine Division
Commanding General   MajGen Graves B. Erskine
3rd Regiment*   Col James A. Stuart

(*This regiment did not land on Iwo Jima and did not actively participate in that operation. The 3rd Regiment remained in the area as Ex Trp Pac Reserve until March 5, 1945, when it returned to Guam.)

9th Regiment   Col Howard N. Kenyon
  1st Battalion   LtCol Cary A. Randell
  2nd "   LtCol Robert E. Cushman
  3rd "   LtCol Harold C. Boehm

21st Regiment	Col Hartnoll J Withers
1st Battalion	LtCol Marlowe Williams
2nd "	LtCol Lowell E. English
3rd "	LtCol Wendell H. Duplantis

4th Marine Division

Commanding General	MajGen Clifton B. Cates
23rd Regiment	Col Walter W. Wensinger
1st Battalion	LtCol Ralph Haas
2nd "	Maj Robert H. Davidson
3rd "	Maj James S. Scales

24th Regiment	Col Walter I. Jordan
1st Battalion	Maj Paul S. Treitel
2nd "	LtCol Richard Rothwell
3rd "	LtCol Alexander A. Vandegrift, Jr.

25th Regiment	Col John R. Lanigan
1st Battalion	LtCol Hollis U. Mustain
2nd "	LtCol Lewis C. Hudson, Jr.
3rd "	LtCol Justice M. Chambers

5th Marine Division

Commanding General	MajGen Keller E. Rockey
26th Regiment	Col Chester B. Graham
1st Battalion	LtCol Daniel C. Pollock
2nd "	LtCol Joseph P. Sayers
3rd "	LtCol Tom M. Trotti

27th Regiment	Col Thomas A. Wornham
1st Battalion	LtCol John A. Butler
2nd "	Maj John W. Antonelli
3rd "	LtCol Donn J. Robertson

| 28th Regiment | Col Harry B. Liversedge |
| 1st Battalion | LtCol Jackson B. Butterfield |

2nd   "   LtCol Chandler W. Johnson
3rd   "   LtCol Charles E. Shepard, Jr.

Of the battalion commanders who landed on D-Day, only seven remained unwounded and in command at the end of the battle.

US Task Force Organization

Overall Command of Iwo Jima Operation	Adm Raymond A. Spruance
Task Force 51 (Joint Expeditionary Force)	V/Adm Richmond K. Turner
Task Force 52 (Amphibious Support Force)	R/Adm William H. P. Blandy
Task Force 53 (Attack Force)	R/Adm Harry W. Hill
Task Force 54 (Gunfire & Covering Force)	R/Adm Bertram J. Rogers
Task Force 56 (Expeditionary Troops)	LtGen Holland M. Smith
Task Group 56-1 (Landing Force)	MajGen Harry Schmidt
Task Force 58 (Fast Carrier Force – 5th Fleet)	V/Adm Marc A. Mitscher
Task Force 93 (Strategic Air Force – Pacific Ocean Area)	LtGen Hillard F. Harmon
Task Force 94 (Forward Area – Central Pacific)	V/Adm John H. Hoover

APPENDIX NO. 2

JAPANESE COMMAND AND STAFF LIST

Commander in Chief	LtGen Tadamichi Kuribayashi
Chief of Staff	Col Tadashi Takaishi

Army Units

109th Division	LtGen Tadamichi Kuribayashi
145th Infantry Regiment	Col Masuo Ikeda
17th Mixed Infantry Regiment	Maj Tamachi Fujiwara
26th Tank Regiment	LtCol (Baron) Takeichi Nishi
2nd Mixed Brigade	MajGen Sadasue Senda
Brigade Artillery	Col Chosaku Kaido
Army Rocket Unit	Capt Yoshio Yokoyama

Navy Units

Commanding Officer	R/Adm Toshinosuke Ichimaru
Naval Guard Force	Capt Samaji Inouye
125th Naval Antiaircraft Defense Unit	Lt Tamura
132nd Naval Antiaircraft Defense Unit	En Okumura
141st Naval Antiaircraft Defense Unit	Lt Doi
149th Naval Antiaircraft Defense Unit	Not known
Operations	Comm Takeji Mase
Communications	LtComm Shigeru Arioka
Engineering	LtComm Narimasa Okada
Supply	LtComm Okazaki
Suribachi Commander	Capt Kanehiko Atsuchi

Total number of Japanese forces on Iwo Jima – February 19, 1945 (D-Day) – 21,060.

APPENDIX NO. 3

FLAGS OVER SURIBACHI

World War II produced many outstanding photographs – Cecil Beaton's picture of the dome of St Paul's Cathedral surrounded by a ring of fire during the London Blitz, the mushroom cloud over Hiroshima, General Douglas MacArthur wading ashore in the Philippines, and the horrific pits full of emaciated bodies at Belsen concentration camp to name a few – but none of them achieved the fame of Joe Rosenthal's picture of US Marines raising the flag on the summit of Mount Suribachi.

When it was first seen in America it became an instant sensation and lent itself to an issue of three-cent stamps that had the largest sale in history. A painting was used for the 7th War Loan drive that raised $220,000,000. The photo appeared on 3,500,000 posters, and 175,000 car cards, was portrayed in films, re-enacted by gymnasts, and a float won first prize in the Rose Bowl Parade. The greatest accolade was the 100-ton bronze statue by Felix de Weldon that stands near the northern end of Arlington National Cemetery in Washington, DC, as a memorial to the United States Marine Corps.

Because of its outstanding composition and the fact that it was the second flag to be raised that day, there has always been speculation that the picture was posed, a view compounded by many books and magazine articles over the years. In

Associated Press photographer Joe Rosenthal with his Speed Graphic camera stands atop Mount Suribachi minutes after taking the picture that was to make him famous. (USMC)

correspondence with Derrick Wright, Joe Rosenthal gives the true story of the events of that day and clears up the misconceptions for good.

On the February 23, Joe boarded an ICT along with Bill Hippie, a magazine correspondent, and landed near Mount Suribachi where the boatswain told them that a patrol was going up Suribachi with a flag. They went to the 28th Regiment command post and learned that a 40-man detachment had already left following two patrols that had reached the top at 0940hrs. At the command post were Bob Campbell, a combat photographer, and Sergeant Bill Genaust, a cine photographer (killed nine days later at Hill 362); Rosenthal, Genaust, and Campbell started the tough climb, stopping occasionally while Marines dealt with enemy troops holed up in caves.

About half way up they met four Marines coming down. One was Lou Lowery, a photographer for *Leatherneck*, the Marine Corps magazine, who told them that a flag had been raised on the summit and that he had photographed the event. Joe was in two minds whether to continue, but decided to press on and take a picture anyway. Reaching the top of the volcano, he saw the flag flying and also saw a group of men dragging a long iron pipe and holding another neatly folded flag. "What are you doing?" he asked. "We're going to put up this bigger flag and keep the other as a souvenir," they said. This second flag came from IST 779 which was beached at the base of Suribachi. Ensign Alan Wood who was aboard told Wright: "A dirty, dusty, battle-worn Marine (2nd Lieutenant Albert Tuttle) asked for a flag. It was one that had been salvaged from a supply depot at Pearl Harbor. I hadn't the slightest idea that one day it would become the symbol of one of the war's bloodiest battlefields."

Private Robert Campbell took this photograph of the first flag being lowered as the second flag was raised. Rosenthal and Genaust were standing a few yards to his left. (USMC)

Rosenthal toyed with the idea of a shot showing the first flag coming down and the second one going up, but left that to Campbell and concentrated on a picture of the second flag being raised. He moved back, but the sloping ground masked his view and he had to build a platform of sandbags and stones (he is only 5ft 5in/1.65m tall). With Genaust standing on his right, he saw the men start to raise the flag and shouted, "There she goes," and swung his camera and caught the scene. He also took pictures of a group of Marines under the flag waving and cheering before he and Campbell made their way back to the 28th Regiment command post.

Back on the USS *Eldorado*, he wrote captions for the day's pictures and handed them in to go on the daily mail plane to Guam. When his picture reached the United States via radiophoto, it was an immediate sensation. Ironically, Joe was not to see it for another nine days when he returned to Guam where he was congratulated by a group of correspondents. "It's a great picture," they said. "Did you pose it?" "Sure," he said – he thought that they were referring to the shot with the waving and cheering Marines, but then someone showed him the picture. "Pose that one?" "Gee," I said. "That's good alright, but I didn't pose that one." It was here that the first misunderstandings about the picture started. Someone heard him say that he had posed a picture and wrote that the shot was a phoney and that Rosenthal had posed it.

Joe Rosenthal's life was completely changed by that photo. He was recalled to America by Associated Press where he became a celebrity, got a raise in salary, was awarded the Pulitzer Prize, and met President Harry Truman. Speaking engagements followed, at one of which he was bizarrely introduced as "Mr. Joe Rosenberg who raised the flag at Okinawa."

The accusations of a posed photograph have been a sore point since the end of the war as the old misconceptions continued to reappear in books and magazines over the years. The "posed" myth is easily discounted by looking at Bill Genaust's five-second cine film taken at the same time which shows one frame identical to Rosenthal's photograph. Joe Rosenthal's final words on the subject are: "I can best sum up what I feel by saying that of all the elements that went into the making of this picture, the part I played was the least important. To get that flag up there, America's fighting men had to die on that island and on other islands, and off the shore, and in the air. What difference does it make who took the picture? I took it, but the Marines took Iwo Jima."

The six flag raisers in the picture are all now deceased. They were from left to right: Pfc Ira Hayes, Pfc Franklin Sousley, Sergeant Michael Strank, Pharmacist's Mate 2nd Class John H. Bradley, Pfc Rene A. Gagnon, and Corporal Harlon H. Block (Sousley, Strank, and Block were all killed on Iwo Jima). Both flags now hang in the Marine Corps Historical Center in Washington, DC.

APPENDIX NO. 4

THE MARINE CORPS MEMORIAL

Directly inspired by Joe Rosenthal's famous Iwo Jima photograph, a memorial to the United States Marine Corps was erected at Arlington National Cemetery in Washington, DC, in 1954. The sculptor, Felix de Weldon, chose the Iwo Jima image as the Marine Corps symbol most familiar to the American public although the memorial of course represents the nation's tribute to the dead of the Corps since its formation in 1775. Three years in the making, the figures are 32ft (9.7m) high and stand on a Swedish granite base surrounded by polished black granite blocks listing the names and dates of all major Marine Corps engagements since the Corps was founded. Also engraved on the base is Admiral Chester Nimitz's famous tribute to the Marines of Iwo Jima: "Uncommon Valor was a Common Virtue."

The memorial was officially dedicated on November 10, 1954, by President Dwight D. Eisenhower, accompanied by Vice President Richard Nixon and the then Commandant of the Marine Corps, General Lemuel C. Shepherd, Jr. Also present at the ceremony were the three surviving flag raisers from Rosenthal's picture, John H. Bradley, Ira Hayes, and Rene A. Gagnon. Surprisingly, Rosenthal's name was not mentioned on the monument and it was many years before it was acknowledged that the statue was based on his photograph and a plaque was added to the base.

Pharmacist's Mate 2nd Class John H. Bradley (US Navy) seldom spoke of his part in the flag raising, even to his family, and lived a quiet postwar life in his home town of Antigo, Wisconsin. The longest surviving member of the six who raised the second flag on Mount Suribachi, he died aged 70 in January 1994.

Corporal Ira H. Hayes, a Pima Indian from the Gila River Reservation in Arizona, enlisted in the Corps in 1942 as a member of the Parachute Regiment. When this unit was disbanded in 1944 he was transferred to the 5th Division, with which he served at Iwo Jima. Ordered back to the US after the flag raising to promote a War Bond selling tour, he found the publicity overwhelming and welcomed the return to his unit. In later life he had major problems with alcoholism and died aged 32 in 1955 and is buried in Arlington National Cemetery.

Rene Gagnon, a 5th Division Marine, was also co-opted to the Treasury Department to promote the 7th War Loan Drive and, after he returned to his unit, served with the occupation forces in China until his discharge in 1946. He died in 1979 and was buried in Manchester, New Hampshire. In 1981 at the request of his widow he was re-interred in Arlington Cemetery.

This 100-ton bronze statue designed by Felix de Weldon is the memorial to the United States Marine Corps at Arlington National Cemetery in Washington, DC. (USMC)

All three survivors had posed for de Weldon who modeled their faces in clay. Photographs of the deceased flag raisers were used to depict their likenesses. The castings of the figures took almost three years to complete and were made at the Bedi-Rassy Art Foundry in Brooklyn, New York.

The monument was funded by US Marines, reservists, friends of the Marine Corps, and members of the Naval Service at a cost of $850,000 – no public funds were used. Now one of Washington's major tourist attractions and certainly the most striking war memorial in the capital, the monument has stood for over four decades in tribute to the Corps.

A major controversy arose recently when the US Air Force attempted to secure an area near the Memorial for its own monument. It was rightly judged that another large structure so close to this one would be obtrusive and detract from the Marine Corps Memorial. After much inter-service and political in-fighting, the Air Force was obliged to find a location elsewhere on the Arlington site.

APPENDIX NO. 5

THE MEDAL OF HONOR – UNCOMMON VALOR

The United States' highest decoration, the Medal of Honor, was awarded to 27 combatants at Iwo Jima, a figure that represents a third of the total number of awards to members of the United States Marine Corps during the whole of World War II. Admiral Chester Nimitz's words: "Among the Americans who served on Iwo Jima, uncommon valor was a common virtue," could not have been more appropriate.

Corporal Charles J. Berry – 1st Battalion, 26th Regiment, 5th Division (Posthumous)

On the night of March 3, Berry and two other riflemen were in a foxhole close to Nishi Ridge. A group of Japanese made an infiltration and lobbed a hand grenade into the foxhole, whereupon Berry immediately threw himself on to it and was killed instantly, saving the lives of his comrades.

Aerial picture of the Marine Corps Memorial on the day of the dedication ceremony, November 10, 1954. The ceremony was conducted by President Dwight D. Eisenhower accompanied by Vice President Richard Nixon and the then Commandant of the Marine Corps, General Lemuel C. Shepherd, Jr. (USMC)

Pfc William Caddy – 3rd Battalion, 26th Regiment, 5th Division (Posthumous)

North of Airfield No. 3, a Japanese sniper had Caddy and his two companions pinned down for two hours in a shell hole. Around 1600hrs one of the Marines scrambled to the edge of the hole to try to locate the enemy but was spotted. The sniper threw a hand grenade, and Caddy threw himself onto it and took the full blast in his chest and stomach, dying immediately.

Lieutenant-Colonel Justice M. Chambers – 3rd Battalion, 25th Regiment, 4th Division

At 38, "Jumpin' Joe" Chambers was one of the old men of the battle. Determined to take "Charlie Dog Ridge," he called in a salvo of rockets and rushed to the head of his men in a wild charge towards the summit, but was hit in the chest by a burst of machine-gun fire and was dragged back to his observation post. After a long convalescence in America, Chambers received his medal from President Truman at the White House.

Sergeant Darrell S. Cole – 1st Battalion, 23rd Regiment, 4th Division (Posthumous)

Storming the beaches on D-Day, Cole's platoon came under very heavy fire from pillboxes on Yellow Beaches 1 and 2. Armed with hand grenades and a .45-cal. pistol he silenced six positions, returning to his lines twice for more ammunition before being killed by an enemy grenade that exploded at his feet.

Captain Robert H. Dunlap – 1st Battalion, 26th Regiment, 5th Division

Dunlap's company were pinned down near Airfield No. 1 under a hail of mortar fire. Grabbing a field telephone he advanced to an isolated position only 50 yards (46m) from the enemy and for the next 48 hours called in devastating fire on the Japanese positions from various directions, playing a significant role in clearing the western section of the island.

Sergeant Ross F. Gray – 1st Battalion, 25th Regiment, 4th Division

When his platoon became bogged down in fighting around Airfield No. 2, Gray grabbed a satchel charge and silenced the nearest emplacement. In short order he repeated the process until all six adjacent positions lay silent and the way was clear for an advance. Later in the day Gray cleared a path through a dangerous minefield single-handedly.

Sergeant William G. Harrell – 1st Battalion, 28th Regiment, 5th Division
Manning a frontline foxhole near Nishi Ridge, Sergeant Harrell and Pfc Carter were attacked by night-time infiltrators. Four of them were swiftly disposed of before a hand grenade was thrown into the position and almost blew off Harrell's left hand and caused other serious injuries. Carter's gun had jammed and he left to get another. Meanwhile, two more Japanese charged into the foxhole, one placed a grenade next to Harrell and attempted to leave. Harrell shot him with his pistol and lobbed the grenade out, but it exploded, blowing off his right hand. The indomitable sergeant was evacuated next morning and after the war, with the aid of mechanical hands, became a rancher in his native Texas.

Lieutenant Rufus G. Herring – USNR LGI(G) 449
The first of Iwo Jima's medal winners, Herring was the captain of Gunboat 449 which was laying down a carpet of rockets in support of frogmen two days before D-Day. A direct hit from Japanese artillery killed 12 of the crew and seriously wounded Herring. Bleeding profusely he struggled for 30 minutes to steer his vessel and wounded crew away from the enemy barrage and alongside the destroyed USS *Terror*, remaining propped up by empty shell cases until all of his men had been evacuated.

Pfc Douglas T. Jacobson – 3rd Battalion, 23rd Regiment, 4th Division
Battling to take Hill 382, 19-year-old Jacobson seized a bazooka and began to wage his own war on the enemy. For 30 minutes he ran from blockhouse to blockhouse, blasting each one in turn until 16 positions fell silent and 75 of the enemy lay dead, opening up a gap for his company to reach the top of the hill. Using a bazooka is a two-man operation, but Jacobson achieved his remarkable feat alone.

Sergeant Joseph R. Julian – 1st Battalion, 27th Regiment, 5th Division (Posthumous)
In vicious fighting around Kitano Point on the 18th day of the battle, Julian silenced four enemy emplacements and a machine-gun nest. Dashing back to his lines he collected demolition charges and a bazooka and once more charged the enemy, this time destroying four more strongpoints before being killed by a burst of machine-gun fire.

Pfc James D. LaBelle – 2nd Battalion, 27th Regiment, 5th Division (Posthumous)
It seems that LaBelle was destined to die on Iwo Jima. On D-Day he missed death by inches when three companions were mown down by machine-gun fire; three days later

he was the only one unhurt when a grenade landed in a shell hole he was sharing with four other Marines; and on day ten his best friend died at his side near Nishi Ridge. While they were standing behind an outcrop of boulders with two friends, a solitary Japanese soldier lobbed a grenade into their midst. Shouting a warning, LaBelle threw himself on the grenade, saving the lives of the others.

2nd Lieutenant John H. Leims – 1st Battalion, 9th Regiment, 3rd Division

Attacking Hill 362C, east of Cushman's Pocket, Leims and his company were cut off. He personally advanced and laid telephone lines across an exposed expanse of fire-swept terrain. Later, learning that several casualties were still behind enemy lines, he made two trips under heavy fire to bring back his wounded.

Pfc Jacklyn H. Lucas – 1st Battalion, 26th Regiment, 5th Division

A born rebel, Lucas had enlisted in the Corps when he was only 14; now at 17 he was wanted by the Military Police in Hawaii for being AWOL. On D+1 near Airfield No. 1 he was one of three men pinned down by enemy fire. When grenades fell among them he grabbed one and smothered it with his body and then grabbed a second and pulled it underneath him. Miraculously he survived the blasts and after spending months in hospital recovered with only a partially paralysed arm.

1st Lieutenant Jack Lummus – 2nd Battalion, 27th Regiment, 5th Division (Posthumous)

Determined to keep up the momentum while attacking a complex of enemy caves and bunkers near Kitano Point, Lummus, a 29-year-old ex-professional football star from Texas, spearheaded an attack and was soon blown to the ground by a grenade. Jumping to his feet, he attacked the position to his front killing the occupants. Waving his men forward for another charge, he stepped on a mine and both legs were blown off. As the debris settled, his men were horrified to see him upright on his stumps still urging them forward. He died several hours later in a field hospital.

1st Lieutenant Harry L. Martin – 5th Pioneer Battalion (Posthumous)

Before dawn on the March 26, between 200 and 300 Japanese troops, the remnants of General Kuribayashi's command, launched a massed attack against a rest area occupied by aircrews, Seabees, and other non-combat troops west of Airfield No. 2. Martin immediately formed a defense line manned mainly by African American troops and held many of the enemy in check. He recovered a number of wounded and attacked a machine-gun position, killing four of the enemy before being seriously wounded by a grenade. As dawn revealed the carnage, the body of Martin was recovered from among the hundreds strewn around the camp.

Captain Joseph J. McCarthy – 2nd Battalion, 24th Regiment, 4th Division

Another "Jumpin' Joe", 33-year-old McCarthy, rallying his men on the approach to Airfield No. 2, filled bags with grenades, mustered a three-man flamethrower team, and headed for the enemy yelling: "Let's get the bastards before they get us." Thrusting grenades through the firing vents, he personally silenced four pillboxes, allowing his company to advance.

Pfc George Phillips – 2nd Battalion, 28th Regiment, 5th Division (Posthumous)

On the very day that Iwo Jima was officially declared "secure," Pfc Phillips, an 18-year-old replacement who had only landed on the island two days earlier, threw himself onto a grenade and died instantly, saving the lives of the three companions that he barely knew.

Pharmacist's Mate 1st Class Francis Pierce, Jr. – 2nd Battalion, 24th Regiment, 4th Division

Corpsman Pierce and a party of stretcher-bearers were ambushed while evacuating wounded on March 15. He engaged the enemy with rifle fire and carried a wounded Marine to safety, returning for another while under constant fire from Japanese snipers. Badly wounded the following day, he refused aid and continued to minister to casualties until he collapsed. Pierce's actions were typical of Iwo Jima's Corpsmen, and show why they were held in such high regard by the Marines.

Pfc Donald J. Ruhl – 2nd Battalion, 28th Regiment, 5th Division (Posthumous)

Twenty-one-year-old Ruhl showed conspicuous gallantry from the day that he landed on Iwo Jima. On D-Day he killed nine of the enemy while charging a blockhouse. The following morning he dragged a wounded Marine to safety across 40 yards (37m) of ground swept by heavy fire and later occupied an enemy gun emplacement and secured it overnight to prevent the enemy from re-occupying it. He met his death on D+2 when he and his platoon sergeant were in a camouflaged bunker bringing fire to bear on the enemy. A grenade landed between the pair, and without a thought for his own safety he threw himself upon it to protect his companion.

Private Franklin E. Sigler – 2nd Battalion, 26th Regiment, 5th Division

In the final stage of the battle in "Death Valley", Sigler took command of his leaderless squad and led an attack against a gun emplacement that was causing chaos among the 2nd Battalion. In the face of murderous fire he silenced the position with hand grenades, killing the entire enemy crew, but was severely wounded by fire from nearby caves. Continuing the attack, he sealed several caves before withdrawing to his lines. Refusing medical treatment, he carried three wounded Marines to safety and continued to direct rocket and machine-gun fire at the enemy until ordered to the rear for medical treatment.

Corporal Tony Stein – 1st Battalion, 28th Regiment, 5th Division

During the advance across the island at the base of Mount Suribachi on D-Day, Stein, armed with an improvised aircraft .50-cal. machine gun that he called his "stinger," attacked five enemy positions killing at least 20 of the enemy. When his ammunition ran out he made repeated trips to the beach for more, carrying a wounded Marine back each time. Although wounded by shrapnel, he continued to fight, supervising the withdrawal of his platoon although having his "stinger" twice shot from his hands. Stein was killed near Hill 362A later in the battle, never knowing of his citation.

Gunnery Sergeant William G. Walsh – 3rd Battalion, 27th Regiment, 5th Division (Posthumous)

During the attack on Hill 362A, Walsh led his platoon to the summit in the face of heavy enemy fire, but his success was short lived when they were forced to withdraw under devastating machine-gun fire from three enemy positions. Undeterred, Walsh mounted a counterattack, again reaching the top where the six men in his squad took cover in a trench. The Japanese retaliated by lobbing hand grenades and when one fell in their midst Walsh threw himself upon it and died instantly.

Private Wilson D. Watson – 2nd Battalion, 9th Regiment, 3rd Division

Two hills, codenamed "Peter" and "Oboe," near Airfield No. 2 were formidable stumbling blocks for the 3rd Division. Watson was the first man atop Hill Oboe, having silenced a bunker and a machine-gun nest on the way. Aided by only one other Marine, he staved off repeated enemy attacks for thirty minutes until reinforcements arrived in support. Pressing forward, he destroyed another bunker and was attacking a second when he was wounded by mortar fire and had to be evacuated for treatment. In two days he had killed over 90 of the enemy.

Pharmacist's Mate 2nd Class George E. Whalen – 2nd Battalion, 26th Regiment, 5th Division

Another of Iwo's gallant Corpsmen, Whalen was wounded on February 26, but continued tending the injured despite intense enemy fire. Wounded again on March 3, he refused aid and was wounded for a third time but crawled among the casualties to administer aid until he had to be carried to the rear for urgent treatment. When evacuated, Whalen had been treating wounded Marines non-stop for five days and nights.

Corporal Hershel W. Williams – 1st Battalion, 21st Regiment, 3rd Division

Confronted with a complex of bunkers and antitank guns adjoining Airfield No. 2, Major Robert Houser called upon 21-year-old Williams, the last of his flamethrower operators. Escorted by riflemen, he incinerated the occupants of the first pillbox and a group of Japanese troops who attempted to shoot him down. Moving from one position to another he burned out bunkers and pillboxes and in four hours had cleared the way for his regiment to move forward. Williams was the first 3rd Division Marine on Iwo Jima to win the Medal of Honor.

Pharmacist's Mate 3rd Class Jack Williams – 3rd Battalion, 28th Regiment, 5th Division (Posthumous)

Williams, a 21-year-old from Harrison, Arkansas, added to the prestige of Iwo's Corpsmen on March 20. Under heavy fire he went to aid a wounded Marine, screening him from enemy fire with his own body while attending to his wounds. Inevitably he was wounded himself, receiving gunshots to the abdomen and groin, but continued treating his patient before attending to his own injuries. He then moved on to a second casualty and although bleeding profusely, administered aid before attempting to return to the rear, but was killed by an enemy sniper.

Pharmacist's Mate 1st Class John H. Willis – 3rd Battalion, 27th Regiment, 5th Division (Posthumous)

Willis had been tending the wounded all day around Hill 362 on February 28 until he was wounded by shrapnel and was ordered to the rear for treatment. Within hours he was back with the troops attending a seriously wounded Marine in a shell hole. With his rifle stuck in the ground, he was administering plasma when a grenade rolled down beside him. He threw it out, but seven more followed in rapid succession and each was quickly thrown out until the last one exploded in his hand, killing him instantly.

BIBLIOGRAPHY

Alexander, Joseph A., *Fellowship of Valor* (HarperCollins, New York, 1997)

Alexander, Joseph A., *Closing In – Marines in the Seizure of Iwo Jima* (Marine Corps Historical Center, Washington, DC, 1994)

Bartley, Whitman S., *Iwo Jima, Amphibious Epic* (USMC Official History, 1954, reprinted by Battery Press, Nashville, Tennessee, 1988)

Berry, Henry, *Semper Fi, Mac: Living Memories of the US Marines in World War II* (Arbor House, New York, 1982)

Brown, Luther A., *The Marine's Handbook* (Naval Institute Press, Annapolis, MD, 1940)

Cameron, Craig M., *American Samurai: Myth, Imagination, and the Conduct of Battle in the First Marine Division, 1941–1951* (Cambridge University Press, New York, 1994)

Canfield, Bruce N., *US Infantry Weapons of World War II* (Andrew Mowbray, Lincoln, RI, 1994)

Cook, Haruko Taya, and Cook, Theodore F., *Japan at War: An Oral History* (New Press, New York, 1992)

Daugherty, Leo III., *Fighting Techniques of a Japanese Infantryman, 1941–1945: Training, Tactics and Weapons* (MBI Publishing, St. Paul, MN, 2002)

Daugherty, Leo J. III., *Fighting Techniques of a US Marine 1941–1945: Training, Techniques, and Weapons* (MBI Publishing, Osceola, WI, 2000)

Forty, George, *Japanese Army Handbook, 1939–45* (Sutton Publishing, Stroud, Gloucestershire, 1999)

Fujita, Masao, *Teikoku Rikugun Senjo no Ishokuju (Life of the Imperial Japanese Army on the Battlefield)* (Gakken, Japan, 2002) – Japanese language

Fuller, Richard, *Shokan – Hirohito's Samurai* (Arms and Armour Press, London, 1992)

Glenn, Harlen, *United States Marine Corps Uniforms, Insignia and Personal Items of World War II* (Schiffer Publishing, Atglen, PA, 2005)

Harries, Meirion, and Harries, Susie, *Soldiers of the Sun: The Rise and Fall of the Imperial Japanese Army* (Random House, New York, 1991)

Hayashi, Saburo, and Coox, Alvin D., *Kogun: The Japanese Army in the Pacific War* (Marine Corps Association, Quantico, VA, 1959)

Henshall, Kenneth G., *A History of Japan: From Stone Age to Superpower* (St. Martin's Press, New York, 1999)

Hewitt, Mike, *Uniforms and Equipment of the Imperial Japanese Army in World War II* (Schiffer Publishing, Atglen, PA, 2002)

Hoffman, Carl F., *Saipan: The Beginning of the End* (HQ Marine Corps, Washington, DC, 1950)

Jones, Wilbur D. Jr., *Gyrene: The World War II United States Marine* (White Mare Books, Shippensburg, PA, 1998)

Krulak, Victor H., *First to Fight: An Inside View of the US Marine Corps* (Simon and Schuster, New York, 1991)

Lane, John, *This Here is G Company* (Bright Lights Publications, Great Neck, NY, 1997)

Moran, Jim, *US Marine Corps Uniforms and Equipment in World War 2* (Windrow and Greene, London, 1992)

Nakanishi, Ritta, *Japanese Military Uniforms, 1930–1945* (Dai Nihon Kaiga, Tokyo, 1991)

Nakata, Tadao, *Imperial Japanese Army and Navy Uniforms and Equipment* (Arms and Armour Press, London, 1975)

Newcomb, Richard F., *Iwo Jima* (Holt, Rinehart & Winston, New York, 1965)

Proehl, Carl W., *The Fourth Marine Division in World War II* (Infantry Journal Press, Washington, DC, 1946)

Ross, Bill D., *Iwo Jima – Legacy of Valor* (Random House, New York, 1985)

Rottman, Gordon L., *World War II Pacific Island Guide: A Geo-Military Study* (Greenwood Publishing, Westport, CT, 2002)

Rottman, Gordon L., *US Marine Corps Order of Battle: Ground and Air Units in the Pacific War, 1939–1945* (Greenwood Publishing, Westport, CT, 2001)

Rottman, Gordon L., *World War II Pacific Island Guide: A Geo-Military Study* (Greenwood Publishing, Westport, CT, 2001)

Tulkoff, Alec S., *Grunt Gear: USMC Combat Infantry Equipment of World War II* (R. James Bender Publishing, San Jose, CA, 2003)

US Army, *Handbook on Japanese Military Forces, TM-E 30-480* (US Army, Washington, DC, September 15, 1944)

Vat, Dan van der, *The Pacific Campaign* (Simon & Schuster, New York, 1991)

Waterhouse, Charles, *Marines and Others* (Sea Bag Productions, Edison, NJ, 1994)

Wheeler, Richard, *Iwo* (Lippincott & Crowell, New York, 1980)

Wright, Derrick, *The Battle for Iwo Jima 1945* (Sutton Publishing, Slough, Gloucestershire, 1999)

INDEX